The Press and Apartheid

Repression and Propaganda in South Africa

William A.
Hachten
and
C. Anthony
Giffard

With the editorial assistance

of Harva Hachten

The
Press
and
Apartheid
Repression
and Propaganda
in
South Africa

The
University of
Wisconsin
Press

Published in the United States of America,
Canada, and Japan by

The University of Wisconsin Press
114 North Murray Street
Madison, Wisconsin 53715

Published in the United Kingdom,
the Continent of Europe, and
South Africa by
Macmillan Publishers

First printing

Printed in the United States of America

**Library of Congress Cataloging in Publication
Data**

Hachten, William A.
  The press and apartheid.

  Bibliography: pp. 311–326.
  Includes index.
  1. Government and the press—South Africa.
2. Freedom of the press—South Africa.
3. South Africa—Race relations. 4. Race
relations and the press—South Africa.
I. Giffard, C. Anthony. II. Hachten, Harva.
III. Title.
PN4748.S58H3 1984 079'.68 84-40150
ISBN 0-299-09940-7

Contents

Introduction

South Africa! That country has virtually become a synonym for anachronism in the twentieth-century community of nations thrusting toward liberation, self-determination, and majority rule. The name alone evokes images of racial strife and discrimination, of a band of determined white men defying both a disquieted nonwhite majority and the opinion of most of the world.

After deadly riots and demonstrations, South Africa in the 1980s has been marked by a rising level of urban terrorism and violence. Bombs have exploded in the busy centers of Pretoria and Bloemfontein, and South African Defense Forces have carried out punitive raids in neighboring Mozambique and Lesotho against suspected bases of the African National Congress, the exiled arm of black opposition. This low-level civil war of majority blacks against entrenched whites has been watched with increasing dismay by the outside world. As one South African newspaper editor put it, "We're the polecat of the world."

In this nation under stress—and South Africa is surely that—the press and mass communication in general are caught up in events and, at times, become actors in the Greek tragedy so inexorably playing itself out at the southern end of Africa.

This is a study both of measures taken by the South African government to control its mass media and of the efforts of its journalists and others to express their views and resist those restraints. Essentially, the media have been—and are being—subjected to two kinds of government controls: coercive and manipulative. Coercion includes legislation that determines who may publish and what may be published as well as less direct measures, such as intimidating the press into self-censorship.

The manipulative controls comprise the extensive state machinery used both to suppress unfavorable information and to promote a positive image of official policies at home and abroad. Some of these activities, like those of the government information services, are overt. Others, like government controls over the broadcasting system, are more subtle. But in the face of hostile world opinion, the South African government has also resorted to illegal and clandestine operations to promote its point of view.

The abrasive relationship between the media and the government must be seen in the context of contemporary social, economic, and political forces rooted deeply in the history of South Africa. For that reason, our analysis of the contemporary conflicts between authority and the different media and the constituencies they serve will be presented in terms of their historical development.

This, in essence, is a case study of official exercises of power over public communication in a modern nation. White South Africa shares many characteristics with other Western societies—parliamentary democracy, an independent judiciary, a tradition of press freedom, and an educated and affluent populace. Yet black South Africa shares many attributes of much of the third world—impoverished, illiterate, malnourished, and politically powerless. And in this context, freedom of the press, as well as civil liberties generally, has been deteriorating. What has happened and continues to happen could occur in other modern societies as well.

In many ways, however, South Africa is a special case—"a very strange society" with its white affluence and black poverty—and hence fascinating to study. The Republic of South Africa is a deeply divided, multiracial society of great complexity, controlled politically and economically by a minority white population. The white minority in turn is broadly split between English speakers, mainly of British heritage, and the Afrikaners of Dutch, French Huguenot, and German descent. The Afrikaners' National party has held political power for over thirty-six years. A tangle of laws, administered by a mammoth bureaucracy of civil servants, police, and security forces, has since 1948 maintained harsh and enforced separation of the races, known as *apartheid*, that has assured continued white privilege and prerogatives in an increasingly affluent economy in which comparatively few nonwhites share.

Because race or skin color permeates all aspects of South African life, the population totals of ethnic groups involved are important. There are about 5 million "whites" of whom about 2.5 million are Afrikaans-speaking Afrikaners, and about 1.5 million are ESSAs (English-speaking South Africans). In addition there are about 1 million other "Europeans," mainly recently arrived Portuguese, Italians, and Greeks, who are largely inactive politically. Among nonwhites or "blacks" are about 21 million Africans (Zulus, Xhosas, Sothos, Tswanas, Swazis, Vendas, Ndebeles, Shangaans, etc.), 2.7 million racially mixed "Coloureds," and 840,000 "Asians," mostly Indians.

To help retain political domination of both the privileged white minority and the unfranchised majority of nonwhites, successive National party governments have implemented wide-ranging restrictive controls over all forms of public communication (see Chap. 5). Most have been directed at the print media, the principal means of expressing political opposition and dissent. (Radio and television broadcasting have long been firmly in the hands of government supporters, and hence require few controls.)

Historically, the mass media in South Africa have mainly served the whites, and the earliest newspapers, started in the nineteenth century, were in English. In fragmented, cellular South Africa, the media have long reflected linguistic and ethnic divisions as well as white domination. The first radio service in 1927 was directed at white English speakers, and the first television service introduced in 1976 was for whites only. Through much of its media history, the "non-Europeans" have been eavesdroppers. That has changed. Today, a majority of newspaper readers and radio listeners are Africans, Coloureds, and Asians. Special publications and separate radio and television channels are directed at different racial groups.

Diverse South Africa is served by twenty-one general daily newspapers, eight Sunday or weekly papers and a hundred weekly or biweekly country papers. About five hundred periodicals, from specialized journals to family entertainment magazines, are published in South Africa. In addition, hundreds of publications are imported from Britain, the United States, and Western Europe.

Newspaper publishing is dominated by four groups—two each publishing mainly in English or Afrikaans. Largest and most powerful is the Argus Printing and Publishing Company which controls seven dailies—the Johannesburg *Star*, Durban *Daily News*, Cape Town *Argus*, *Pretoria News*, Bloemfontein *Friend*, Kimberley *Diamond Fields Advertiser*, and the *Sowetan* which is edited for Africans in the Johannesburg area. Argus also puts out two weekend papers, the *Cape Herald*, oriented toward Coloured people in the western Cape, and the *Sunday Tribune* of Durban.

The other English medium group, SAAN (for South African Associated Newspapers), includes four dailies, the *Rand Daily Mail* of Johannesburg, the *Eastern Province Herald* and *Evening Post*, both of Port Elizabeth, and the *Cape Times*, plus two weekend papers, the *Sunday Times* and *Sunday Express*, and the *Financial Mail*, a weekly. The daily *Natal Mercury* of Durban is mostly owned by SAAN. There are two independent dailies, the *Daily Dispatch* of East London and the *Natal Witness* of Pietermaritzburg.

Argus and SAAN are financially linked, with Argus holding 40 per cent of SAAN stock and SAAN holding a somewhat smaller part of Argus. Both publishing groups are financially tied to mining and industrial interests, and their interlocking ownership makes them vulnerable to government charges of monopoly and concentration of ownership.

The two Afrikaans press groups, Perskor and Nasionale Pers, not only are financially unallied but are highy competitive and represent different factions within the National party. Nasionale Pers owns the dailies *Die Burger* of Cape Town, *Die Volksblad* of Bloemfontein, *Beeld* of Johannesburg, and *Oosterlig* of Port Elizabeth. Perskor had long owned the Johannesburg dailies *Die Transvaler* and *Die Vaderland*, as well as two small dailies in Pretoria, *Hoofstad* and *Oggendblad*. As a result of the intense competition between *Beeld* and *Die Transvaler*, *Die Transvaler* was moved to Pretoria in early 1983 to merge with and replace *Hoofstad* and *Oggendblad*. Both groups jointly own the successful weekend newspaper *Rapport*.

A significant characteristic of the South African press is the clear predominance of the English-language newspapers. Although Afrikaans-speaking whites outnumber English-speaking whites by a ratio of six to four, the English papers account for three-quarters of total daily circulation and two-thirds of Sunday circulation. A great many Afrikaners, as well as nonwhites, read the English press, but few English speakers or nonwhites read Afrikaans papers.

The only English paper supporting the Nationalists was *The Citizen*, which was started in 1975 with secret government funds. After the government involvement was revealed during the Muldergate scandal (see Chap. 10), it was taken over, at least ostensibly, by Perskor.

The black press has been severely eclipsed in recent years (see Chap. 6). Yet weeklies aimed by white publishers at specific racial groups have been a fast-growing aspect of South African journalism. The *Cape Herald* intended for coloureds in the Cape Town area had a 1982 circulation of 50,000. The *Post/Natal* in Durban was edited for Asians and had a circulation of 34,000. *Ilanga*, published in the Zulu language, sold 107,000 copies a week in 1982, and *Imvo Zabantsundu*, a Xhosa-language paper in the Eastern Cape, had 50,000 circulation the same year.

Historically, various groups in South Africa—mainly some English-speaking whites, the defeated Afrikaners after the Boer War, the urban Africans, and, to a lesser extent, the Coloureds and Asians—have utilized newspapers and the printed word to express their political aspirations and to contest at times either English or Afrikaner domination. This political discord is further reflected in three distinct concepts or theories of the press—Afrikaner, English, and African—coexisting uncomfortably within South Africa. The Afrikaner press has historically been an instrument of National party political aspirations; it served to bring the National party to power and generally supports goals of the Nationalists. The English press concept, anchored in private ownership and reflecting Anglo-American traditions of press freedom, calls for an informational and critical role. The English press regards itself as the unofficial "opposition"—a check on the abuses of authority. However, radical critics, including some blacks, argue that the English press is itself a part of the white power structure and by its token opposition actually legitimizes the apartheid regime. This is one reason black journalists have become alienated from the English papers which both employ them and oppose apartheid. Finally, the African press, harassed and suppressed by the apartheid regime, has in recent years increasingly identified with "the struggle" and sees the printed word as one tool for bringing about basic political change and ending white hegemony. The conflicts and clashes between these three irreconcilable approaches to journalism are themes running through this study. (See Chap. 4 for a more extended analysis of the three concepts.)

For South Africa, it may be argued, has never become a true nation, in large part because the xenophobic, closely knit Afrikaner "tribe" has never really accepted the hated British or the despised blacks. (In this study, the term "blacks" usually will be used for all those discriminated against under apartheid: Africans, Asians, and Coloureds. The frequently used terms "nonwhites" or "non-Europeans" carry a negative connotation but will be used occasionally for clarity.) For that matter, Afrikaners have not welcomed any other "Uitlanders" encroaching on their exclusive "volk" concept of nationhood. The National party government, in fact, emphasizes differences among ethnic groups, especially between the African tribes, as part of a strategy of divide and rule. The mass media further this policy; for example, vernaculars are used in radio broadcasting, and there are separate television channels for white and black viewers.

Although this study focuses on government pressures and strictures on the press and mass communication since the Nationalists took power in 1948, newspapers have been embroiled in South Africa's divisive and complex politics since they were first established a century and a half after the Cape settlement was founded in 1652. The origins of the dispute between press and government go back to the early days of the white settlement at the Cape and the historical hostility between the Dutch and English settlers. In the early nineteenth century, for example, some English journals at the Cape campaigned against slavery—the abolition of which was one reason for the Boer trek to the interior in 1836. Later, when the discovery of gold brought a flood of immigrants to the republic the Boers had established in the Transvaal, the English-language newspapers there became a mouthpiece for immigrant grievances. In the events leading up to the Boer War, the leading English paper, *The Star*, was implicated in a conspiracy to invade the Transvaal Republic and overthrow Afrikaner control. After the Jameson Raid failed in 1896, the Kruger government passed a law giving the president the right to ban the distribution of newspapers that were "contrary to good morals or dangerous to peace and order in the republic." Through the years, newspaper owners and editors—British, Afrikaners, and blacks—were far more than passive chroniclers of events; they were politically engaged and used their presses to pursue their own economic and political goals.

For their part, the various rulers, whether British colonial governors, presidents of Boer republics, or Afrikaner prime ministers, provided ample precedents for the official suppression of expression. Chapter 2 shows that when the National party took control of the government in 1948, the rules of the game already were well established. The censorious and repressive measures that followed were not something new, but a continuation of a historical process.

Through more than a hundred laws, Nationalist-controlled parliaments have closed off from press and public scrutiny large areas of important information, especially concerning police, prisons, military, and security matters. Political critics have been harassed, banned, detained, or imprisoned under a policy that equates normal (by Western democratic standards) criticism, dissent, or even repeated expressions of black political aspirations with disloyalty, subversion, or treason. Black journalists and black newspapers have been singled out for particularly harsh treatment.

One tragic consequence of this continuous repression of expression has been the near demise of any kind of meaningful public dialogue between the white minority and the nonwhite majority. Another result is the virtual obliteration of any black political expression through either print or electronic media that is of, by, and for the 24 million-plus Africans, Coloureds, and Asians. Furthermore, the opposition English-language newspapers have been subjected to mounting pressures and restrictions from newly passed or threatened legal controls or from governmental intimidation and harassment.

The long saga of the Press Council, discussed in Chapter 3, illustrates the presures and intimidations directed against the press by successive National party governments and the newspapers' responses to those pressures. From 1952 to 1982, the same political drama has been played out again and again: first come harsh official criticisms directed at newspapers, followed by threats of new statutory controls if the press does not "discipline" itself. The newspaper publishers have responded by first establishing a press council and then modifying it over time to fit government requirements. Some regard this as abject self-censorship by the newspapers to appease their Afrikaner masters and so protect their financial interests. By "feeding cookies to the tiger," the press has placated the government on each occasion, but at the same time has given away more and more of its freedom and independence.

As for other important forms of expression—books, motion pictures, ephemera, and university publications—they have long been subjected to censorship, based primarily in the past on the religious and moral precepts of the Afrikaners as taught by the Calvinistic Dutch Reformed church and several fundamentalist offshoots. More recently, censorship of erotic and literary expression has eased somewhat while suppression of politically relevant expression has increased. (see Chap. 7, Censorship under the Publications Acts.)

In the area of official information and propaganda, National party governments have used public communication to persuade and influence, both at home and abroad. Traditionally, the Afrikaans-language newspapers, as primarily political instruments of Afrikaner nationalism, have been financially supported by Afrikaner interests and regional party groups and, therefore, have operated without the commercial constraints of the independent English-language newspaper enterprises. Major National party leaders, including Daniel Malan, J. G. Strijdom, Hendrik Verwoerd, and P. W. Botha, have been closely identified with newspapers such as *Die Burger, Die Transvaler,* and *Die Vaderland,* longtime steadfast advocates of National party policies. Since becoming more successful as commercial enterprises, the Afrikaans papers are showing more editorial independence on specific issues, but are still essentially loyal to the National party. Two small but notable exceptions are *Die Patriot* and *Die Afrikaner*, mouthpieces for ultra-right-wing Afrikaner parties defying the Nationalists. (See Chap. 8 for an analysis of the changing Afrikaans press.)

Similarly, the South African Broadcasting Corporation (SABC) has long functioned as a propaganda tool of the National party. Though the SABC is operated by a nongovernmental body patterned after the British Broadcasting Corporation, the dominant Afrikaner elites, operating through the secret *Broederbond*, gained control of it years ago and have used the radio and, since 1976, the television broadcasting monopoly to further the goals and interests of the government and the National party. SABC's pervasive and technically efficient broadcasting system runs sixteen radio services and three television services broadcasting a total of 2,269 hours a week in seventeen languages, making it a powerful force for molding public opinion in South Africa. (See Chap. 9).

The National party has also drawn on the full resources of its government to influence opinion at home as well as abroad and to counter what it considers hostile and distorted news and information about South Africa's system of apartheid. (The American and British press and their correspondents based in Johannesburg are particularly blamed today for South Africa's negative image in the world.) The surprising dimensions of these covert and often illegal propaganda efforts were revealed by the opposition English-language press in the Information Department scandals of 1978–79, popularly known as "Muldergate." The Muldergate revelations showed the English press at its investigative best, but the price of its journalistic enterprise has been increased hostility from National party leaders as well as further restrictions on news gathering. (See Chap. 10).

Today's mass media of communication, whether independent of or closely identified with government, are business enterprises that seek ever wider audiences, that sell advertising, and that try to make profits for their proprietors or stockholders. Changes in the sales, readership, and circulations of newspapers and other publications or in the audiences and use of radio and television have important political implications since these factors often determine what kinds of media will prosper and survive to tell what version of events. Not all pressures on the media are political and direct; some are subtle, indirect influences of a financial and economic nature. Some newspapers are finding that their profits diminish when they strongly criticize government policies or report what some white readers and advertisers consider "too much" news about the black community or about continuing racial tensions. (See Chap. 11).

A central thesis of this study is that freedom of the press—the right to talk serious politics and to report and criticize government with impunity—now nonexistent for the black majority, has been steadily declining for the white population as well. Some South African journalists believe that the indistinct line between meaningful press freedom and unacceptable government control has already been crossed.

The general election of April 1981 revealed the strong hold that the most reactionary and intransigent elements of the Afrikaner elite hold over the National party. And the car bomb attack of May 20, 1983, in downtown Pretoria, which killed 17 people and wounded 188, was only one of a series of events that have escalated the deadly confrontation and hardened the lines between two nationalisms—Afrikaner and African. For to the beleaguered Afrikaners, survival is first and foremost. Further, it must be survival on *their* terms—with no basic dismantling of the apartheid apparatus and no real sharing of political power. But the black majority will settle for nothing less and is supported in its political goals by all of black Africa and much of world opinion.

White South Africa, in its unswerving maintenance of its "way of life," has been evolving into a militaristic state, with totalitarian overtones. Prosperous and technologically sophisticated though it may be for a minority of its citizens, the only freedom of expression may in time be the freedom to support and applaud an increasingly repressive and arbitrary government whose racial policies have made it a unique pariah of the contemporary world.

How government and media relationships have evolved to this current state of affairs is what this book is about.

**The
Press
and
Apartheid**

Repression
and Propaganda
in
South Africa

1 | "Total Onslaught" against the Press

The persistent tensions between the ruling National party and the press are rooted in South Africa's turbulent history of long-standing economic, ethnic, and political cleavages. The press, reflecting as it does the clashing views and political differences within the Republic, becomes inextricably enmeshed in the news and comments it reports and, in so doing, becomes the target of repressive efforts designed to resist change. For as the South African government comes under increasing pressures from opponents of apartheid at home and abroad, so does freedom of expression within South Africa diminish.

The government of Prime Minister P. W. Botha has invoked new catchwords to describe these tensions. South Africa, Botha has asserted, is in peril from a "total onslaught" by its enemies foreign and domestic; to survive, the nation must adopt a counterattacking "total strategy." "Total strategy" requires, among other measures, a supporting and conforming press; for to the ruling Nationalists, critical and carping newspapers have become part of "the enemy."

In recent years, a series of seismic events have rocked the Republic, and these in turn have hardened government attitudes toward its critics and dissenters and have led to tougher and more restrictive measures against expression.

Uprising in Soweto

Major shocks were set off by the Soweto riots which began in June 1976 as a peaceful protest by black youths against the use of the Afrikaans language as the medium of instruction in the schools. By

3

the time the tear gas and the gunsmoke had cleared, more than six hundred were dead; unofficial estimates went as high as one thousand. Because white reporters and photographers were sealed off from the sprawling black ghetto near Johannesburg by the police and by African suspicion, only black journalists were able to report the facts of this major event, which assumed the proportions of an insurrection. The opposition English-language papers, especially the *Rand Daily Mail* and the black-oriented *World*, thoroughly covered the events as reported by the black journalists on their staffs. For the opposition papers, Soweto was primarily a major news story, in part because it validated their warnings about where apartheid policies were taking South Africa. The depth of black anger and despair reverberated throughout the Republic, and this shocked most whites who interpreted the events as a direct and immediate challenge to the stability and continuity of white rule.

Besides suppressing the protesters, the police and military cracked down on those reporting the event. Black reporters were beaten or arrested and held without charges. Journalists and photographers literally disappeared, and their families, as well as their editors, did not know whether they were alive or dead. Even months later, some black journalists were still in detention, and still others were being arrested on charges of having helped ignite the uprising. Many were arrested under the Terrorism Act, and most were eventually released without trial. Within the journalism profession and the black community, however, black journalists gained new status. As Benjamin Pogrund, deputy editor of the *Rand Daily Mail*, said at the time, "Without the courage and determination of the black journalists, the world would never have known what really happened in the Soweto riots."[1]

Authorities blamed the press for fomenting the riots and exacerbating an already dangerous situation, but the government's own Cillie Commission later exonerated the press, deciding it played no part in causing the unrest. The commission indeed expressed appreciation for the balanced reportage of newspapers at the time. The commission also gave an official toll of that tragedy and its aftermath: 575 people dead—494 Africans, 75 Coloured people, 2 whites, and 1 Indian.

Police action resulted in 451 of these deaths; 124 others were killed by other than police. Of the total dead, 134 were under eighteen, 113 of them dead by police action.[2]

Ironically, the Soweto riots were the first major news story for the newly established television service of the South African Broadcasting Corporation (SABC), which went on the air in January 1976. Television reports about Soweto rioting confirmed that television news, like that of SABC radio for decades before, would serve the propaganda interests of the National party.

Radio and television deliberately underplayed the Soweto events. SABC's annual report for 1976 claimed that "every effort was made to place the disturbance in the black townships in the proper perspective and to control passions." (However, anxious South Africans, assured each evening by SABC-TV that all was quiet, read next morning in their newspapers that all hell had broken loose the night before.)[3] Foreign television cameras were barred from Soweto, and so, for this story of worldwide interest, foreign broadcasters had to rely on carefully edited film provided by the SABC. Even so, television reportage of Soweto, beamed by communication satellite around the world, had a powerful impact and contributed significantly to world reaction to the uprising. As a watershed event in race relations, Soweto set off racial political tremors that have rumbled through South Africa ever since.

1977 Crackdown on Apartheid Foes

In response to the unrest over the death in police custody of Black Consciousness leader Steve Biko and the closure of Soweto schools following a walkout of teachers and students, the South African government on October 19, 1977, resorted to its most drastic actions to date under the Internal Security Act. Eighteen organizations, including the Black People's Convention, the Christian Institute, and the South African Student's Organization (SASO), were declared unlawful under the Internal Security Act; three publications, including the *World*, were prohibited; forty-seven black leaders including *World* editor Percy Qoboza and Dr. N. H. Motlana, a spokesman for the people of Soweto, were arrested and held in preventive detention, and seven prominent whites, including Dr. Beyers Naude, director of the Christian Institute, and Donald Woods, editor of the *Daily Dispatch* of East London, who had campaigned editorially for a full-scale probe of Steve Biko's death, were banned.

Qoboza, and *Weekend World* news editor Aggrey Klaaste, were arrested and their newspapers closed for "contributing to a subversive situation." Woods was pulled off a plane bound for the United States and banned from practicing journalism for five years. Although more liberal than most, Woods was a well-regarded establishment editor. The banning of a newspaperman of such repute was unprecedented. Woods later fled the country.

These severe measures were significant in that the *World* and *Weekend World* were not typical of the many small black publications that had been suppressed over the years. Although edited for blacks and largely staffed with blacks, these successful newspapers were owned and managed by the profitable Argus company.

A Scandal Called Muldergate

If Afrikaner self-confidence was shaken by the events set off by Soweto, then it was rocked to its very foundations by the accumulation of newspaper revelations called "Muldergate." During 1978, a series of exposures in the English newspapers, mainly the *Rand Daily Mail* and the *Sunday Express*, showed a widespread pattern of secret and illegal expenditures of vast sums of government monies ($74 million was placed in a 1972 secret fund) to win friends and punish the enemies of South Africa both at home and abroad. The press disclosures covered a wide range of covert and illegal activities of the Information Department, directed by Information Secretary Eschel Rhoodie, that spread over several continents. The scandal went right to the uppermost seats of power implicating Prime Minister John Vorster, Information Minister Connie Mulder (heir apparent to Vorster as prime minister), and other cabinet members.

Of the two hundred or so secret projects, of which only a small fraction were exposed, the opposition press took a special interest in those directed at the National party's particular "enemy"—the English-language press. An estimated R 32 million (R 1 = $1.15) were put into secret government funding of *The Citizen*, a progovernment newspaper launched in Johannesburg to provide something the National party had never had before: editorial support in an English-language newspaper. The morning market was chosen to place it in direct competition with the *Rand Daily Mail*, long the National party's bête noire.

Other media projects included subsidies for *To the Point*, a conservative newsmagazine with an international circulation, and a loan of about R 10 million to U.S. publisher John McGoff for his unsuccessful attempt to buy the *Washington Star*. The extensive secret efforts to buy media influence around the world reflected the somewhat naive view of many white South Africans (including some high in politics) that if the world only had the full facts about South Africa, then it would understand why "separate development" was necessary to preserve that "bastion of Western civilization on the southern tip of Africa."

A full analysis of Muldergate is provided in Chapter 10, and it shows that the final results were far different from the comparable Watergate scandal in the United States, which also involved official malfeasance and a subsequent cover-up. The thorough and careful investigative reporting of Mervyn Rees, Kitt Katzin, and others showed South African journalism at its best, but the results were somewhat anticlimactic. Two National party giants, Vorster and Mulder, were brought down. But the National party itself survived along with its dominance over South African politics, as Botha and the Cape Nationalists took over from the Transvaal branch of the party. One result of Muldergate, however, was that it tarnished badly the image of Afrikaner leaders as honest, incorruptible, and forthright. However, unlike Watergate, not a single person implicated in the scandal, not even Eschel Rhoodie, went to jail.

Most ominous for the press was the reaction of the government to Muldergate—perhaps the biggest political scandal in South African history. Rather than propose reforms to prevent such abuses from recurring, the government's first response was to take legislative steps to restrict future reporting of government scandals. It was also quite apparent that the various covert and unauthorized projects of the Information Department had not all been terminated. Some were in fact continued, including a number of secret projects never exposed in the first place.

Total Onslaught

With the ascendancy of Minister of Defense P. W. Botha to prime minister in 1979 as a result of Muldergate, something new and threatening was added both to politics and to press/government relationships. Owing to his long and close involvement with the defense forces and with military officers, particularly Gen. Magnus Malan (later Botha's minister of defense), the influence on government policies of the military and its perceptions became more apparent. Gen. Malan had earlier interpreted the rolling tide of black nationalism and decolonization in southern Africa as a Soviet-inspired "total onslaught" seeking by all available means to spread Marxist influence through the neighboring black countries with the ultimate purpose of attaining Soviet dominance over South Africa and its strategic minerals. The South African response, he argued repeatedly, had to be a "total strategy" that would meet the threat in the political, economic, and psychological spheres as well as the military one.

Both in their rhetoric and their actions, Botha and his small circle of advisers have been markedly influenced by this military thinking. The message was apocalyptic since it suggested that the white man's very existence in South Africa was threatened. But both Botha and Malan were not unaware that a "total strategy" required black cooperation, and therefore white South Africa would have to change to meet the political and economic challenges of the black majority. And so Botha added another catch phrase, "adapt or die," to his political lexicon. The implications of the enunciated need to adapt or die, coupled with Botha's promises to end some "petty" aspects of apartheid, such as the Immorality Act, led many to believe that significant changes in the whole apartheid structure were imminent. This has proved to be largely a false hope so far; for one thing, any amelioration of apartheid evokes opposition from right-wing Afrikaners inside and outside the National party.

It soon became apparent that "total strategy" also meant that opponents and dissidents were expected to get "on side" and support uncritically the policies and actions of the National party regardless of where they led the country. All elements of society, Botha argued—business, working people, the churches, various political groups, and especially the press—must work together for the national interest of withstanding the Soviet threat and maintaining white control. Consequently, "total strategy" has brought with it an accelerating official intolerance of much criticism and reporting.

Straightforward press reports of labor unrest or strikes or of ordinary black activities, for example, are increasingly regarded as subversive and disloyal, and, in the final analysis, treasonous. This paranoid *laager* mentality, which views much of the English-language press as "aiding the enemy," has exacerbated the already poor relationships between journalists and those running South Africa.

Botha and his colleagues not only demanded uncritical support for Nationalist policies but also reserved the right to define the limits of reporting. The public need not be kept informed of all government actions in pursuance of "total strategy," even when South Africa undertakes armed conflict beyond its borders. As Anthony Mathews has pointed out, South Africa's 1975 intervention in Angola "more than anything else, starkly revealed official information practices and the impotence of the press to inform the public about a matter as momentous as the invasion of a neighboring country by South African forces."[4] At the time, P. W. Botha was minister of defense.

The incursion on the National Union for the Total Independence of Angola (UNITA) side of the Angolan civil war, which was urged by the U.S. government and from which the South Africans finally withdrew under U.S. pressures, had enormous implications for South Africa, and, hence, the public clearly had a right to know what was happening. But the majority of South Africans were kept in ignorance until after their forces were withdrawn from Angola. Though constrained by laws and harassed by military censorship, some papers tried to inform the public about these events, but could only hint at the real situation and allude to "rumors" of the invasion printed abroad.[5]

Several other military adventures have followed, including the Cassinga massacre in Angola in 1978 in which six hundred refugees, mostly women and children, perished; the raid of African National Congress headquarters in Maputo in early 1981; the September 1981 strike into Angola in which a reported one thousand SWAPO (South West Africa Peoples Organization) supporters were killed and a large cache of Soviet arms and equipment captured; and the night assault into Maseru, Lesotho (December 1982), directed, as the military announced, at recently arrived African National Congress "terrorists," which killed forty-two people, including twenty-nine black South Africans, some of whom were legitimate political refugees.

These foreign incursions, along with the protracted low-level guerrilla war for Namibian independence in which the South African Defense Force has roamed at will into both Angola and Zambia, gave a distinctly military cast to the Botha government. The unmistakable indications were that the government was thinking more and more of military solutions to its problems, both internally and externally. Some called it a militarization of the South African government and society. In all of these cross-border incursions, information to the press was carefully controlled and orchestrated, with the South African public finding out well after the fact and then only from official sources. Journalists were occasionally taken on official conducted tours of combat areas in Namibia, but no independent reporting of military activities was permitted. The press, of course, was expected to support these activities and most newspapers did or, at least, withheld criticism.

Ten days after the Maseru raid, bombs exploded in the Koeberg nuclear power station twenty-five miles from Cape Town, and the African National Congress claimed credit for the sabotage. This incident suggested that sabotage initiated by the ANC, a legal organization for nearly fifty years before it was banned and forced underground in 1961, would increase. Before 1983, most ANC sabotage had been aimed at installations, not people. But more recent incidents indicate a change of tactics. In February 1983, a bomb explosion in Bloemfontein injured 76 blacks, and two months later a car bomb explosion in Pretoria killed 17 and injured 188; both indicated that the ante had been raised and that urban terrorism would become more deadly. Few doubt that sabotage and terrorist attacks against whites will escalate, as will the government's preemptive strikes against ANC bases outside South Africa. Further, assassination by gunmen, letter bombs, and car bombs have all befallen ANC leaders in exile during 1981–82, which may push the ANC into further terrorism. These events have contributed to an increasing polarization between the white and black communities and have had the effect of pushing some of the opposition newspapers closer to the Nationalists' positions.

In press/government relations, the attitude of the prime minister himself as the political leader of the National party has always been a key factor. P. W. Botha not only was clearly hostile toward the English-language newspapers but, in the opinion of many journalists, did not understand the press. He gave lip service to press freedom, they said, but felt strongly that the press should *always* support government aims and policies. One outspoken critic, Joel Mervis, former editor of the *Sunday Times*, says that Botha's expectations of what the press should be doing are a distortion of what good journalism is all about, that he apparently does not understand that the press has an obligation to report all the news, including that which reflects badly on the government. Even normal journalistic practices are in Botha's view a breach of responsibility. Mervis does not believe that Botha wants the government to take over the press or institute official censorship, but thinks Botha is looking for a lever or formula to accomplish the same thing. According to Mervis, Botha has crystalized the conviction that the press has the obligation to support the "total strategy" and that a "responsible" press will do so.[6]

The continuing and rising tensions between the races and, by extension, between the government and the press have been as much a fact of life in the 1980s as they were in the 1970s. Unquestionably, black militancy rose sharply in the first years of the new decade as manifested by continuing school boycotts, labor unrest and strikes, and deadly acts of urban terrorism. Some National party leaders felt that the newspapers, by merely reporting these news events, were provoking the blacks to even more opposition and violence. As one government official said: "We can't see ourselves governing this country as long as some newspapers go on as they do."[7]

The prime minister, cabinet ministers, and other officials clearly enunciated the government's perception of the press as an instigating factor in black activism. Marais Steyn, minister of Coloured and Indian affairs, for instance, asserted that "propaganda" carried by the English-language papers exaggerated the extent of the 1980 school boycott, thereby encouraging more students to join in. Newspapers, he said, would have to "decide whether they were on the side of law and order or whether they were on the side of those attempting to bring about change by force."[8]

In Parliament, the prime minister said he would curb the press if newspapers continued to give prominence to "activities of subversive or revolutionary elements" and that he would order the SABC-TV "not to headline subversive or revolutionary elements."[9] (The television reference raised a few eyebrows because the government has long claimed the SABC was independent of government controls.) Later the prime minister charged that the outlawed ANC had intensified its efforts to infiltrate certain sections of the mass media which were playing a leading role in the "total onslaught" on South Africa.

And the government acted. During the June 1980 unrest following the commemoration of those who had died in Soweto in 1976, police banned journalists from entering townships and other "operational areas," i.e., areas where police and security forces were active. Foreign journalists also were barred because, police claimed, foreign television cameramen had been seen inciting people in Soweto to riot, a charge vehemently denied by the foreign correspondents. On June 20, 1980, with widespread strikes in Uitenhage, the industrial area near Port Elizabeth, the entire town as well as the surrounding townships was declared an operational area. Journalists could enter only with police permission and under police escort. Photographs were prohibited. These developments culminated in the announcement on June 27, 1980, of the establishment of the Commission of Inquiry into the Mass Media under the chairmanship of Justice M. T. Steyn, who had headed an earlier commission that looked into the reporting of security matters (see Chap. 4).

Meanwhile, harassment of journalists, black and white, continued. Newsmen were brought before the courts to disclose their sources of information, detained in prison for questioning, or charged with various offenses. Journalists' applications for passports were routinely refused. In addition to these administrative actions, the government, although already armed with numerous laws to retrict press coverage, indicated that further restrictive legislation was in the offing. In a way, these threats were unsurprising. From the earliest days of his tenure as prime minister, Botha had sought press conformity through legislation, some of which was passed, some just threatened.

Perhaps most press outrage was expressed over the government's response to the Muldergate scandal of 1978–79—the controversial Advocate General Act. Journalists called it the "gagging act," since it clearly was designed to eliminate the watchdog function of the press in relation to official corruption and misconduct. As proposed, once the newly appointed "advocate general" started an investigation of official conduct, the matter would become *sub judice*, and the press could no longer comment on it. The exposure of Muldergate probably would have been impossible if the Advocate General Act had been in effect. According to Allister Sparks, former editor of the *Rand Daily Mail*, this act was "part of an emerging pattern which is beginning to characterize the P. W. Botha administration; a pattern of military style leadership, with tighter and more direct state control in all spheres."[10]

The lengthy, acrimonious public debate over the Advocate General Act showed a marked change of attitude by the Afrikaans newspapers, once described as showing "dogged, all-weather loyalty to the National Party." The Afrikaans press opposed the legislation as vigorously as the English papers and resumed their party-supporting role only when the legislation was watered down. This was the first time in thirty-one years that the Afrikaans press had openly defied its National party leadership. At least some Afrikaans editors apparently felt that the government had gone too far in its efforts to shackle the press.

Another Botha-sponsored law with restrictive press provisions was the Second Police Amendment Act, which prohibited publication of stories about police movements and methods of combating terrorism. Journalists considered the Police Act particularly egregious because it placed significant police matters beyond the reach of press or public scrutiny. One newspaper executive said, "It's the first step toward the Gestapo. Once a person falls into the hands of the police, we will not be able to obtain information about a person's arrest, trial, or disposition."[11] For three important areas of public concern—police, defense, and prisons—the principle had, in effect, been established that the press cannot report anything unless cleared by government authorities.

This power to control information was further strengthened by the passage in June 1982 of the Protection of Information Act which provided jail sentences of up to ten years for the unauthorized disclosure of information about a security matter involving terrorists. (See Chap. 5 for more details on this and other recent legislation.)

Often legislation or threats of legislation have been accompanied or followed by specific actions against newspapers and journalists. The black press, for instance, suffered a series of crippling blows from the government in early 1981. The *Post* (Transvaal) and *Sunday Post*, the only two black newspapers in the country with significant daily and weekly circulations, were suspended from publication, and the security police served banning orders on several leading black journalists who were officers of the black journalists trade union. The *Post* had a daily sale of 112,000, but its actual daily readership was estimated at 907,000. The *Sunday Post* had a sale of 118,000, and an estimated readership of more than 1 million.

Before the ban, the government had been playing a curious cat-and-mouse game with the *Post* newspapers and their owner, the Argus company. The papers' troubles began with a strike by black journalists demanding better pay and working conditions that kept the papers off the streets for two months. After much wrangling, Argus and the black union, the Media Workers Association of South Africa (MWASA), finally reached an agreement. At that point, the government informed the management that its licenses to print had lapsed because the papers had failed to appear for two months. Upon appeal, a judge upheld this ruling. Still it seemed only an annoying technicality until, unexpectedly, Minister of Internal Affairs Chris Heunis and Justice Minister H. J. Coetsee informed Argus company chief Hal Miller that if the company insisted on proceeding with a reregistration application, the government would ban the papers forthwith under the Internal Security Act. There is no right of appeal against such a banning, and Argus did not proceed. Miller said: "We have no power to prevent the government's action, no redress against the course it has chosen to follow. We think that by acting this way it diminishes us all—that another bar has been added to the cage which is beginning to circumscribe our freedom."[12] Why the authorities chose to take this drastic measure was difficult to understand, especially at a time when the government was trying to present a more moderate image to the world as the new Reagan administration was taking office in Washington.

Shocked and angry reaction within and from outside of South Africa followed these actions. Dave Dalling, a Progressive Federal party spokesman, was blunt: "The banning is a fascist step that is bringing the revolution nearer." Even the Afrikaans press joined the worldwide outcry. Editorials in both *Die Transvaler* and *Beeld* questioned the necessity of closing the papers, and *Die Transvaler* said the banning of the journalists smacked of arbitrary action against individual freedom. Overseas critics condemned the closures and bannings as part of a further attack on press freedom in South Africa.

The government was indeed hard pressed to justify its actions. Justice Minister Coetsee said the government was convinced that the actions of the *Post* and *Sunday Post* were "aimed at creating a revolutionary climate in South Africa." The editorial offices of the papers, he claimed, "were used as a venue for the final briefing of prospective terrorists before they left South Africa." The *Post* newspapers had provided much propaganda for the African National Congress and had become vehicles of activism, militancy, radicalism, and subversion, the minister said. But many found it hard to believe that the conservative Argus company would permit two of its own newspapers to be used for such purposes. Harvey Tyson, editor of Argus's *The Star*, said, "If the State has evidence of this attempted subversion, it should have prosecuted those responsible. Instead it closed down the newspapers, breaking a fundamental principle of freedom and bringing opprobrium on South Africa from even the most conservative democratic nations." The charge that the papers were fomenting revolution was challenged even by *Beeld*, the prime minister's mouthpiece in the Transvaal. Its editor, Ton Vosloo, said, "As regular and critical readers of the newspapers, we saw no sign of this in their published editions."[13]

The concurrent banning of prominent black journalists in early 1981 was equally chilling. Zwelakhe Sisulu, president of MWASA, and Marimuthu Subramoney, the union's Natal vice-president, were restricted to their hometowns and forbidden to take part in any journalistic or political activities. (Sisulu was later held in detention for over eight months.) Several weeks later, banning orders were served on Mathata Tsedu, Phil Mtimkulu, and Joe Thloloe, all of whom had worked for the *Post* and had been officers in MWASA. Both Tsedu and Thloloe were detained in 1982.

These actions against the black press illuminated several strongly held attitudes of the National party leadership. Whenever black political expression occurs, even in such a bland forum as that of a white-owned newspaper published for blacks, the government can and often will act ruthlessly to suppress it. The government is also quite willing to endure harsh condemnation at home and abroad when it decides to suppress black political expression. Yet at the same time, Botha and his colleagues reveal a perhaps paranoid and exaggerated fear of any expression that runs counter to their own political and moral beliefs. In incidents like these and the 1977 banning of the *World* and *Weekend World*, the prime minister and his cabinet appeared to be captives of the fears and suspicions of their police and security advisers about the power of the media to sway the country's political and social outsiders.

This concern about black political expression carries over into the application of the nation's basic censorship law, the Publications Act of 1974. The law, and its predecessor, the Publications and Entertainments Act of 1963, provide an elaborate mechanism for censorship of virtually all expression except for the thirty or so daily and Sunday newspapers and eighty-eight other periodicals belonging to the Newspaper Press Union.

Pressures from an increasingly sophisticated and worldly urban public have resulted in less and less censorship of books and motion pictures on grounds of obscenity and blasphemy. At the same time, however, restraints on political expression, especially that of blacks and university students, markedly increased during the years after

Soweto. Well-known fiction writers, such as Nadine Gordimer and André Brink, found it easier to get their antiapartheid novels published within South Africa. But black writers and anyone dealing with black nationalism faced official suppression of their works. For as Chapter 7 explains, official control of expression through censorship is regarded as an essential instrument with which to maintain Afrikaner political dominance as well as Calvinistic religious and moral values.

And the threat of censorship has sometimes led to self-censorship. The white press of South Africa enjoyed a rare, if brief, moment of consensus when all segments informed the Steyn Commission during 1980–81 that further legislation to restrict news gathering was unneeded. But the deep differences remained between the Afrikaans and English papers, exemplified by the absence of an organization of journalists that would include both linguistic groups. Within the English press itself, significant splits exist, none more divisive than that between the publishers' group, the Newspaper Press Union (NPU), and the Southern Africa Society of Journalists (SASJ), the professional organization of English-speaking journalists. (Afrikaans journalists chose not to belong to SASJ and most black journalists identify with MWASA.) Besides the usual differences between management and labor, the two groups are split in their positions with regard to self-censorship in the face of government pressures.

Working journalists and some editors feel that the newspaper publishers and managers have been far too willing to censor themselves in order to placate National party critics and head off further statutory press restraints. Instead of continuing to appease the government critics, thereby giving up their freedom a little at a time, management should, many in SASJ (and in editors' chairs as well) believe, draw a line and resist all efforts to restrict press freedom. Central to the dispute is the proper role of the Press Council—an instrument for self-regulation if not self-censorship. (Such self-censorship is a central concern of this study and is discussed in Chap. 3.)

Self-censorship takes many forms and is not easily identified. Failure to report certain news stories is the usual manifestation, but why a particular news story was not used is often difficult to determine. A story about, say, dislocation of blacks may not be reported because it may offend the government, or is of little interest to white readers, or simply because an editor decides it is not news. Whatever the reason, some observers feel that even the most outspoken papers, such as the *Rand Daily Mail* and *Cape Times*, have pulled their punches on occasion.

The removal in mid 1981 of Allister Sparks as editor of the *Rand Daily Mail* was a case in pont. Several reasons were offered for his dismissal, all reflecting the ambiguity of the situation. The paper had been losing money, and the South African Associated Newspapers (SAAN), the owners, hoped that a change of editors might help in Johannesburg's highly competitive situation. The *Mail*'s outspoken opposition to apartheid and its aggressive reporting of the black community and the inequities it suffers are often cited as a primary reason for the *Mail*'s financial problems. A good many white readers (and advertisers) do not particularly enjoy reading about such unpleasant realities; Sparks's firing was possibly designed to moderate the paper's voice. By replacing the liberal editorial line with a more soothing conservative one, management perhaps felt that more white readers would become attracted to the paper once again. However, some observers interpreted Sparks's ouster as an act of political appeasement by the SAAN board in a bid to dissuade the government from introducing more antipress legislation. Whatever the real reasons for Spark's dismissal—and there are probably several—the aroma of self-censorship hangs over the whole affair, and many in South Africa working for peaceful change were dispirited by Sparks's departure.

To survive in the marketplace, newspapers cannot be too divergent politically from their readers or advertisers. *The Star* of Johannesburg, the biggest and most financially successful daily in the Republic, is more moderate in tone and strives to reassure its white readership. As a result, *The Star* makes money and the *Rand Daily Mail* has been a losing operation for years.

Another national debate in the press (and about the press) was set off in early 1982 when the Steyn Commission finally submitted a 1,400-page report to Parliament.[14] As expected, the commission recommended a number of sweeping proposals for yet further controls over the opposition press. When the hearings first began in 1980, journalists had predicted that the commission would recommend a register of journalists—a system of licensing similar to that of the medical profession. Many journalists regarded the register as another Botha proposal to "tame" or control the press without actually placing a government censor in every newspaper office. Even the Afrikaans newspapers had opposed the register.

The Steyn Commission's proposal for a legally enforced "professionalization" of South African journalism with a code of conduct was contained in its proposed Journalists Bill. However, following public and press criticism, the government hesitated to push the bill through Parliament. The solid front of opposition from both Afrikaans and English newspapers was undoubtedly a major reason.

A compromise was reached in mid 1982, and the newspaper publishers agreed to set up a new media or press council of their own with powers to fine and reprimand journalists, but not to strike newspersons from any register of journalists. But in the final hours of the 1982 parliamentary session, the Registration of Newspapers Amendment Act was pushed through by the Nationalists. The act provides that the minister of internal affairs may cancel the registration of any newspapers if the publishers of such newspapers do not subject themselves for disciplinary purposes to a body concerned with journalistic standards. Thus, the two right-wing newspapers, *Die Patriot* and *Die Afrikaner*, which did not belong to the NPU, would come under the jurisdiction of the new Media Council. So, once again, the newspapers, threatened by tough new laws, agreed to further regulate themselves and yield a little more of their freedom, and once again the government backed off. (See Chap. 4 for more on the Steyn Commission.)

The future of press freedom in South Africa will be determined not only by the government's intimidating "total onslaught" policies and additional legal rstraints, but also by the willingness of white South Africa to support a press relatively independent of government influence. Here again, the prognosis is not good. The majority of the affluent, privileged whites, who still enjoy a monopoly of political power, put their own economic and political survival first. This is most clearly shown in the overwhelming majorities the National party has enjoyed in Parliament since coming to power in 1948 and retained again in the 1981 election. Obviously many English speakers supported the Afrikaner-dominated Nationalists, and Botha himself seems more concerned about the apprehensions of the far right than those voiced by the more moderate Progressive Federal party.

As a group, white South Africans show little understanding of or concern for freedom of the press and do not feel that their own freedoms are jeopardized when black newspapers are closed down or journalists arrested. The white public, with the exception of a comparatively few liberals, are far more concerned about the vague "total onslaught" than what has happened to civil liberties of fellow South Africans. And the majority blacks, of course, find little reason to support the whites' freedom of the press because they have none themselves.

2 | The Roots of the Conflict

As immediate as are the tragic difficulties facing the diverse peoples and the press of South Africa, it is important to realize that the causes are embedded in South African history. The further one goes back in South African press history, the clearer it becomes that little has changed. From the earliest days of the colonial press, newspapers in South Africa have been identified with one or other of the dominant white language groups, with their very different cultures, political philosophies, and economic interests. They have reflected, and been a part of, the struggle for power between these groups. No matter what government happened to be in power at any given time, one section felt it was not represented, and expressed its opposition vociferously through its newspapers. The continuing gulf between the population groups has meant that the country's newspapers have never outgrown the stage of a highly partisan press. (The black press—newspapers and other publications primarily intended for the African, coloured, and Asian communities—developed along such different lines that its historical background will be considered in Chap. 6, Suppression of the Black Press.) So conflict between the government of the day and the newspapers has been inevitable. At first, this conflict was essentially an internal dispute between the English settlers at the Cape in the early 1800s and their own colonial government over press freedom. No sooner had independent English newspapers been established at the Cape, however, than the earlier Dutch settlers, whose interests were threatened by the newcomers, felt a need for journals to express their point of view.

Unable to regain political ascendancy at the Cape, many of the Dutch farmers trekked beyond the borders of the colony into the interior, there to set up republics conducted to their own liking. They were not left long to their own devices. The discovery in the interior of fabulous deposits of first diamonds then gold attracted a horde of alien fortune seekers. They brought not only their own ideas as to how the Boer republics should be run, but their own newspapers to back up their demands. The conflict between the English-language newspapers in the Transvaal and the Boer government prior to the Boer War at the turn of the century offers some remarkable parallels with the present situation in the modern Republic. One ever-present issue has been policy toward the black, coloured, and Asian populations. At first the dispute was largely over slavery. Later it centered on what role, if any, blacks should have in the governance of "white" South Africa. Certainly by the end of World War II the issues and their protagonists had been identified, and the battle lines clearly demarcated.

Cape Town was the arena for the initial struggle for press freedom. As the only large population center in the colony and as the only major seaport, it was a natural communications center. News was brought from overseas by seafarers, from the interior by travelers and by farmers coming to market their goods. Being a trading center, it had a merchant class large enough to support a newspaper with advertising revenue. In addition, it was the seat of the government and the social and cultural hub of the colony. Under Dutch rule, there was no attempt to establish newspapers, although there was a move to import a press to print government notices. Nothing came of this, as the Colony was handed over to Britain soon after.

In 1800 the British governor authorized a Cape Town firm to operate as government printer. This was by no means a licence to run a newspaper—the same proclamation forbade private printing under penalty of a fine and confiscation of the press. The *Cape Town Gazette and African Advertiser* made its debut on August 16, 1800. Although devoted largely to government notices, it did carry some paragraphs of news. News fit to print was hard to come by. In the first edition, the editor lamented that "in consequence of the non-arrival of any ships from England for a long time, we feel disappointed at not being able to lay before our readers anything particularly interesting, especially to those who reside in and about the capital of the Colony." The paper had a short run, however. Within three months the governor had withdrawn the printing monopoly and bought the press, which was moved to the Castle where the paper was printed every Friday. During the restoration of the Cape to Dutch rule from 1803 to 1806, it was published in Dutch as the *Kaapsche Courant*. With the return of the British it again became bilingual. The *Courant* enjoyed a monopoly at the Cape for more than twenty years.

The first major impetus to a free press in South Africa came with the arrival of the British Settlers in 1820. The Settlers, who numbered about 4,000 in all, were encouraged to emigrate to the eastern frontier by the British government, partly to create a buffer between Xhosa and Dutch cattle farmers. They came to South Africa from a Britain in which the principle and practice of free expression were firmly rooted. In London the press was already pursuing its independent course, and the ruling Tory party was under constant attack from a growing pack of "popular" journals that championed the exploited, restless factory workers and farm laborers.

The Settlers, in fact, arrived in South Africa fully expecting to continue their cherished right as British subjects to voice their grievances. One even brought his press with him, with the intention of launching a newspaper on the Eastern Frontier. Robert Godlonton and his companion, Thomas Stringfellow, had worked for a printer in England. When they emigrated he gave them a complete printing plant. They arrived in Table Bay aboard the Settler ship *Chapman* in March 1820. The authorities soon learned of the press aboard the *Chapman*, and Godlonton discovered that conditions in the Colony were less permissive than in the mother country. Colonial authority, in the person of Sir Rufane Donkin, acting governor of the Cape in the absence of Lord Charles Somerset, intervened. Although the Settlers were generally not allowed ashore in Cape Town lest they fall in love with the fair Cape and not want to continue to the frontier, Stringfellow was summoned before Donkin, who told him that allowing them to proceed "would be equal to scattering firebrands along the Eastern

Frontier." The press was seized and, to keep it out of harm's way, was sent to the remote village of Graaff-Reinet and used to print government forms.

The Settlers found the restrictions on them at the Cape intolerable, and the colony's official gazette at best a bore. William Wilberforce Bird, controller of customs at the Cape in 1822, wrote that "the liberty of the press is a feeling so congenial to the heart of a British subject, that it is mortifying to describe such a degraded establishment as the Government Printing Office at the Cape of Good Hope. The annual circle of its duties consists in printing the Cape Calendar and Almanac, and a weekly newspaper called the *Cape Gazette*, which is in fact a mere list of proclamations, of civil and military appointments and promotions, marriages, births, christenings, deaths, the price of articles of produce, and advertisements of sales. . . . The public is rarely indulged with a scrap of European intelligence; and when such a circumstance does take place, it consists of matter suited to the submissive state of the colony . . . here are no extracts from Parliamentary debates, nothing breathing opposition or leading to discussion, for this might create the habit of thinking; nothing scientific, for that might enlighten; but the whole is a mass of uninteresting, tasteless stupidity." Bird said sixteen hundred copies of the *Gazette* were printed every Friday, of which six hundred were sent free of charge by government dispatch to officials in the colony and to government departments in Cape Town. The rest, Bird said, were bought by Cape merchants and other dealers "to guide them in their attendance upon the daily sales, and to inform them of the government regulations." The free distribution of so many papers through the colony, containing all the government advertisements, gave the *Gazette* an advantage against which no other paper could stand. This was unfortunate, Bird felt, because "a free press, bearing hard upon the vices and absurdities of mankind, is the grand corrective of the present times. Since there was little hope of a free press in Cape Town, Bird looked to the new settlers on the Easter Frontier. They would, he wrote, "not be content to bear their fanciful and real grievances without the English luxury of grumbling in print . . . it is therefore to the east that the Cape must look for liberty of the press."[1]

And within a short time one of the Settlers, Thomas Pringle, did start the colony's first independent newspaper, but not on the frontier, where the stuggle for survival in the first years was more pressing than the need for a free press. Pringle, before coming to the Cape in 1820, had been involved in Edinburgh literary circles that included the fiercely critical *Edinburgh Review*. Pringle headed the Scottish party of Settlers, who were located on the Baviaans River in the Eastern Cape. He helped the party—many of them his relatives—to establish themselves, but the lure of a literary career became too strong, and in September 1822 he left the frontier for Cape Town.[2]

His acquaintance with the influential author Sir Walter Scott procured him a post as sublibrarian at the public library. Soon he had launched an academy for English-speaking pupils in Cape Town. In November 1822, Pringle wrote to a friend in Scotland, John Fairbairn, inviting him to come out to help run the academy and suggesting they establish a journal. "There is not even a decent newspaper" in the Colony, he lamented. While awaiting Fairbairn's arrival, Pringle and a Dutch clergyman, the Rev. A. Faure, planned a monthly periodical to be called the *South African Journal*, with a Dutch edition to be known as *De Zuid Afrikaansche Tydschrift*.

By this time the governor, Lord Charles Somerset, had returned from leave in England. He ruled the Cape as a despot, tolerating no dissent, and ruthlessly persecuting those who dared inquire into his sometimes dubious dealings. Typical of his style was a proclamation issued in May 1822, prohibiting public meetings "for the discussion of public measures and political subjects" without prior permission, and stating: "It is my firm determination to put down, by all the means with which the law has entrusted me, such attempts as have recently been made to disturb the public peace, whether by inflammatory or libellous writings, or by any other measures." It is small wonder then that Somerset reacted with alarm to the news that Pringle proposed an independent journal. "I forsee great evil," he wrote to Lord Bathurst, the secretary of state for the colonies. And he took an instant dislike to Pringle, whom he described as "an arrant dissenter who had scribbled" for a journal in Scotland.[3] Pringle's application to the governor to proceed was refused. He then raised the matter with the commission of inquiry that had been sent to the Cape in 1822 by the British Parliament to investigate the strained relations between Somerset and the Settlers. The commissioners advised

Pringle and Faure to wait. Some months later, under instructions from the Colonial Office, Somerset summoned Pringle before him and, in Pringle's words: "After some admonitory remarks of his own, Lord Charles gave, with obvious reluctance, and with a very ill grace, his sanction for us to proceed with the publication." The first number appeared soon after.[4]

Meanwhile, Somerset was being badgered an another front. George Greig, a printer who had been employed in the King's Printing Office in London, arrived at the Cape bringing a press and the determination to start a periodical, which would "combine the ordinary topics of a magazine, and more particularly such as are interesting to the commercial and agricultural parts of the community." It would, he promised Somerset when asking permission to go ahead, exclude "personal controversy and all discussion of matter relating to the policy or administration of the Colonial Government." Permission was refused, but Greig, finding that there was no law against such a publication, went ahead anyway. The first issue of his *South African Commercial Advertiser* appeared on January 7, 1824. Greig edited the first two editions himself, after which Pringle and Fairbairn became joint editors.

The two journals soon ran into trouble. Although there was never any direct criticism of the governor, the *Commercial Advertiser* printed proceedings of a court case that dealt with allegations of corruption in Somerset's administration. The Cape fiscal, or magistrate, under orders from Somerset, demanded that Greig submit proof sheets of the next issue of the newspaper to him before publication. The issue duly appeared under these conditions but also with a notice declaring that "His Majesty's Fiscal having assumed censorship of the South African Commercial Advertiser . . . we find it our duty as BRITISH subjects to discontinue the publication for the present in this colony." Angered, Somerset had the press sealed.[5]

Pringle, too, refused to submit to censorship. The second number of his *South African Journal* carried an article by the editor, "The Present State and Prospects of the English Emigrants in South Africa," which listed the causes of the failure of "this ill-planned and ill-conducted enterprise." The fiscal warned Pringle that his article had displeased the governor, and demanded that he pledge not to make similar comments in future. Rather than submit, Pringle abruptly suspended publication. Pringle was summoned before the governor, whom he found with the *South African Journal* lying open before him. As Pringle records it: " 'So, Sir,' he began, 'you are one of those who dare to insult me and oppose my government,' and then he launched into a long tirade of abuse; scolding, upbraiding and taunting me, with all the domineering arrogance of mien and sneering insolence of expression of which he was so great a master."[6]

From then on the struggle was carried on in London. A petition asking for press freedom at the Cape was sent to the colonial secretary in December 1824. Greig himself took his case to London, where he was given permission to resume publication of his newspaper—provided he adhere to his original prospectus. Within a month of Greig's return, his *Commercial Advertiser* reappeared, this time under the sole editorship of John Fairbairn.

Despite further difficulties, the fight for an independent press at the Cape had in effect been won. Final victory came in April 1829, after Somerset's recall, when the new governor removed the last irritating restrictions on the press. From then on, expansion was rapid. New newspapers were started in Cape Town, then Grahamstown, and quickly spread north and east as the Settlers penetrated the interior. A list of newspapers filed with the Colonial Office in Cape Town in 1881 includes the names of more than 125 assorted journals. The Eastern Province had more than its share. In the words of Anthony Delius: "The bush positively bristled with guardians of the rights, liberties and morals of the citizens."[7]

The "Settler press" confiscated from Godlonton in 1820 was auctioned off at Graaff-Reinet to Louis Henry Meurant, who started up a newspaper in the fast-growing center of Grahamstown. The first issue of his *Graham's Town Journal* appeared in December 1831, with the motto, "Open to all parties, influenced by none." Godlonton became a partner in the firm and bought the business from Meurant five years later. Under his editorship the *Graham's Town Journal* became the spokesman for the settlers on the frontier, defending their interests against the sometimes sneering attacks of philanthropists in Cape Town and London.

To the frontiersmen the terms philanthropist or negrophilist had the same loaded meaning as the modern "nigger lover." And therein lies the genesis of the conflict that has plagued relations between the

English press in South Africa and its adversaries ever since. The views expressed by Pringle, who after leaving the Cape became secretary of the Anti-Slavery Society in London, and of the equally liberal Fairbairn, were in tune with enlightened opinion in London and to some extent in Cape Town. In politics they were identified with the philanthrophic missionaries and advocates of the native tribes. But to the settlers on the frontier, faced with the reality of stock theft, raids, and occasional all-out war with the black tribes, their ideas were wildly unrealistic. Thus when an article in the *Commerical Advertiser* in December 1834 criticizing the high-handed treatment of frontier tribes reached Grahamstown as it was girding for another war, it had an explosive effect. Nearly five hundred infuriated frontiersmen signed a declaration denouncing these and previous "false statements," and alleging that Fairbairn's visit to the frontier was among the causes of a confederacy among the Kaffir chiefs that "threatens the total ruin of a large part of the colony."[8] To the frontiersmen, Fairbairn (whose father-in-law was the controversial missionary John Philip) represented a clique of fanatics obsessed with the idea of outrages on the defenseless natives.

The frontier residents were also concerned about the effect of Fairbairn's writings on opinion abroad. Godlonton, in the *Graham's Town Journal*, complained: "The future safety and well-being of the colony depended upon the British public and government forming correct and decided opinions on the power and character of the native tribes on our border. To misapprehension on this point might be attributed all the existing disorders . . . The temerity which was displayed in giving publicity, and that within the colony, to such barefaced fabrications, excited equally the surprise and indignation both of the public and of the local government."[9] Thus the concern about the effect of South African newspapers on public opinion abroad, which was later to become a major criticism of the English-language press, can also be traced back to the colony's first independent newspapers.

If Godlonton's was representative of the reaction of English speakers, it can be understood that the Dutch were even less enamored of Fairbairn's liberal views. As one Dutch historian noted: "Although his ability was always recognized, his views regarding the native question could not be accepted by people to whom slavery had been an institution which they regarded as justifiable and not at all immoral."[10]

One reaction of the Dutch colonists was to set up a journal to counteract Fairbairn's paper. *De Zuid Afrikaan* appeared in 1828 and, according to an Afrikaans historian, was obliged from the outset not only to fight against "the radicalism of the negrophilist philanthropists," but also frequently "to defend the good name of the Dutch residents against the libels of a hostile English party at the Cape and in England."[11] To the Dutch, the terms "free press" and "independent press" came to mean organs hostile to their philosophy and way of life.

From a very early stage, then, the English press was identified with the humanitarian views of white liberals in South Africa, while the Dutch (and later Afrikaans) press represented the more conservative views of that language group. The opposing positions of the English and Afrikaans newspapers regarding the role of the press in South Africa likewise crystalized almost from the start. A Dutch newspaper, *De Mediator*, established in Cape Town in 1837, complained that "despite all the advantages that the press has brought us, which we readily acknowledge, it has done a great deal of harm to this community." *De Mediator* blamed the imported British concept of freedom of the press not only for the bloody frontier wars in the eastern Cape, but for the Great Trek of 1836, when hundreds of Dutch farming families, seeking new pastures for their stock and freedom from British rule, left the colony to found the Boer republics of the Orange Free State and the Transvaal. According to *De Mediator*, the oldest and most respected farmers "left their pastures, their hearths, the land of their birth, to trek to a wild and unknown region of the interior, because the government was no longer able to protect them."[12] The cause of all this, says *De Mediator*, was "the liberal, philanthropic, independent press." A subsequent issue of *De Mediator* objected to local reformers who were "incapable of distinguishing between freedom and responsibility"—a dichotomy that has echoed down through the years in discussions of the function of the South African press.

Despite these upheavals, Cape Town continued to flourish. By 1858 the city had eight newspapers. Among them were the revived

South African Commercial Advertiser, the *Cape Monitor*, the *Standard and Mail*, the *Cape Mercantile Advertiser*, and the *Cape Argus*. Of these, only the *Argus* has survived. In time it was to spawn Africa's largest newspaper chain.

The *Argus*, founded in 1857, was a typical commercial paper of the colonial period. It was a time of expansion at the Cape, which then had a population of about 140,000. The colonists had a growing degree of self-rule and hence a stake in public affairs. After representations from both Dutch- and English-speaking colonists, the British government granted the Cape representative government in 1853, with an elected legislative assembly. A member of the first assembly, Bryan Henry Darnell, anxious to give wider expression to his ideas, decided to start a newspaper. He approached Richard William Murray, then editor of the *Cape Monitor*, to join him as joint proprietor of the publication to be printed by Saul Solomon, owner of the largest printing establishment in Cape Town. A leaflet advertising the new paper promised, among other things, that the paper would not be beholden to any one party, and that "its first cause will be to secure free expression for the opinion of all." The first copy appeared on January 3, 1857. Before long the *Argus* was the only triweekly in the Cape and claimed the largest circulation. Each week when Parliament was in session the *Argus* produced a supplement containing an almost verbatim report of debates, virtually a Hansard for the Cape legislature. The paper printed a special supplement, prepared by a correspondent in London, whenever the mailship arrived in Cape Town.[13]

The next major phase in the South African press came with the discovery of diamonds in the interior in 1869. Mining camps sprang up all over the diggings. Notices in the Cape Town, Grahamstown, and Bloemfontein papers carried advertisements offering transportation to the diggings—and news of local people who had struck it rich there. Newspapers soon followed. The first, the *Diamond Fields*, was launched in October 1870, in Kimberley. Only three days later it was followed by the *Diamond News*. During the 1870s there were no fewer than six papers serving the diggings. Only one of these has survived— the *Diamond Fields Advertiser*, established in March 1878. The paper later was acquired by the Argus company.

The diamond fields, South Africa's first industrial community, gave a tremendous impetus to newspapers. A year after the rush began, Kimberley was the most populous center in South Africa outside of Cape Town, with two churches, a theater, a hospital—and the six newspapers. By 1871 there were fifty thousand whites and blacks on the diamond fields. The influx of population and of capital diversified the political, social, and economic life of the colony. Nor was the growth limited to the diamond fields. Imports through the Cape and Natal ports soared.

The country's increased commercial activity, and the change from an agricultural- to an industrial-based economy, made the growth of newspapers not only possible, but inevitable. Their role in the economic system can be seen in the huge increase in advertising in newspapers over this period.

Previously, newspaper activity outside the western and eastern Cape had been limited. The first newspaper to be established across the Orange River was the *Friend of the Sovereignty and Bloemfontein Gazette*. This paper, which survives today as the *Friend*, was started as a bilingual weekly in June 1850 by Robert Godlonton, owner of the *Graham's Town Journal*. A press and a few cases of type were loaded onto an ox wagon and taken to Bloemfontein from Grahamstown to start the paper.

The first newspaper in Natal, the *Witness*, was founded in Pietermaritzburg by a young teacher and lawyer, David Buchanan, in 1846. Pietermaritzburg at the time was a village with a population of about three hundred whites and about seventy or eighty houses. Buchanan, who set up a legal practice in the town, ran the paper himself, printing it on a small hand press he had brought with him. He and a black assistant ran off the weekly paper by hand at a rate of two hundred copies an hour.

Meanwhile there were new developments in Cape Town. The *Cape Argus* encountered some stiff competition in 1876 when the *Cape Times* appeared as a penny paper. In April 1880, the *Argus* was forced to heed the challenge, switching from thrice-weekly to daily publication, and also selling for a penny instead of 3d. The editor of the *Argus* at the time was Francis Dormer, a British-born teacher. After various teaching jobs and experience as a journalist on the *Queenstown Representative*, he joined the *Argus* as a subeditor, soon rising to the position of editor.

Saul Solomon, then owner of the *Argus*, had meanwhile lost interest in the paper and wanted to leave South Africa. Dormer was able to borrow the six thousand pounds Solomon wanted for the *Argus* from Cecil John Rhodes, the mining magnate, who desired support of a newspaper to further his political ambitions. Dormer took control in July 1881. Five years later, Solomon's shop, now run by Solomon's nephews, had to sell its assets to avoid bankruptcy, and the buyers were a group of Cape Town businessmen headed by Dormer. Together they formed the Argus Printing and Publishing Company, with Rhodes as a major shareholder. Thus began the powerful Argus group with its close association with mining and commercial interests.

The next major impetus to the spread of newspapers into the interior came with the discovery of gold in the Transvaal, though the republic had not been entirely without newspapers before. A small weekly paper had appeared at Potchefstroom in 1857, was taken over by the government in 1859, and became the republic's official gazette. Different political factions in the Transvaal also had their own news sheets, most short-lived. The government gazette moved to the new capital, Pretoria, in 1863. The discovery of gold in the 1870s, first in the eastern Transvaal and then on the Witwatersrand, brought hundreds of prospectors and fortune seekers. The diggers were, for the most part, aliens—or "Uitlanders" as the Dutch called them—with little sympathy for the established Boer government, which they regarded as corrupt and inefficient. Before long the diggers had a press to support their views. The *Gold Fields Mercury* appeared at Pilgrimsrest in the eastern Transvaal in 1873, and from the beginning was strongly critical of the Boer government. Two other pro-digger papers began publication at Barberton.

The influx of the Uitlanders coincided with a change in British policy toward the Boer republics. Britain, for economic and philanthropic reasons, now wished to incorporate the independent Boer countries into a federation with the Cape Colony and Natal. The idea met with strong opposition from the republicans, and from the Dutch press at the Cape. But it was supported by merchants in the Cape and

Natal, and by "liberals" who charged that the Transvaal still prac-
ticed slavery. Uitlander newspapers in the Transvaal also pressed
hard for British rule, and the president of the republic, T. F. Burgers,
realized the need for a good Dutch newspaper to support the Boer
cause. The result was the founding of *De Volksstem* in 1873, a paper
that vigorously supported the Boer government against England's
imperialistic designs. When Britain annexed the Transvaal in 1876,
De Volksstem was a major factor in inciting the Boers to armed
resistance. Sir Theopolis Shepstone, administrator of the Transvaal
during the annexation, confided to the high commissioner of the Cape
Colony that "I am afraid I shall have to prosecute *De Volksstem* for
sedition; it has been, and still is, most persevering in its efforts to stir
up the Boers to do mischief."[14] Encouraged, among other things, by
the urgings of *De Volksstem*, the Boers revolted in 1880 and defeated
the British in a series of engagements that culminated in regaining
their republic's independence.

The peace did not last. Discoveries of rich deposits of gold on the
Witwatersrand brought a new flood of Uitlanders. Within months
there were 3,500 people in "the camp," as Johannesburg was then
called, and on February 6, 1887, only four months after the Johannesburg diggings were proclaimed, ox wagons loaded with printing
equipment rolled into the camp from Aliwal North in the eastern
Cape. The proprietor, Will Crosby, put up his tent in Market Square
and produced the first issue of the *Diggers News and Witwatersrand
Advertiser* on February 24, 1887. A day later C. W. Deecker produced
the first issue of the *Transvaal Mercury Argus*—no relation to the *Cape
Argus*. R. S. Scott, formerly of Queenstown, arrived in March to set
up the *Standard and Transvaal Mercury Chronicle*, also produced
under canvas on a Columbian hand press. Scott's *Standard* and Crosby's *Diggers News* were amalgamated in 1889 as the *Standard and
Diggers News*. The paper was sympathetic to President Kruger's
government rather than to English-speaking mining interests.

None of these pioneer papers survived. But one, published a few
months later, did. Like the other pioneers, *The Star* was moved to the
Transvaal from elsewhere, in this case Grahamstown. Thomas and
George Sheffield's paper there, the *Eastern Star*, was in tough competition with the well-established *Graham's Town Journal* and *Gro-*

cott's Penny Mail, founded in 1870. Thomas Sheffield visited the Rand in 1887 and decided to move his paper up there—staff, plant, and all—via train to the railhead at Kimberley, then three hundred miles overland to Johannesburg in ox wagons. The first number of the *Eastern Star* to appear in Johannesburg came out in October 1887. The triweekly evening journal was an immediate success. By March 1888, its circulation, the paper noted, was "exceeding we believe by many hundreds that of any newspaper published in Johannesburg."[15]

Other people were also interested in the new diggings. Francis Dormer, manager of the first Argus company, had visited the Rand and was determined to launch a paper there. In view of the established six or seven journals, Dormer decided it would be better to buy an existing paper, and chose the *Eastern Star*. The Sheffields agreed to take part in the formation of the new Argus Printing and Publishing Co., Ltd. (1889), which absorbed both the old Argus company and the *Eastern Star*. In addition the company had stationery establishments in Cape Town and Kimberley and published a weekly edition of the *Cape Argus* in London. Mining financiers, including Rhodes, were strongly represented among the shareholders. The name of the paper was changed to *The Star*, soon becoming a daily, with four to eight large, eight-column pages.

Trouble was brewing, however, between the Boer government of the Transvaal under Paul Kruger, and the Uitlanders in Johannesburg. It was a conflict that was to lead to the Jameson Raid and culminate in the Boer War. From a homogeneous, pastoral, and—by Western standards of the time—a backward country, the Transvaal was transformed virtually overnight by the rush of new settlers to the goldfields. Ten years after the diggings were proclaimed, there were seven Uitlanders for every three burgers. The rural republic now had a world industry in its midst and a new population that was politically and socially indigestible.

Issue was joined over the question of political rights for the Uitlanders, once it became clear that the goldfields would support a major mining industry for years to come, unlike the temporary phenomena of the gold rushes of California, Alaska, and Calgoorlie. The new settlers were not transients. However, citizenship of the Transvaal Republic was based on land tenure and, faced with the numerically and financially superior Uitlanders, Kruger made the franchise laws so strict after 1882 that newcomers had virtually no chance of getting the vote. Restrictions on franchise were accompanied by others: English was not permitted in courts or in schools, nor were the Uitlanders permitted to hold public meetings.

The Transvaal's impostition of high customs and rail tariffs and its system of monopolies and concessions, including its monopoly on the manufacture of dynamite, placed economic pressures on the mining companies. From the Boer point of view, these restrictions were justifiable. They saw the huge influx of foreigners and foreign capital (most of it British) as a threat to their independence and way of life. They believed the British, and Rhodes in particular, coveted their wealth. The experience of the Diamond Fields, which had been annexed by the British after the discovery of gemstones there, made the Boers doubly suspicious. Thus economic and political forces made conflict inevitable. In all this the press played a vital role. As prospects for political reform became fainter, the English papers adopted a more critical and aggressive tone. The idea of forceful intervention from outside on behalf of the Uitlanders began to take form with secret meetings and smuggling of arms. The Uitlanders formed an organization called the Transvaal National Union in 1892 to demand change in the franchise system. Petitions they sent to the government in Pretoria demanding redress of their grievances were rejected. *The Star*, along with other papers like the *Critic*, strongly backed the National Union's demands. The government point of view was expressed, in English, by the *Standard and Digger's News*, which received a subsidy from President Kruger, and was intended to drive a wedge between two sections of the Uitlander community, the miners and their capitalist backers. Rhodes threw the vast resources of the Consolidated Gold Fields company behind the reform movement in 1895.

When it became clear that there would be no reforms, Rhodes decided to promote an Uitlander uprising in Johannesburg to be led by his friend and lieutenant governor of the Cape, Dr. Leander Starr Jameson. Dissention among the conspirators, personality conflicts, and poor timing doomed the enterprise, and on January 2, 1896, Jameson and the remnants of his five-hundred-man force surrendered. The leaders of the Reform Movement were arrested and brought to trial. Four were sentenced to death; others received heavy fines. But the death sentences were commuted on the payment of fines of twenty-five thousand pounds sterling each.

The Jameson Raid damaged relations between the Transvaal government and the British and their supporters beyond recall. The raid also had its effect on the press. In 1896 the Kruger government passed a new press law to protect itself from attacks by newspapers. The new law required the disclosure of the names of printers and publishers, and it gave the state president the right to ban the distribution of publications which were "contrary to good morals or dangerous to peace and order in the Republic."

The first paper affected by the new legislation was the outspoken Johannesburg journal, the *Critic*. In Novemenber 1896, the entire staff of the *Critic* was arrested for contravening the article of the Press Law that required publication of the names of printers and publishers. But the state was unable to prove that any one of the accused was responsible for the alleged contravention, and the case was dismissed. The editor and proprietor of the *Critic*, Henry Hess, refused to tell the court the name of the responsible editor or proprietor. This led to the suspension of the *Critic* for six months, though Hess was permitted to continue the paper under another name, the *Transvaal Critic*. Nevertheless the suspension of the *Critic* was attacked by English newspapers. The *Cape Times* said that suppression of the *Critic* "will be resented by the entire free press of South Africa." *The Star* pointed out "the danger of liberty to thought" which the proceedings demonstrated. It said: "The President has at all times the power to prohibit the circulation of any newspaper, with no right of trial accorded to the parties responsible for its publication and no possiblity of appeal."[16]

These restrictions on the Uitlander papers did little to curb their hostility to the Boer government. As one contemporary observer, Sir William Butler, noted, "The English journals in the Transvaal were outrageous in their language of insult and annoyance. Threats and menaces were being used every day against the government of the republic and the people of the Dutch race." In some instances the

Uitlander press stopped barely short of sedition. The *Transvaal Leader*, for example, commented that the president was "incompetent to maintain the honour and dignity of the state"; that there was discontent among all groups of the population and especially among the ten or twelve thousand Uitlanders "who have raised the country from a state of bankruptcy." These men, said the *Advertiser*, had large interests in the land, yet the government ignored their claims to be heard except as suppliants. The pro-Boer press saw things from a very different perspective. The *Standard and Diggers' News* proclaimed that it "stood up for the Boer, for his right to be master in his own house and to hold what he had." It defended the Boer against "the agitator, against the covetous encroachments of Capital with its dollar-dominion and tyranny of millions."[17]

There is little doubt that these newspapers served to exacerbate the conflict between the Dutch and the English communities they represented. A journalist who had worked for newspapers supporting both sides commented later that the Transvaal had been "particularly unfortunate in its newspaper press." This, he said, applied to both sections of the press, Boer and Uitlander alike.

Given this dichotomy, conflict was inevitable. *The Star*, for example, carried a cartoon in March 1897, that showed President Kruger in a chair having his head examined by a phrenologist, with a caption that commented sarcastically on the president's moral and intellectual qualities. A week later a government officer served a warrant on the editor, signed by Kruger, banning the circulation of *The Star* for a period of three months "on grounds that the contents of the said newspaper are in my judgment dangerous to the peace and quiet of the Republic." That evening *The Star* reported its own suppression at great length. The next day another journal, in every way identical to *The Star*, appeared under the masthead, the *Comet*. *The Star* decided to appeal the banning to the Supreme Court. Counsel for the paper argued that the law under which the paper was suppressed was contrary to the Transvaal constitution, which assured the liberty of the press. Article 19 of the constitution read: "The Liberty of the Press is conceded, provided the printer and publisher remain responsible for all publications of a libellous character." It argued further that even if the law were valid, it gave power to suppress only what had been printed, not what had not yet been printed. The court upheld the appeal, and *The Star* reappeared the next day.

This ruling brought only a temporary respite. Boer and Briton were on a collision course. The day hostilities began in October 1899, the Uitlander press in the Transvaal was shut down by order of the Kruger government.

The war was a setback for some sections of the press. At the Cape at least four editors, including D. F. Malan, were jailed for seditious libel after printing a letter claiming that a British general had fired on Boer homes occupied only by women and children. Two others went to jail for reprinting the letter. Dutch journals were banned from districts in which martial law had been proclaimed, in effect restricting their circulation to Cape Town and cutting them off from their constituency in the interior.

In the Orange Free State, the local paper was forced to do an abrupt about-face. The *Friend* of the Free State had served the English-speaking merchant community in Bloemfontein since 1850. But when war broke out its editor, Thomas Barlow, threw his support to the Boer side. "It is our country, and as loyal Free Staters we must stand by it," he declared. But within six months, the British had captured Bloemfontein, and editorship of the paper was entrusted to a group of British war correspondents, the best known of whom was Rudyard Kipling. The paper now stood for "the maintenance of British supremacy in South Africa." When the British forces moved on to attack the Transvaal they made sure the paper would not revert to a pro-Boer stance: it was put under the control of the Argus company.

Post–Boer War Press

The present structure of the English-language press has its roots in the immediate post–Boer War period. At the end of the war in 1902, the muted papers in the Transvaal found their voice anew. English papers flourished in all the major cities, their circulations spurred by interest in news of the conflict and its resolution. The cities, including those in the former Boer republics, were the domain of English-speaking merchants, tradesmen, professionals, and administrators, and the papers reflected their interests. Cape Town had three English-language papers: the *Cape Argus*, the *Cape Times* and the *South African News*, which was founded in 1899 and folded after fifteen years. Durban was served by the *Natal Mercury* (1852), and Port Elizabeth, East London, Bloemfontein, Pretoria, Kimberley, and Pietermaritzburg already had papers that still exist today.

An important development of this period was the founding in Johannesburg of the *Rand Daily Mail* in 1902. The *Mail*, edited at first by the British author Edgar Wallace, pledged to support "the imperial ideal" and "progress in the Transvaal and South African affairs."[18] Just two years later the paper's founder, Freeman Cohen, died, and a bid by what the editor called "a small band of men of Dutch leanings" to take over (the first of several attempts by Dutch nationalist interests to buy it and change its editorial policies) was thwarted when Sir Abe Bailey, a mining magnate and financier, put up the money to keep the paper going. Bailey left control of the *Mail* in the hands of a syndicate that, in 1906, launched another significant paper, the *Sunday Times*. Like the *Mail*, it professed to be "loyal to the fingertips, and Imperialistic to the backbone." But it vowed to steer an "independent course during the coming political storm in the Transvaal."[19] The *Mail* and the *Sunday Times* were to become the foundation of the South African Associated Newspapers (SAAN) chain.

The Argus group, meanwhile, was expanding. From its base in Johannesburg and Cape Town, it acquired newspapers in every major city or town except Port Elizabeth. It bought the Durban-based *Natal Advertiser* in 1918, and renamed it the *Daily News* in 1937. In 1921 the Argus company bought a controlling interest in Kimberley's *Diamond Fields Advertiser*, and in the *Pretoria News* in 1925. These acquisitions made the Argus group by far the strongest press combine in the country.

The early English newspapers were heavily influenced by British journalistic tradition. Just as many South African schools and recto-ries were staffed by graduates of British universities, so top posts in journalism often went to British journalists. Their limited knowledge of local affairs clearly was thought to be offset by their training on British newspapers. Harry O'Connor, until recently editor of the

Eastern Province Herald, worked under such editors when he entered journalism in the 1930s. They were, he said, well educated and highly literate. Their papers were soundly professional, dedicated to journalistic responsibility and integrity, but in the South African context they had their faults. No matter how hard they tried to hide it, they tended to look down on "colonials" generally, said O'Connor, and expecially on those whom they could not help considering "lesser breeds." The result, he said, is that they were usually quite out of touch with the outlook of Afrikaners and also smugly oblivious of the inequities inflicted on nonwhites: "The newspapers they produced gave few hints that there were grievous wrongs to be righted in a land where, many of them felt instinctively, their most important mission was the perpetuation of British influence in a most conservative form." O'Connor recalled an editor who personified this school of journalism, an erudite man who could thread his way surefooted through Debrett's Peerage and "considered it practically a capital offense to mistake a baron for a baronet." He was well equipped with Greek and Latin quotations, "but his accomplishments did not include the faintest smattering of Afrikaans. Nor had he the slightest inkling of what the Afrikaners thought and felt about matters, although he was aware of their existence as a group which could be a nuisance as harriers on the flanks of advancement of the British cause. But they had, after all, lost the South African War, and their better elements, led by General Smuts, could be depended on to behave sensibly. The Chamber of Mines was in its heaven—all was right in the world."[20]

Such attitudes obviously rankled among Afrikaners. It was not only the pro-British slant of the newspapers that distressed them, but that the papers that portrayed South African reality for internal and external consumption were largely controlled by powerful financial interests, including the mining industry. The connection was evident in both the management of the papers and their editorial policy. The management link was exemplified by the career of John Martin, an Englishman who became general manager of the Argus company in 1916 and managing director in 1922. His successful handling of the newspapers impressed the directors of the mining houses that controlled major shareholdings in the Argus company, and in 1926

Martin was invited to fill the most important position in the industry—chairman of Rand Mines, Ltd., and resident director of the
Central Mining and Investment Corporation. Martin accepted on
condition that he need not sever his links with the newspapers. He
remained chairman of the Argus company until 1949. This cozy
relationship led a former Argus editor, H. L. Smith, to comment that
"it has been the policy of the daily press . . . that *ipso facto* whatever is
best for the gold mines is best for South Africa as a whole, and that end
is kept ever foremost in mind."[21]

By the time the National party came to power in 1948 and began its
long siege of the English-language press, this situation was already
changing. South African-born journalists were becoming more influential in deciding newspaper policy. Proprietors, who likewise
were becoming more South African oriented, were more tolerant of
editorial independence. The newspapers were beginning to question
some aspects of mining company policy.

Whatever the new reality, however, to the Afrikaners the English
newspapers continued to represent all that was inimical to their
interests. They stood for the British imperialism that had overthrown
the Boers' cherished republics. And even after the Afrikaners had
regained a large measure of political independence, they remained
economically subservient to the English financial and mining houses.
The English newspapers' close links to the mines—the original agent
of the destruction of the Boer republics—marked them as enemies not
to be trusted. Long after the last British editors had passed from the
scene, to be replaced by South African-born journalists, Nationalist
politicians were calling for legislation to ensure that senior staff of
South African newspapers be bilingual citizens of the country.

The Afrikaners had emerged from the Boer War a defeated and
impoverished nation. Sir Alfred Milner, British high commissioner
from 1897, worked at resettling the Boers on their farms, many of
which had been laid waste in the fighting. Recovery was slow, however, partly as a result of a five-year drought that began in 1903 and
drove many off the land to a poverty-stricken existence in the cities.
To their economic miseries was added Milner's policy of anglicizing
the country. He forbade the use of Dutch in government schools:
"Dutch should only be used to teach English, and English to teach

everything else." Milner also worked hard at building up the English population by immigration, arguing prophetically that "if, ten years from hence, there are three men of British race to two of Dutch, the country will be safe and prosperous. If there are three of Dutch to two of British, we shall have perpetual difficulty." Milner's immigration policy never did achieve the English dominance he hoped for, and his attempts to ensure British political and cultural domination were a major spur to Afrikaner nationalism—and to the development of Afrikaner nationalist newspapers.

The Afrikaners were quick to mobilize their political power against Milner's policies. They refused to serve on his proposed legislative council, declaring that self-government alone would satisfy them. In 1904 several hundred Afrikaners gathered in Pretoria to establish their first major political organization, Het Volk. A similar group, the Orangia Unie, was formed in the Free State in 1905. Both focused on Afrikaner grievances over restrictions on the use of Dutch and over the administration of relief funds.

The establishment of the Union of South Africa in 1910 was intended to achieve reconciliation of Boers and British in a unitary state. And indeed the first cabinet under Gen. Louis Botha was about evenly balanced between the two groups. The new constitution also called for equal status for Dutch and English in official business and for a bilingual civil service. But it did little to quiet the republican sentiments of many Afrikaners. Led by Gen. Barry Herzog, a member of Botha's cabinet, the more militant Afrikaners continued to campaign for bilingual education of all white children in public schools. Also, while the new constitution made South Africa independent in many respects, it was still subservient to the British crown in external relations, including matters of war and peace.

Herzog, in a series of speeches in 1912, promoted the theme of "South Africa first," to the embarrassment of Botha, who was seeking an accommodation with the English elements in South Africa. Herzog, forced out of the cabinet, formed a new party, the National party, dedicated to compulsory bilingualism in the civil service, dual-medium education, and the priority of South African interests.[22] The latter issue was sharpened in 1914 when war broke out between England and Germany. Most Afrikaners favored neutrality;

many actually sympathized with Germany, hoping that a German victory would hasten the reestablishment of a Boer republic in South Africa.

This renewed nationalism gave birth to the Afrikaans press as it exists today. At the time of union in 1910 there were no Afrikaans daily papers, as earlier ones had succumbed during the Boer War. Then in 1912, Harm Oost founded *Die Week* in Pretoria, dedicated to supporting the political, cultural, and economic agencies being developed to rehabilitate the Afrikaner people. *Die Week* lasted less than two years before going bankrupt, but Oost then became associated with a new paper, *Het Volk*, that enthusiastically backed Herzog's National party. The paper rallied support for a pure South African nationalism, based on the three pillars of church, language, and school.[23] It demanded that Afrikaans be given equal status with English, with parents having the right to determine their children's education. It argued forcefully against the integration of different cultural and racial groups, asserting that God's purpose was to have different nationalities develop in their own separate ways. This theme was to mature into the apartheid doctrine of later Nationalists.

Given the political tensions of the time such extreme views could hardly be tolerated, and in 1914 the government suspended *Die Week* and jailed Oost for taking part in an armed rebellion against its authority. The crisis had begun when England, having declared war on Germany, asked Botha to invade the German territory of South West Africa. Botha, and his minister of defense, Gen. Jan Smuts, went along with the request, perhaps hoping eventually to incorporate the territory in the Union. But Herzog's party wanted no part of Britain's war, preferring neutrality. Several Boer leaders who supported the German cause went into open rebellion. It was quickly suppressed, and for the most part the rebel leaders received light sentences. They soon were ensconced in the Nationalist pantheon, however, and several who had died in the rebellion became full-fledged martyrs. One of the ringleaders, Jopie Fourie, condemned to death for shooting at government forces under a flag of truce, died facing the firing squad without a blindfold and singing a psalm.[24]

Such events exacerbated nationalist fervor as nothing had before. And into this atmosphere was born a paper that was to play a crucial part in the nationalist movement. The story of *Die Burger* is perhaps the best example of the history and function of the Afrikaans press. Two days before Fourie's execution, a group gathered in Cape Town to discuss the founding of a newspaper.[25] The idea was to provide the Herzog group with a mouthpiece of its own in the Cape. There were few individual Afrikaners who could muster the resources to start a newspaper. In any event, tactically it was considered essential to involve large numbers of ordinary Afrikaners in the undertaking. The principle of popular support for a nationalist cause was already established: thousands had contributed small amounts to the Helpmekaar society to pay the fines of leaders of the rebellion. Thus an appeal was launched for the people to buy shares in the newspaper company. Its capital grew in driblets, but by April 1915 there was enough on hand to appoint an editor. The man chosen was Dr. D. F. Malan, at the time a Dutch Reformed church minister in the town of Graaff-Reinet and already a leading nationalist thinker and activist. Significantly, Malan's brief was not only to edit *De Burger* (its original Dutch name), but to lead the National party in the Cape.

The paper began in less than promising circumstances. The country was under martial law and *De Burger*, suspected of pro-German leanings, had to be exceptionally cautious to avoid suppression. Few Afrikaners were accustomed to reading newspapers—some could read English more easily than Dutch. The paper's readers, predominantly a rural people or city dwellers of modest means, had little purchasing power to attract advertisers. *De Burger* was overshadowed by its well-established competitors, the *Cape Argus* and the *Cape Times*. The *Argus* alone was printing about fifteen thousand copies a day to *De Burger*'s three thousand. Circulation slowly picked up, however, particularly in the Afrikaner-dominated hinterland.

From the start there was no mistaking *De Burger*'s political purpose. Six days a week (it was years before the Calvinist Afrikaners would accept Sunday papers) *De Burger* developed and propagated the policy of the National party in its news and editorial columns. Malan saw no distinction between his roles as editor and as party leader. Malan made *De Burger* the shield and sword of Afrikanerdom. It encouraged steps to improve the lot of the poor whites. Although initially published in Dutch, it played a crucial role in the language movement that eventually resulted in Afrikaans being accepted as an official language in 1925. The proportion of Afrikaans in the paper was gradually increased until in 1922 its name was changed to *Die Burger*, and it began printing all its leading articles in Afrikaans.

Nasionale Pers, the publishing house that controlled *Die Burger*, soon extended its influence to other centers. In 1917 it bought *Die Volksblad*, a nationalist newspaper in Bloemfontein that had moved there from Potchefstroom to support the Herzog cause in the Free State. Nasionale Pers also launched popular agricultural and general interest magazines for Afrikaners and a subscription series of books that boosted the Afrikaans language and literature.

There were similar developments, for similar reasons, in the Transvaal. Afrikanerdom had been split down the middle by Malan's defection in 1934 from the Herzog-Smuts United party. Malan took with him the support of the Nasionale Pers publications. The Herzog faction, left without a mouthpiece in the Cape, nevertheless had an organ in the Transvaal. Afrikaanse Pers, controlled by the Herzog group, published a paper called *Ons Vaderland* in Pretoria. For tactical reasons the paper was moved to Johannesburg in 1936, and renamed *Die Vaderland*. Malan's national party, needing an organ of its own in the Transvaal, set up Voortrekker Pers the same year. It produced a Johannesburg daily, *Die Transvaler*. At about the same time Nasionale Pers established a paper in Port Elizabeth, *Die Oosterlig*, also to support the National party. As in the case of *Die Burger*, these papers were funded largely through small individual contributions from the party faithful.

Die Transvaler's first editor was Dr. H. F. Verwoerd, an uncompromising nationalist who later became prime minister. Like Malan, he made little distinction between his roles as theologian, politician, and journalist—and later grand architect of apartheid. His paper was a staunch supporter of segregation—not only of whites from all other hues but of Afrikaners from their English-speaking compatriots. To survive, Verwoerd asserted, the Afrikaners had to be culturally isolated. *Die Transvaler* pressed for a Boer republic, independent of what Verwoerd called "the British-Jewish form of mock democracy." An

Afrikaner republic outside the British Empire, he believed, was an essential precondition for improved relations between Afrikaans and English speakers in South Africa.

Afrikaner-English relations became increasingly strained as the Union once again was faced with the dilemma of whether or not to support Britain in a war with Germany. The country was split down the middle. The English-language newspapers naturally sided with Britain—and when one paper strayed from that position it was quickly brought back into line. The policy of the Argus company, in the period immediately preceding the Second World War, was that its papers should take care not to undermine Britain's position as she strove for peace in Europe. The editor of the *Cape Argus*, however, became increasingly critical of Neville Chamberlain's policy of appeasement, accusing him of selling out Czechoslovakia to Germany under the Munich agreement. The editor, D. McCauseland, was fired. The incident was a clear demonstration of the close links between the English press and the mining houses and, through them, with Britain. McCauseland's successor, L. E. Neame, wrote later that "news agencies and the correspondents of some of the English newspapers cabled the strongest parts of McCauseland's articles to London as a South African view of the situation in Europe and the policy of the British government. The extracts gave the impression that a paper owned by the chief gold-mining groups, with a chairman (John Martin) who was a director of the Bank of England, was opposed to the attitutde of the British prime minister."[26] H. L. Smith commented that the amazing point about the incident was that McCauseland was fired for criticizing the British, not the South African government. The firing was not, said Smith, at variance with the general policy of the mining press: "The newspapers do not in many instances criticise the British government. To do so would immediately give that section of the Afrikaans press which is bitterly opposed to anything British an added incentive to make the most of it. Criticism of the British government is therefore taboo in the general interests of the mining industry, which is anxious to attract capital into South Africa, and to do nothing that might tend to repel it."[27]

The Afrikaans papers took a very different view of the conflict. Those that supported the National party, with its pro-Nazi sympathies, were opposed to South Africa's assistance to Britain. The papers that supported Herzog also favored neutrality. The five-year-old coalition between Herzog and Smuts split over the issue, with Smuts favoring a South African role in the war. Smuts, with the collaboration of the Labor and Dominion parties, formed a new government and led South Africa into World War II. There was no direct censorship of the press during the war years. Instead, to ensure that information that might be useful to the enemy not be published, Smuts asked editors for their cooperation. This was promised, but his patience must at times have been sorely tried.

Extremist elements of the National party had formed an organization called the Ossewa Brandwag. It started as an Afrikaner cultural movement, but inspired by events in Germany, it became a paramilitary group with its own storm troopers. By 1942 the group was engaging in acts of sabotage to hinder the government's war effort and bombing the homes and businesses of Jewish merchants. Many of its members, including several who later became Nationalist cabinet ministers—or in the case of B. J. Vorster, prime minister—were interned by the government. The leader of the Ossewa Brandwag, J. F. J. van Rensburg, challenged Malan for leadership of the National party. The republican ideals of the Afrikaners, van Rensburg declared, would not be achieved through political means. Malan, who had a much stronger commitment to democracy, disagreed. At first *Die Burger* treated the Ossewa Brandwag with kid gloves—its adherents were, after all, at the very heart of Afrikaner nationalism. Gradually, however, *Die Burger* weaned the party away from an explicit commitment to Hitler's National Socialism.

The attitude of *Die Transvaler* was even more ambivalent. Like *Die Burger*, it had followed Malan's lead in attacking those in the party who openly sided with the Nazis. But Nazi Germany's propaganda radio station was broadcasting to the Union in Afrikaans, encouraging the Ossewa Brandwag movement. Some of the arguments made in the columns of *Die Transvaler*—like that for a separate peace between the Union and Germany—appeared to be remarkably similar to those of Nazi radio. In October 1941 the flagship paper of the Argus group, *The Star*, ran an editorial headed "Speaking up for Hitler," saying that *Die Transvaler* "this week gave a rather better example than usual of the process of falsification which it applies to current news in its support of Nazi propaganda." Citing the way in which *Die Transvaler* had treated a statement issued by the South African Bureau of Information, *The Star* added: "Its dishonesty is too easy to expose, and it identifies *Die Transvaler* so closely with Nazi propaganda that it must assist in opening the eyes of those who read the paper in question as to the extent to which it is a tool of malignant forces from which this country has everything to fear."[28]

Verwoerd sued *The Star* for defamation—and lost. In finding for *The Star*, the court ruled that Verwoerd's right to publish what he did was not in question: "The question is whether, when he exercises this legal right the way he does, he is entitled to complain if it is said of him that what he writes supports Nazi propaganda and makes his paper a tool of the Nazis." On the evidence, said the court, Verwoerd was not entitled to complain: "He did support Nazi propaganda, he did make his paper a tool of the Nazis in South Africa, and he knew it."[29]

The issue that divided the two white language groups, and the newspapers that spoke for them, was thus centered on the external policies of the government. The Afrikaans press came to realize, however, that it was more profitable to focus on internal policy—and specifically on questions of race. Although Smuts had taken the country into the war against racist Germany, his government was far from liberal in its approach to race relations. The difference between its attitude to the country's traditional segregationist policies and that of the Nationalists was one of degree, not kind. However, the country's booming wartime economy, spurred by industrial development to produce arms and munitions, had drawn increasing numbers of blacks into the labor market. A shortage of white workers meant many were doing jobs previously reserved for whites. In 1942 a government commission recommended important reforms in the educational, social, and health conditions of urban Africans. It also eased its enforcement of the pass laws that restricted black influx into the cities. The English newspapers, with their close links with a wider Anglo-American social reality, began to reflect the West's growing revulsion against Nazi racism and authoritarianism and to press for more liberal policies at home.

At the same time the Smuts government appeared to be losing its ability to keep the blacks in their place. Newly industrialized Africans quickly formed trade unions, often supported by the small but then still legal Communist party. The influx into the cities created an acute shortage of housing with accompanying social problems. Squatter movements, and subsequent clashes with police, led to a series of strikes, boycotts, and riots. Black nationalists demanded their own bill of rights, including "the freedom of all African people from all discriminatory laws whatsoever." Afrikaans newspapers made the most of these issues. As historian Rodney Davenport notes of the Nationalists: "With the help of a dedicated press and some brilliant cartoonists they won the propaganda battle even though their opponents had a call on the loyalties of newspapers with far greater circulations."[30] To the surprise of most, including Malan himself, the National party came to power in the general elections of 1948.

3 | The Press Council: Self-Censorship through Intimidation

Few things illustrate more graphically the pressures on the South African press than the continuing saga of the Press Council. The council was established in 1962 in an attempt to forestall direct government control of the press. Threatened with legislation to establish a statutory press council, the Newspaper Press Union (NPU), an organization representing most of the country's newspaper publishers, decided that self-discipline was preferable to government censorship. The first body they set up was the essentially harmless Press Board of Reference. It could impose no sanctions; the code of conduct it administered comprised little more than a series of platitudinous statements no self-respecting journalist could object to.

Nevertheless, not all journalists supported the move. Many feared that even a voluntary disciplinary body would be the first step toward ever more restrictive measures. Few were prepared to forge their own fetters. However, as this chapter will demonstrate, the government was determined to impose some form of discipline on the press. While publishers and journalists may have differed over the need for, and nature of, the self-disciplinary measures required to appease the government, they were united in opposition to statutory control. But the fears of those who saw in the Press Council a first and dangerous step along a slippery path were justified. As internal and external pressures on the country grew with the implementation of apartheid, the Nationalists felt obliged to impose ever more restrictive conditions on the press. By bluster and sheer intimidation, it forced the industry to amend the constitution and code of the Press Council, until it largely resembled the kind of disciplinary body the Nationalists had had in mind all along. Yet, because it still functions as a voluntary body, the government has been able to point with pride to the fact that South Africa has the freest press on the continent.

The history of the Press Council goes back to the years immediately after the Second World War, when a worldwide demand for improvement of democratic institutions led, among other things, to an examination of the power of the press. In the United States, the privately financed Commission on the Freedom of the Press was set up in 1942. Its report, *A Free and Responsible Press*, recommended "reform from within" the industry.[1] In Britain, the new postwar Labour government appointed a royal commission to inquire into the press. Its report, released in 1949, suggested among other things that a press council be established.[2]

Similar questions were being asked about the press in South Africa, where the matter was debated in the Parliament in 1948. The major theme of the debate was criticism of the Argus group's dominance of the newspaper industry.[3] But the minister of the interior, H. G. Lawrence, after listening to charges against the press, replied that the United party government did not believe the matter justified an inquiry. Soon after, in the general election of 1948, the Nationalists were elected to power—a position they have not relinquished since. That victory brought an all-Afrikaner government to power for the first time since the defeat of the Boer republics.

The new government immediately began implementing racial segregation, or apartheid, through a series of laws that stirred a storm of protest at home and unremitting hostility in the media abroad. The Prohibition of Mixed Marriages Act of 1949 made all future marriages between whites and members of other race groups illegal. The Population Registration Act of 1950 allocated every South African to a specific racial group. The Immorality Act made sexual relations across the color line a serious offense. The Group Areas Act separated the different population groups into separate geographical areas. Political segregation was achieved by withdrawing the token franchise extended to the Indian population by the Smuts government, by abolishing the Native Representative Council, and by a bitter consti-

tutional campaign to remove Coloured voters in the Cape from the
common electoral roll. Resistance to these laws was stifled by such
repressive measures as the Suppression of Communism Act.

The bitter political conflict these measures generated was reflected
in the press. English-language newspapers were outspoken in their
opposition, views mirrored in coverage of the Union's affairs abroad.
The human suffering brought on by the apartheid legislation made for
sensational headlines: prominent people committing suicide after
being arrested under the Immorality Act; families split up under the
Population Registration Act; people being left homeless after evic-
tions under the Group Areas Act; arrests and bannings under the
Suppression of Communism Act. Stung by the criticism, the minister
of defense, F. C. Erasmus, told Parliament in 1949 that although
South Africa was the only country in which the experiment of a white
and a nonwhite race living together had succeeded, and although the
conditions of the indigenous population were "nowhere better,"
there had been a "slanderous campaign" against the Union and that
no previous government had ever been attacked by the opposition
press with "such fury." He said attempts were being made to incite
English-speaking South Africans against Afrikaans-speaking South
Africans, and "what is worse," nonwhites against whites. News
reports sent abroad, he said, had "grossly slandered" South Africa
and its people.[4]

A year later a Nationalist member of Parliament, A. J. R. van
Rhyn, called on the government to set up a commission to investigate
the press. Van Rhyn's motion asked for an inquiry into monopolistic
tendencies in the press; into internal and external reporting—and the
advisability of "control over such reporting." The debate that followed is significant in that it articulated themes that were to recur
through the years and do much to explain the Nationalist government's subsequent actions against the press.[5]

Introducing the motion, van Rhyn accused British and other overseas newspapers of sensationalism, of misrepresenting South African
affairs, of misleading people by false reports, and of inciting public
opinion overseas against South Africa. The effect on black readers
was a concern, too. Noting the large nonwhite population who read
the newspapers, he pointed out that only the continued respect of the

nonwhite population maintained white superiority, and when non-whites noted distortions and omissions in their newspapers they began to have their suspicions about white honor. Citing the recent takeover of a newspaper company in Port Elizabeth by a British proprietor, van Rhyn condemned foreign ownership because it allowed the molding of black opinion by outside interests.[6] Van Rhyn called for an investigation into monopolistic tendencies in the control of the press, citing the Argus group, which owned nine of the seventeen daily papers in the Union. The freedom of the press was "limited by those who control it," he said.

Replying to van Rhyn, H. G. Lawrence, by then an opposition MP, maintained that deliberate falsifications in the press were rare and blamed the government's apartheid policies, rather than the newspapers, for blacks' loss of faith in the integrity of the whites. Other opposition members attributed the distrust of the government abroad not to a hostile press but to the attitude of the Nationalists during the war, a suspicion that they had fascist tendencies, and to their attempts to abolish the representation of nonwhites in Parliament.

The minister of external affairs, Eric Louw, said that much harm had been done by slanderous newspaper reports about South Africa. He mentioned hearing these reports quoted at the United Nations against the Union as though they were facts. Louw called for deportation of foreign journalists who abused South Africa's hospitality. The minister of posts and telegraphs, Dr. Albert Herzog, alleged that the South African Press Association, the cooperative news agency, had a monopoly in the supply of news, which was first passed through London where it was "filtered" and sometimes "twisted."

The prime minister, Dr. D. F. Malan, insisted that even in peacetime comment ought to be restrained by patriotism. He called the South African press the "most undisciplined in the world," comparing it with the press in countries like Britain, where a considerably greater self-discipline was exercised, and the Netherlands, where he said journalists were registered and could be struck off the register for breaching the official code of conduct. Whereas other countries had proper organizations of journalists and editors, with suitable codes of professional conduct, South Africa had no such organization.

Moreover, while the correspondents of overseas newspapers in Britain had drawn up their own code, foreign correspondents in the Union were nearly all members of the staff of local English-language newspapers, but remained outside the latter's control with news they sent abroad. They therefore wrote reports for foreign newspapers which they would not dare to write in the South African press.

It was after this debate in 1950 that newspapers appear to have made their first conciliatory gestures, making it known that English-language editors were prepared to meet with the prime minister to discuss their differences. Gen. Jan Smuts, leader of the opposition, told Parliament that "the whole matter can be settled in a friendly way by the Prime Minister of the country and the press of the country."[7] But the government was determined to act, and nothing came of the suggestion.

The Press Commission was set up in March 1950. Its charge included the concentration of control of the press and its effect on editorial opinion and comment and presentation of news. It was to investigate accuracy in the presentation of news in South Africa and abroad by correspondents in the Union, having particular regard to, among other things, "use of unverified facts or rumors as news or the basis of comment" and "reckless statements, distortion of facts or fabrication." The commission was directed also to study "the adequacy or otherwise of existing means of self-control and discipline by the press." The very formulation of the commission's tasks suggested that the findings most likely would be negative. Implied in the establishment of the commission was the threat that its findings might lead to some kind of government action against the press. At the very least, the press was served notice that its activities were under close scrutiny—and that it had better watch its step.[8]

Against this background, D. H. Ollemans, chairman of the Argus company, proposed in 1951 that a voluntary press council be set up. Though the suggestion found little immediate support, Ollemans continued to press for the idea, and in 1955 he arranged two informal meetings, attended by representatives of virtually every daily and Sunday paper and by a number of editors. No decision emerged; it was generally felt that any action should await the report of the Press Commission. Nevertheless, Ollemans drafted a code of conduct for a proposed press council and outlined the procedures for its observance. These he discussed with his colleagues in the NPU.[9]

Meanwhile, although the Press Commission's report was pending, the English-language press came in for increasingly virulent criticism from Nationalist politicians. The English papers were outspoken in their condemnation of apartheid legislation, comments often picked up and echoed by newspapers abroad. Thus one finds the minister of lands, J. G. Strydom, telling a Nationalist rally in August 1954 that the English-language newspapers were writing things "the effect of which must be that the Natives are incited against the laws of the land." If the editors of the various English newspapers were chased out by Native uprisings which their writings had fomented, they would shake off the dust of South Africa and return "home." To people who urged racial equality, said Strydom, "whether they are newspapers, ministers of religion or anything else, I say that the white race has been here for 300 years. As previous generations of English and Afrikaans frontier farmers alike fought and shed their blood, so we in this generation will fight to the death to maintain the white man's leadership in South Africa."[10]

J. G. Strydom succeeded Daniel Malan as prime minister in 1954. He had little regard for constitutional restraint if it delayed implementation of apartheid. During his tenure thousands of blacks were removed from urban areas rezoned for whites. Segregation was enforced in almost all public places: libraries, churches, theaters. The Extension of University Education Act set up four ethnic colleges, but severely restricted the admission of other race groups to the traditionally white universities. These measures met with increasingly violent protests and equally violent suppression. The government's decision to compel African women to carry reference books, or passes, gave rise to widespread protests, burning of reference books, and stoning of the officials sent to distribute them. When the multiracial Congress of the People adopted a charter demanding a democratic, nonracial system of government, the state responded with a severe crackdown. Police arrested 156 people of all races and all walks of life and charged them with high treason. Their trial lasted more than two years and ended in acquittals for all the accused—but not before incalculable damage had been done to race relations at home and the country's image abroad. Inevitably the press reflected in its reporting and comment the growing polarization in the land. Strydom's response, in the classic "kill the messenger" syndrome, was to attack the English newspapers in 1957, accusing them of always giving publicity to the views of left-wingers and of stirring up nonwhites against whites. The English-language press, he said, was South Africa's greatest enemy.[11]

This political mudslinging was criticized by the leader of the South African Society of Journalists at its annual congress in 1957. "If it is calculated to bring one section of the press into disrepute, it can only be to the detriment of the press as a whole and of the country," SASJ President M. A. Johnson said, warning that a press council might be instituted and some form of control imposed over those journalists who sent reports to newspapers abroad.

The attacks on the English-language press continued, both in an out of Parliament. Strydom's successor as prime minister, H. F. Verwoerd, speaking at a political rally in May 1959, blamed the economic depression in South Africa on the irresponsible and unpatriotic behavior of the English press. A Nationalist MP, F. S. Steyn, told the House of Assembly that the law should be changed, making it treasonable to advocate any steps that would overthrow apartheid. In September that year, the South African Information Department released an "analysis of British newspapers" which purported to show that three-quarters of the items published in the British press about South Africa concerned "negative subjects," which created an unfavorable impression on the British reader. Most of the objectionable articles, said the report, were concerned with race relations and politics.[12]

Matters came to a head in 1960, a year of spectacular turmoil in which South Africa probably came closer to revolution than ever before or since. The government had announced that in 1960 the white electorate would be asked to decide whether to change the country's form of government. Ever since the defeat of the Boer republics, a cherished Afrikaner goal had been the reestablishment of a republic, free of formal links with the British crown. The proposal met with strong resistance from English-speaking whites, who valued their ties with Britain and the Commonwealth. The largely English-speaking province of Natal threatened to secede if a republic were declared.

Blacks, who would not be consulted in the decision, saw in the republic a further entrenchment of Afrikaner domination and a weakening of what little protection the links with Britain afforded them. Led by the Pan-Africanist Congress, a militant offshoot of the African National Congress, they launched a passive resistance campaign against the pass laws, a hated symbol of their subjugation. Political and racial tensions ran high. In January 1960 a police raiding party in Cato Manor, a black township near Durban, was set upon by an irate mob. Nine policemen were killed. These events received prominent coverage in South Africa and abroad. The situation exploded into large-scale violence on March 21, the day the Pan-Africanist Congress had set for protests against the pass laws. Blacks were urged to go peacefully to the nearest police station, report they did not have their passes with them, and ask to be arrested. A large crowd surrounded the police station in Sharpeville Township, near Vereeniging in the Transvaal. The besieged policemen, mindful no doubt of what had happened at Cato Manor, panicked and opened fire with Sten guns. By the time the firing stopped 69 people lay dead and 180 were injured. Many victims were shot in the back as they fled, others were hit while in their nearby homes. Police in the black township of Langa, near Cape Town, opened fire on a crowd the same day. The violence quickly spread to other centers. The government responded by declaring a state of emergency, calling up civilian reserve units, arresting hundreds of people suspected of sympathizing with the black aspirations, and banning the ANC and PAC.

These events turned the international spotlight on South Africa as never before. The country's turmoil dominated the world's headlines as media and news agencies sent correspondents to cover the unrest. Their news reports led to South Africa's being roundly censured abroad, including a condemnation by the UN Security Council, called into session by Afro-Asian delegates who were widely reported as calling the shootings an "inhuman massacre," a "barbaric act," and "uncivilized behavior." Hundreds of demonstrators scuffled with police outside the South African embassy in London. The state of emergency prompted heavy selling of South African securities on the world's exchanges. In Johannesburg, stock prices took their worst losses in years. Movements flourished abroad to boycott South African goods, to isolate her politically, to ban sports and cultural exchanges.

Ironically, in many cases readers abroad were better informed about what was happening in South Africa than South Africans themselves. The emergency regulations included restrictions on reporting so far-reaching that if interpreted literally would mean a complete ban on publishing anything relating to the crisis. The regulation prohibited, on pain of severe penalties, the publication of "subversive statements," presumably including photographs or cartoons. "Subversive statements" were defined as anything likely to have the effect of "subverting authority . . . inciting any section of the public to resist or oppose the Government . . . engendering or aggravating feelings of hostility in any person or section of the public . . . causing panic, alarm or fear . . . weakening the confidence of the public in the successful termination of the state of emergency, unless the statement is proved to be a true and complete narrative."[13]

The result was that South African editors, unsure about what they could print, had to exercise a large measure of self-censorship. The Star, for example, carried a long extract from an editorial in the Times of London dealing with the situation. Alongside this was a panel headed "CANNOT BE PUBLISHED," that read: "Many other London newspapers today gave great prominence to the situation in South Africa, but their news reports and editorial comment are of such a nature that it is impossible to publish them in South Africa under the emergency regulations."[14] Because local publications largely toed the line, there were no prosecutions, although the police did raid the officers of Drum and Golden City Post, publications with large black circulations. A number of black journalists were held under the emergency regulations; others fled the country.

But reports appearing overseas could not be controlled. Even the normally moderate Times of London was moved to write that the South African government had seized with alacrity "the chance to put into practice the brutal, undemocratic methods which have always had the backing of a powerful minority of the Nationalist Party. The unquestioned duty of every government to maintain law and order has been prostituted. This week alone 1,200 Africans have been detained or arrested. Savage fines, out of all proportion to anything that would be tolerated in a civilized country, have been inflicted on many of the Africans for offenses against the intolerable pass laws . . . the extent of the reign of terror, deliberately created, is harder to estimate because its architects, wisely from their point of view, are keeping it imprecise. The Press in the Union has not been bludgeoned by censorship into silence, but is having to work daily under the shadow of the axe." Coverage like this led *Die Burger* to lament that comment abroad on South Africa was "practically a catastrophe . . . when [British] newspapers like the *Times* and the *Daily Telegraph* become practically hysterical in their vehemence, then it has become for us far, far later than 12 o'clock on the propaganda front."[15]

Now the annual flagellation of the press in Parliament took on a new note. Blaar Coetzee, Nationalist MP for Vereeniging in whose constituency Sharpeville was situated, said "the news the outside world gets from us it gets through the English press . . . the English language and the English press is the window through which the outside world views us. This is the case 90 per cent of the time. If they paint these false pictures, what chance has the Minister of Information? . . . we are reaching a point where criticism stops and treason starts, and the English press often exceeds that point." Another Nationalist MP, Carel de Wet, declared that the time had arrived for the government to provide some means of holding newspapers responsible for what they were doing and saying.[16]

By 1961 South Africa had become a republic and, in the face of unprecedented hostility on the part of other members, had withdrawn from the British Commonwealth. It was encountering increasing pressure at the United Nations and sanctions abroad. Nationalist politicians were inclined to see these developments as the result, not of universal opprobrium of their policies, but of lies and distortions in the mass media in South Africa and abroad. This was the context of a speech in Parliament by Prime Minister Verwoerd, who claimed that

the position in which we have landed, both in the Commonwealth and at the UN, is to a large extent the result of inaccu-

rate reports and a wrong interpretation of the policy of the
Government . . . I would like to see members of the press
coming together . . . to ensure that they apply self-control and
discipline themselves, and to ensure that their patriotism also
serves as a background for them jealously to supervise their
own profession . . . the press in South Africa is not, like other
professions, organized to apply self-discipline. There is not a
single method by which exact reporting can be ensured . . .
South Africa cannot be allowed to suffer continuously, particularly in view of the fact that it now finds itself in a crisis, as the
result of inaccurate reports and distorted interpretations of policy and motive . . . I therefore insist that the press, in the interests of South Africa, particularly in the times in which we
live, should exercise care and that they should keep an eye on
each other.[17]

English-language newspapers responded with some alarm to this
threat.

The *Rand Daily Mail*, making the point that any action against the
press would damage South Africa's reputation abroad even further,
said of the prime minister:

In his warning to the press yesterday there is an ill-concealed
note of panic. He implies possible government action not only
against the presentation of news but also against the publication
of comment. Let him stop to consider what such warnings may
themselves do to the country. If he does so, he cannot fail to
realise that any action he takes to curb the freedom of the press
will everywhere be interpreted as only the first step towards a
general muzzling of speech and opinion in South Africa.[18]

It was clear that if the press did not act to discipline itself, the
government would step in. In March 1962, the Newspaper Press
Union held a special meeting in Johannesburg, attended by representatives of all the principal papers, country papers, and consumer
and trade magazines. Also present were editors, representatives of the
South African Society of Journalists, and non-SASJ journalists. The
SASJ objected strongly to the proposed code of conduct and press

board of reference because it considered the scheme "a first (and disastrous) step towards censorship over political reporting and comment."[19]

At the end of the joint discussions, the NPU adopted the constitution for the Press Board of Reference and a code of conduct. Members were not unanimous in accepting the board. Support came from the Argus group and Afrikaans newspapers. Most of the South African Associated Newspapers were opposed. *The Star* (Argus group) argued that "self-discipline is preferable to state discipline." The *Rand Daily Mail* (SAAN) said: "Some of our colleagues have managed to rationalize acceptance of the code by considering its merits unrelated to the background of political pressure . . . others are franker and say it is preferable to statutory press control. But we have come to regard the 'lesser of two evils' approach as surrender by installment."[20]

The NPU went ahead anyway, and formally accepted the proposals in April 1962. The then chairman of the NPU, M. V. Jooste, managing director of Afrikaanse Pers, said that "any suggestion that outside interference or pressure has in any way influenced the formulation and contents of the proposed code is quite erroneous."[21]

The constitution stipulated that the board's objectives were to maintain the character of the South African press "in accordance with the highest professional and technical standards"; to consider alleged infringements of the code of conduct, and to publish periodical reports on the work of the board "and on any developments which the board regards as inimical to the continuance of a free press in the Republic of South Africa."[22] The board comprised a chairman and an alternate chairman, both retired judges, and two members, also with alternates. All were to be appointed by the executive committee of the Newspaper Publishers Union—in other words by the publishers of the newspaper groups. The board was to adjudicate any complaints that newspapers had contravened the code of conduct.

The code was essentially similar to those in other countries with press councils and contained nothing that a conscientious journalist would not normally observe. It stipulated that in presenting news there should be no willful departure from the facts through distortion, significant omissions, or summarization. If the accuracy of a report was doubted, it should, where possible, be checked before publication. Headlines and posters should fairly reflect the content of reports. It enjoined the use of obscene or salacious material and of excess in the reporting and presentation of sexual matter. The code stipulated that comment should be clearly distinguishable from news. Comment should be made on facts truly stated, free from malice, and not actuated by dishonest motives.

The code did differ from those of other press councils in two material ways. Journalists were not required to observe professional secrecy to protect their sources of information, and a specific injunction that "comment should take cognisance of the complex racial problems of South Africa and the general good and safety of the country and its peoples" was included. The accompanying rules of procedure set up a rather cumbersome machinery for adjudication of complaints. Anyone with a grievance was first obliged to approach the publication concerned. If satisfactory redress was not obtained, the person had to submit his complaint in writing to the board, along with supporting documents and a small deposit that was forfeited if the complaint was deemed trivial or frivolous. A copy of the complaint was sent to the editor concerned, who would be invited to reply within twenty-one days. The editor's reply, in turn, was sent to the complainant who was given a further fourteen days to respond. The case was then considered by the board, which met quarterly. Either party could appear before the board to be examined under oath and could be represented by legal counsel. If the board found that the publication had violated any code provision, it could reprimand the proprietor, editor, or journalist, require its findings to be published in the offending newspaper, and require a correction to be published where necessary. Adherence to the code and the jurisdiction of the board was voluntary, and a publication could withdraw at any time—unless a complaint was pending against it.

The first report of the board, for the period June 1962 to February 1964, listed six complaints adjudicated, five from politicians and the sixth from a political organization. Four were complaints by Nationalist politicians against the English-language press. The board ruled in favor of the press twice, against it four times.

Several principles providing guidance for editors in interpreting the code emerged from the early cases. In three instances, it ruled that when an editor realized that a report was incorrect he should, spontaneously and immediately, publish a full correction and in a position "equally prominent" as the original incorrect report. Further, the board stipulated that a correction should be accompanied by an "admission of error" and an apology to the wronged party. Concerning access, the board ruled that a person or organization attacked in a newspaper was entitled to an opportunity to defend itself. Thus a newspaper was obliged to carry a letter replying to such an attack. Three of the rulings took a relatively liberal line. Regarding confidentiality, the board said that newspapers were in no way bound to refrain from using information regarded as confidential between third parties. The fact that matters were discussed in secret or appeared in a confidential document did not oblige a newspaper not to publish them. On the gathering of news, the board ruled that it had no authority to adjudicate on the manner in which news was obtained; its jurisdiction was confined to news and comment as published. Ruling on a complaint that a report had contravened the clause in the code requiring the press to "take cognisance of the complex racial problems of South Africa," the board said that the code was not intended to stifle all criticism of the government's race policy. At the same time, the board thought "that editors will be well advised to heed the restrictions envisaged in the clause when racial problems are dealt with in their columns." The board chairman, H. H. W. de Villiers, a former judge of the appellate court, noted in a preface that the board had no inherent powers. It could impose no fine nor cite for contempt. This made it highly desirable that the board should have the full cooperation of all sections of the press: "The alternative is the risk that instead of control by consent, the press may have legislative control forced on it."[23]

Meanwhile, the Press Commission presented the first part of its long-awaited report to Parliament in February 1962.[24] It comprised two volumes, totaling 700 pages, and seventeen appendices running to a further 1,566 pages. This first report, which said nothing about a press council, was devoted largely to an analysis of the coverage of

South African news in foreign media—which it characterized as "extremely undesirable." It recommended changes in the constitution of the SAPA, the cooperative news agency, to give the Afrikaans newspapers more say in its affairs. But even at the time of presentation the report was out of date and was tabled without any action being taken on its recommendations.

In the second part of its report, however, the Press Commission did deal with the whole quesiton of control of the press and specifically the NPU's new Press Board. The report, presented to Parliament in May 1964, commented that the Board of Reference "does not satisfy the fundamental requirements of a body designed to discipline or encourage self-control of the press." The commission's major objections were that only owners were represented on the board, not journalists or members of the public. Second, the board had no real disciplinary power—it should have authority to redress wrongs that had been suffered. In other words it should have statutory authority, backed by the power of the state. Third, the code of conduct was not comprehensive enough. For example it did not cover invasion of privacy or secrecy by journalists in search of news. The commission objected also to the fact that the board had no power to deal with individual journalists. Therefore, the Press Commission recommended that a statutory press council be set up. It would, among other things, be expected to maintain press freedom; to encourage accurate reporting; to encourage informed and responsible comment; to encourage the press to "maintain the dignity of the state and its officials," and to receive complaints and "try such matters and give judgement thereon." This council should include proprietors, journalists, the general public, and political parties. Every newspaper and every journalist would be required to register with the council yearly and pay a registration fee. Copies of all news reports sent abroad would have to be filed with the council and be made available to the public a week after their dispatch. The council could try those accused of breaching its code, reprimand any person found guilty and order the judgment be published. It could impose a fine of "unlimited amount."[25]

The commission recommended further that there should be no appeal from the decisions of the press council; that contempt of the press council would be an offense triable by the courts; and that provision should be made for the press council to be financed, at least in part, by a levy on the press.

The press council envisaged by the commission differed in several repects from the Press Board established by the NPU. First, the Board of Reference was a voluntary body, while the Press Commission's recommendation meant that a press council would be created by statute. Second, the Board of Reference had jurisdiction only over members of the NPU who wished to adopt the code of conduct; the Press Commission's press council included all journalists, local and foreign. Third, the commission recommended the registration of journalists, and of all cables sent overseas. Fourth, whereas the Board of Reference had only the power of publicity, the press council envisaged by the Press Commission would have far greater powers, with fines of "unlimited amount." And finally, the proposed press council differed greatly from the composition of the Press Board. The government, however, appeared willing to give the NPU's new board a chance to prove itself, and the recommendations of the Press Commission were not implemented, although its ideas were by no means forgotten and were to emerge again later.

Meanwhile, the Press Board continued to function. Its second report, for March 1964 to January 1968, appeared in October 1968. During this period only eight complaints reached the board, all involving politically active individuals or organizations or government departments and all concerning essentiallly political issues. Four were dismissed, three were upheld, and one was partially upheld. No new principles were involved. In his report, de Villiers noted that, as chairman of the Press Board for six years, "I have come to the conclusion that, generally speaking, we have an excellent press in South Africa that compares favorably with any press in the world." In regard to errors, he said, the remarkable fact was not they they occurred, but that they did not occur more frequently.[26]

The board's third report, for July 1968 to June 1972, listed only 13 complaints that required adjudication. Of these, eight were upheld, four dismissed, and one partially upheld because the newspaper involved, while printing a correction, did not also apologize and express regrets. In the first ten years of the council's existence, therefore, it had adjudicated only twenty-eight complaints—an average of about three a year. While the judgments went against newspapers in fifteen cases, only twice were newspapers reprimanded.[27]

The relatively moderate tone of the Press Board's decisions during its first few years of operation helped allay some misgivings of liberal journalists. The S.A. Society of Journalists was sufficiently reassured as to change its mind about recognition. At the SASJ congress in 1971 the society's president, Roy Rudden, said he had initially opposed the board because of the political threat that had motivated its establishment. "But the Press Council, in its actions and decisions, has done a first-class job. We are very impressed by it," said Rudden. The delegates voted to recognize the board.[28]

But not everyone was happy. The board's lack of impact on newspapers, while appealing to journalists, did not impress critics of the English-language newspapers. Continued press criticism of apartheid led to counterattacks by Nationalist politicians. In October 1971, Prime Minister Vorster accused the press of "stabbing South Africa in the back." A few weeks later Interior Minister Theo Gerdener suggested that the press council be given far wider powers, including the ability to impose heavy fines on offending newspapers. He suggested also that the council should be able to take action on its own. "I would suggest that the Press Council be given the power to take the initiative in any case which it believes should be investigated," he said. The press came in for further criticism, particularly at the Transvaal congress of the National party in September 1972. The newly elected Transvaal leader, Dr. Connie Mulder, declared that "if the press acted irresponsibly, it did not deserve the freedom it enjoyed and the government would act, even if the price was the freedom of the press."[29]

The following year, addressing the National party's Cape congress in September 1973, Vorster said that the government would amend the Riotous Assemblies Act to enable the courts to "deal properly" with people who were sowing enmity between the races. Newspapers clearly were the target. "If South Africa ever finds itself in the position in which Rhodesia now is, we will not allow the newspapers to play the same role as they did in Rhodesia," he said, referring to the Rhodesian press's outspoken opposition to the Smith government. Vorster said

there were people, newspapers, and organizations who, out of frustra-
tion, would not hesitate to do all in their power to cause a confrontation between white and nonwhite South Africans. The country's race
relations were so delicate that the government could not allow them to
be disturbed. Vorster repeated his allegations at the Transvaal party
congress later that month. He said the press was trying to bring about
a racially explosive situation, and quoted a letter from a black that had
appeared in the *Rand Daily Mail*, saying separate development led to
poverty and disease and to enslavement of blacks. Such a letter, said
Vorster, should never have been published. He said he had warned
newspaper directors and editors and was not going to warn them
again; either they must come to heel now, or he would step in and
bring them to heel. And he gave the press an ultimatum: It had until
January 1974 to "clean up its house."[30]

   These threats provoked a strong reaction from all the English-
language newspapers, the SASJ, and even from some Afrikaans newspapers. The *Rand Daily Mail* huffed that a proud and healthy press
"was not going to be intimidated into self-censorship." The *Mercury*
remarked that Vorster "does not say how they [the newspapers] must
put their house in order. It's no good asking him, because the time for
talking is finished . . . For its part, *The Mercury* does not know what
the Prime Minister is talking about . . . if the Prime Minister does not
like what the *Mercury* prints, he must make the next move." Even Dr.
Willem de Klerk, editor of *Die Transvaler*, defied the official line. De
Klerk wrote that it was the politicians who were irresponsible. At the
very congress where calls for press responsibility met with loud
applause, he said, the delegates themselves were saying reckless
things, like "I am a racist," "Immigrants are the scum of the earth,"
and "African children should be washed so they would not smell."
Some delegates, he said, had made statements about the press that
amounted to a plea for dictatorship. He pointed out that the press is
"the mirror that reflects what goes on in society . . . but where the
mirror correctly reflects what has been said or done you cannot blame
the mirror, if when you look into it, the face you see there is an ugly
face." De Klerk's defiance was staggering in that previously his
newspaper had seldom if ever deviated from the party line. In later
years, the Afrikaans papers showed even more independence.[31]

The newspapers' response angered Vorster even more, and in September he announced his intention to introduce legislation that would force off the streets any newspaper that persisted in publishing articles that incited racial hatred. Vorster said that when a newspaper said to him, as the *Rand Daily Mail* had done, that it was not prepared to censor itself, and that he should do whatever he wished, it was looking for a confrontation. "I am looking at legislation now which will contain a clause providing that if a newspaper continues to be guilty of publishing articles inciting racial hatred it will simply not appear on the streets." And Vorster indicated he was not concerned about reaction abroad—a reaction the English-language newspapers had long felt would stay the governments' hand. "People who are looking for a confrontation with the Government will get it," he said.[32] This new threat again evoked a flood of comment. Newspapers pointed out the almost impossibility of defining "racial incitement," and if it could be defined, who would be to blame—the politician who made the remark, or the newspaper that reported it?

The newspaper publishers, their very existence threatened by Vorster's pledge to ban papers that displeased him, were far more conciliatory than their editors. In October 1973, the NPU asked Vorster for a meeting. Vorster refused, saying he had made his position "perfectly clear." The editors who had rejected self-censorship, he said, presumably had done so with the approval of their directors, so any further discussions would serve no useful purpose. "Under the circumstances," Vorster wrote to the NPU, "I have no option but to finalize the contemplated legislation and to proceed with my plans."[33]

In an attempt to dissuade Vorster, the S.A. Society of Journalists organized a symposium on press freedom in Cape Town in July 1974, to commemorate the stand taken 150 years earlier by Thomas Pringle and John Fairbairn in support of press freedom. Furthermore, the symposium was timed to coincide with the opening of Parliament and so gain maximum publicity. Virtually all major English newspaper editors were present; notably absent were the editors of the Afrikaans papers. Raymond Louw, editor of the *Rand Daily Mail*, saw this as "yet another example of the Afrikaans Press' dedication to the interests of their own political party rather than to journalism." Their absence, said Louw, "saddens me, because if representatives of one section of the public cannot congregate with representatives of another to affirm a common loyalty to the ideals of a profession serving the public interest, there seems little hope for all of us in the future." The managing director of the Argus group, Leyton Slater, then chairman of the NPU, said that the NPU would fight any form of control by the government, but did not mention that the NPU was, even at that time, negotiating with the government on steps to strengthen the press council. The NPU had prepared a revised constitution and a more restrictive code of conduct, which had been delivered to Vorster two days before the symposium.[34]

The amended constitution widened the powers of the council, giving it "teeth" by enabling it to impose fines of up to R 10,000. The fines would be imposed on guilty publications whether the infringement was the responsibility of the proprietor or any editor, journalist, or other person associated with the publication. The new constitution required all members of the NPU to accept the jurisdiction of the council, and it gave the council the power to insist on the prominent publication of its findings in the newspaper concerned. Even more controversial than the power to impose fines was the new code of conduct. One change, possibly a sop to the council's critics, stipulated that "the public have the right to be informed and that publications therefore have an obligation to report news." Another new clause decreed that "the presentation of news should be in context and preserve a sense of balance." But two new clauses went considerably beyond the original code in specifying the "standards applying to South African publications." One demanded of newspapers "due care and responsibility concerning matters which can have the effect of stirring up feelings of hostility between racial, ethnic, religious or cultural groups in South Africa, or which can affect the safety and defense of the country and its peoples." The second required "due compliance with agreements entered into between the Newspaper Press Union and any department of the Government of South Africa with a view to public safety or security or the general good."[35]

The announcement of the new constitution and code divided the country's journalists. Leyton Slater spoke for the NPU and Argus when he said the changes represented an effort to keep control of the contents of the newspapers "out of the hands of bureaucrats and politicians." Slater said the NPU believed Vorster was not bluffing about introducing legislation to control the press. "The argument that Mr. Vorster was bluffing was based largely on the theme that the kind of control he envisaged would be too damaging to South Africa's image abroad," said Slater. But he pointed out that the government was introducing legislation to remove the rights of playwrights, authors, publishers, and magazine proprietors from appealing to the courts against decisions of the censors. "Would one more step—action against newspapers—make much difference to South Africa's image abroad?"[36]

The changes were supported in the editorial columns of the Argus group papers while, as before, the most vehement opposition came from SAAN editors. And the new code was rejected by SASJ chapters all over the country, declaring it a capitulation to threats and smears that would dangerously inhibit reporting.

The Afrikaans press took a far more ambivalent line. *Die Transvaler* felt that the NPU's proposals at least deserved careful consideration. "We hope they will be accepted as an honest and sincere effort by the press itself to put right in its own circle what is wrong, and that it will help ensure that the government will not deem it necessary to continue with the envisaged legislation against the press." *Die Vaderland* commented that "the proposed amendments can only benefit the press. Perhaps the government will be less inclined to come forward with its 'take hold' legislation—measures about which we are also a little cagey."[37]

Having forced the NPU to bring its press council more into line with what the government would like it to be, Vorster continued to play cat and mouse with the press, refusing to say whether he accepted the new council or still planned to proceed with legislation. From Vorster's point of view, keeping the press in a state of uncertainty might keep it in line. He clearly believed that the outspoken reporting and comment in the opposition newspapers could jeopardize his politically sensitive plans to divide the country into separate black and white states. There were also security considerations caused by instability in Rhodesia and by Portugal's planned withdrawal from Mozambique and Angola, which would expose South Africa's borders to potentially hostile black governments. By dividing the industry, setting one group of editors against the other, and exacting a self-disciplinary code, Vorster could continue to boast of a free press. And to the beleaguered Nationalists it was important to be able to point north to black Africa and ask critics to mention one country where the press was as free to criticize government policy as it was in South Africa.

While the government kept the NPU in suspense it continued its criticisms. Opening the Free State congress of the National party in November 1974, Vorster hit at the press for "irresponsible reporting." He said that a report in the Johannesburg *Financial Mail* had called a speech by South Africa's ambassador to the United Nations "the most breathtaking falsifications" ever presented to the world body. Writing this about a most important speech displayed a lack of patriotism, said Vorster. "I want to say before my discussions with the Newspaper Press Union that if editors carry on that line then the discussions are a waste of time. That would be a pity because I believe the new code is an improvement on the old one. But it is not worth the paper it is written on if that is the way the editors carry on." In September, Justice Minister James Kruger, angered by the breaking of an embargo on some photographs released by the government, suggested that if the NPU could not discipline its members, he would do so: "If the Press Union is not capable, as it appears to me they are not capable, of disciplining their members, then obviously it would be better for me to rely on a proper act (of Parliament) to discipline the press." The minister of defense, P. W. Botha, threatened to scrap an eight-year-old agreement between the press and the minister of defense because some newspapers were leaving blank spaces in reports for which permission to publish had been withheld by the Defense Department. Adherence to the agreement was covered by a clause in the revised code of conduct. In December 1975, Vorster returned the NPU's amended code, suggesting some changes, which were scheduled to be discussed with the NPU in 1976. But before they could be acted upon, events in South Africa led to a truly draconian set of new proposals to discipline the press.[38]

On June 16, 1976, the worst outbreak of violence in South Africa since Sharpeville began in Soweto. Before the violence ended more than a year later, hundreds would die, thousands would be arrested, and millions of dollars in property would be destroyed. Rioting, looting, and arson quickly spread, not only through Soweto but to other townships in the area, and then around the country.

The government responded with a severe crackdown, rushing through Parliament the Internal Security Act that widened the scope of the 1950 Suppression of Communism Act. It empowered the minister of justice to ban organizations or publications and to imprison or otherwise restrict persons without their being found "Communistic." They could be banned if they were deemed guilty of "expressing views or conveying information the publication of which is calculated to endanger the security of the state or the maintenance of public order."

Once again South Africa dominated the world's headlines. The United Nations Security Council adopted a resolution condemning the South African government for "massive violence against and killings of the African people." Governments expressed their concern or condemnation. Correspondents flocked to the country, sending out a flood of highly unfavorable publicity.

Inevitably the government's attention turned to the press, which many Nationalists believed was responsible for prolonging the unrest. If not agitators themselves, the newspapers were seen as providing a forum, a mouthpiece for the country's enemies. Vorster had still not given the NPU a final answer on its revised press council and code of conduct. Now he was pressing them to accept legislative curbs on the press. In February 1977, the government gave the NPU copies of proposed legislation that would impose direct state control on newspapers. The publishers rejected the proposals out of hand, talks broke down, and a few days later, on March 12, 1977, the government introduced in Parliament its Newspaper Press Bill. The bill embodied the Nationalist ideal of how the press should be controlled—a statutory press council, backed by the authority of the state that would administer a press code of conduct far beyond the restrictions already embodied in the NPU's revised code.

The bill provided for a press council comprising a chairman, who would be a judge or a retired judge of the Supreme Court, and up to four other members, one-half to be appointed from a list of persons nominated by the state president, the other half from a list provided by the NPU. The council would function in much the same manner as a court of law with the complainant and the editor or owner of the newspaper permitted to appear before the council in person or be represented by lawyers. The council could require testimony under oath and was given subpoena and contempt powers. South Africans writing in foreign publications would come under the council's jurisdiction.

The bill gave the council the authority to impose reprimands or fines of up to R 1,000 on guilty individual reporters and up to R 10,000 on newspaper owners. And, as an ultimate step, it could suspend publication for a period. The council's decisions could not be appealed to a court of law, but would be subject to review by three judges of the Supreme Court. The bill prohibited insurance companies from covering newspapers against penalties imposed by the council.

The code of conduct included in the legislation took over the provisions of the NPU's revised code, but went further. A clause in the NPU code calling for "exceptional care and responsibility" in reporting matters that might affect the safety of the state or the peace and good order and the defense of the country was expanded to include reports that might affect the Republic's "economic prosperity." The most far-reaching addition was a section stipulating that newspapers should ensure that "the standards of decency and public morals of the nations and population groups of the Republic are not debased"; that relations between the different groups were not prejudiced; that the name of the Republic was not damaged abroad, and that "the safety of the state, the common weal and the peace and good order are not endangered."[39]

Publication of the bill united the English and Afrikaans newspapers in an unprecedented show of opposition. The outraged reaction of the English papers and newpapers abroad was predictable. *The Star* said the bill "would corrode the confidence of South Africans, along with their right to know what is really happening." The *Rand Daily Mail* warned: "We are all in peril. In proposing to destroy press freedom as it has been known in South Africa, the Government's reason has finally snapped."[40]

More unexpected was the reaction of the Afrikaans newspapers. B. J. Schoeman, a former Nationalist cabinet minister and then a director of Perskor, stated bluntly that "in spite of what the minister [Dr. Mulder] said, the bill is aimed at establishing press censorship." But Willem de Klerk, editor of the chain's senior paper, *Die Transvaler*, took a more conciliatory line, pointing out that self-control was more practical, more fair and better than control by the state.[41] The board of directors of Nasionale Pers, the other large Afrikaans newspaper chain, reacted more conservatively than most of its editors, virtually all of whom were critical of the bill. The SASJ rejected the bill outright, pointing out that abundant legislation already existed to provide for the protection of the individual and the safety of the state through the due process of law.

A week after the bill was introduced, Vorster met with a deputation from the NPU including the union's secretary, G. G. Uys, and the chairmen of each of the four major newspaper groups. Discussions continued for three days. On March 23 Vorster announced that he was withdrawing the bill and would give the NPU one year to test its new self-disciplinary measures.

This was by no means a victory for the press. In exchange, the NPU had to agree to accept a code of conduct, worded almost identically to that in the Newspaper Bill but with some important differences. Unlike the council proposed in the bill, the new NPU body would not have the power to suspend publication or fine individual journalists. And the new clause in the Newspaper Bill code that enjoined newspapers from prejudicing relations between different groups or damaging the Republic's name abroad was dropped. Thus, an essentially toothless council set up only fifteen years previously had evolved into something far more to the liking of the government.

The publicity attendant on the Newspaper Bill and the revision of the Press Board and the procedural changes that made it easier to lodge complaints resulted in a much larger volume of cases being brought before the council. In the first two years after the revisions were introduced in May 1977, the council received almost four hundred complaints. Of these, ninety-five were settled between the parties and only seventeen were adjudicated. The rest were rejected, dismissed, or allowed to lapse. Of the seventeen cases that were heard, eleven were upheld, five were settled, and judgment was reserved on one. With regard to these figures, the NPU noted that the "small number of 17 complaints that reached the hearing stage reflected a healthy press." It suggested also that the sharp reduction from four hundred to seventeen "hard-core" cases implied a certain amount of harassment of the press by frivolous or unsubstantiated complaints. The council's figures for 1978–79 showed a similar trend. Of the eighteen complaints received during the year, only seven were placed before the council. Of these four were upheld—two of them on grounds that later were found to be false—and three were settled at the hearings. The rest were rejected or lapsed because the complainants did not pursue the matters.[42]

Between May 1981 and September 1982, the council received 145 complaints—thirty-four of them from the government. About 25 per cent were dismissed by the chairman; another 65 per cent lapsed or were settled between the parties. Thus only 10 per cent of the complaints were still pending.

This record by no means appeased the Nationalists who could see no change in English press opposition to government policies. A parade of government officials appeared before the Steyn Commission of Inquiry into the Mass Media in 1981, calling for new measures—especially a statutory council and a register of journalists—to bring the press to heel. (See Chap. 4 for a continuation of the confrontation under Prime Minister Botha and the creation in 1983 of the S.A. Media Council to replace the Press Council.)

Clearly the Nationalist government would not be satisfied until it had instituted statutory press control or at least until the press itself had adopted regulations every bit as stringent as the government desired. The history of the Press Council, as Laurence Gandar, former editor of the *Rand Daily Mail* puts it, is not a straightforward example of a profession's submitting itself to the normal process of self-discipline. The council, says Gandar, "is a reluctant response to raw political pressure applied over a long period—an act of appeasement, in fact." Second, he says, the council has little to do with any felt need to codify the ethics of journalism: "It has everything to do with the political clash in South Africa of two fundamentally different outlooks as to the nature of society and how the public good can best be served."[43]

4 | The Steyn Commission and Three Concepts of the Press

Underlying the continuing controversy over the Press Council has been one persistent policy of the Nationalists: to bend the English press to its will, to find a way to make it conform to the concerns, and even the world view, of the ruling Afrikaners. Nationalist prime ministers from Malan to Vorster have sought to "discipline" the pesky opposition newspapers into being "responsible."

The Nationalists have been trying to "find a lever" to control the press without imposing overt censorship, but this is not easy to do because freedom of the press is a long-established value in South African society. Even right-wing Afrikaners give it lip service, and the Afrikaans newspapers have shown increasing resistance to Nationalist efforts to restrict press independence. Further, the opposition English press, financed as it is by major financial and mining interests, represents significant economic power. And, finally, the Nationalists recognize that South Africa's claim to the "freest press in Africa" is one of its few assets in world public opinion.

P. W. Botha's major effort to find a lever was through the mechanism of the "Commission of Inquiry into the Mass Media," usually called the Steyn Commission, which held hearings from November 1980 to April 1981 and issued its final, 1,367-page report, along with draft legislation, to Parliament on February 1, 1982.[1] Prime ministers have used such commissions of inquiry to gather evidence on public policy issues from interested parties and then make recommendations for new laws. In most cases, the recommendations have been propos-

76

als the prime minister had wanted all along; the procedure was a way of preparing the public for the government's action. A commission of inquiry can create the impression that public opinion favors the new legislation. The Steyn Commission was one of several established by P. W. Botha that concerned themselves in one way or another with press performance. Opponents of the government regard such commissions of inquiry as hollow exercises or public relations gimmicks that erect a facade of democratic procedures (at least among whites) for a ruling minority that will usually do what it wishes anyway.

The Steyn Commission was mandated to "inquire into and report on the question of whether the conduct of, and the handling of, matters by the mass media meet the needs and interests of the South African community and the demands of the times, and, if not, how they can be improved."[2] From its inception, the commission was controversial. No representative of the press, not even an Afrikaans journalist, would agree to serve on the five-person commission, and the English press opposed it as unnecessary and worse, an unwarranted intrusion into press prerogatives. Indeed, two major recommendations of the 1982 report of the Steyn Commission—a system of licensing journalists and a proposal to break up ownership of the major newspaper groups, Argus and SAAN—had been advocated for years by government spokesmen. At the same time, this and similar commissions provided revealing insights into the wide differences over political values and goals within deeply divided South African society. This was reflected in the testimony of those appearing before Judge M. T. Steyn and his four commissioners: Dr. Dirk "Das" Herbst, director of the Southern Africa Forum; Klaus von Lieres und Wilkau, a deputy attorney general of the Transvaal; Basil Landau, executive director of the Union Corporation Mining House; and James Hopkins, a Natal educator and vice-chairman of the SABC board.

The differing views within South Africa over the rights and duties of the press and its proper role in that divided society surfaced clearly during the extended hearings. The government used these hearings as a sounding board to express its unhappiness with the press and to lay the groundwork for further legal restraints on newspapers. In a very real sense, the work of the commission was a continuation of the

process of harassment and intimidation that had begun in 1950 soon
after the Nationalists took control.

The parade of government officials and supporters who testified
revealed much about establishment, right-wing attitudes toward the
press and echoed antipress sentiments heard years earlier. Johan
Eysen, press officer of the Department of Cooperation and Development, led off for the state with a call for a statutory monitoring body
with power to act against reporters, editors, and "people who expressed opinions, who were irresponsible and disrupted community
relations," i.e., stirred up the blacks. But Eysen insisted he was
opposed to statutory censorship of the press.[3]

Vlok Delport of the Department of Foreign Affairs and Information said that no South African papers were deliberately disloyal to the
state; nonetheless, they formed part of the "psychological onslaught"
against it, particularly as providers of "negative information" for the
overseas press. According to J. L. Scheepers of the Department of
Manpower Utilization, newspaper reporting on labor matters did
great damage to the economy. Such stories involving blacks, he said,
were presented "as though blacks were being treated unfairly by their
employers."[4]

Press support for the pardon or release of Nelson Mandela, imprisoned ANC leader, was regarded as "subversive" by the military,
according to Brigadier G. Wassenaar, who appeared for the Defense
Force. He also condemned two articles on the ANC in *The Star* which,
he said, gave the impression the group was an effective revolutionary
organization with reasonable demands, driven to violence by white
intransigence. Wassenaar suggested that a statutory council be established to discipline journalists by striking them from a professional
register which should be established. (This was a clear indication of
what the government expected the commission to recommend.)[5]

Brigadier J. Coetzee, chief of the Security Police, said that the
media were not responsible enough in the face of the "onslaught"
against the country and criticized those who, he said, reported that
South Africa was sliding into a revolutionary war. He declared newspaper articles commemorating the banning of Black Consciousness
organizations in 1977 bordered on support for those organizations and
that press reporting of the Steve Biko case had been part of a campaign

to discredit detention without trial. Coetzee urged that journalists
who identified themselves with political groups and so compromised
their objectivity be barred from writing.[6]

Professor Mike Louw, an Afrikaner academic, told the commission
that "some newspapers were in the country, but not of the country.
They are merely present in Johannesburg but they are not South
African." One of the problems, he said, was that the "English press
does not always hold the same view of the national interest as does the
Government, and presents a picture overseas which can be said to be
deliberately distorted."[7]

A right-wing journalist, Ivor Benson, told the commission that the
policies of both the major English newspaper groups, SAAN and
Argus, were controlled by the powers behind the "international
capitalist-communist conspiracy." The two press groups, he said,
were a threat to national security, little more than internal wings of
"foreign interests" waging undeclared war on South Africa. He accused government leaders of showing no clear will to take corrective
action against press "abuses" and cited Taiwan as an example of how
the media could be harnessed for the total strategy purposes of the
authorities.[8]

What emerged from the progovernment testimony, not surpris-
ingly, was the government's craving for a press obedient to its will and
its desire to dictate news coverage. Essentially, the press was accused
of giving aid and comfort to the nation's enemies, and several witnesses suggested what the government had in mind to remedy the
problem. Brigadier Gerard van Rooy, speaking for the South African
Defense Force, said that the "professionalization" of journalism and
the establishment of a statutory body to control reporting were
needed. He said that journalism could possibly be raised to a professional status and journalists registered in the same way as doctors. A
minimum qualification to enter the profession could be established,
and journalists who contravened statutory regulations governing the
profession could be disciplined or disqualified from practicing.[9]

This all added up to a muzzled opposition press, yet, ironically,
most testifying officials went to great lengths to deny they were
advocating press censorship or news control. While there was no
evidence that the submissions of the various departments had been

orchestrated, they all followed the official line enunciated by former
Minister of Interior and Justice Alwyn Schlebusch and by Prime
Minister P. W. Botha in various public statements.

Schlebusch envisaged a press code applicable to all South African
newspapers; a statutory press council, with press and public members, empowered to investigate contraventions of the code and to
discipline transgressors; and a code of conduct for journalists who
could be temporarily or permanently barred from journalism if found
by the press council to have violated the code.

On a number of occasions, Botha had acknowledged the right of the
press to convey the truth to its readers. But he said he was opposed to a
press that caused "confusion." "We cannot afford to confuse our
people in these times," he said at Bloemfontein in September 1980.
These views, according to Chris Freimond of the *Rand Daily Mail*,
were reflected in nearly all evidence from progovernment sources:
they acknowledged the importance of press freedom as stated by
Botha but proposed curbs as outlined by Schlebusch.[10]

Significantly, in spite of the government testimony alleging "negative, subversive, irresponsible, twisted, and unbalanced and incorrect" reporting, none of the officials of seven departments that came
before the commission had referred grievances to the existing Press
Council, whose function it was to investigate just such complaints.
That fact later proved to be one of the stronger counterarguments
given by press representatives before Judge Steyn.

Although they opposed establishment of the Steyn Commission
itself, South Africa's white journalists took the opportunity to respond strongly to the government's views on press freedom and
performance. (No black journalists were willing to appear before the
commission.) Spokesmen from both English and Afrikaans newspapers showed a rare unity in that they all agreed that the South African
press was already bound by too many restrictive laws and that there
was no need for any further legislation, especially a register of journalists. The thrust of the press's testimony was that government denials
notwithstanding, some form of censorship was the ultimate goal.

Harvey Tyson, editor of *The Star*, said restrictive measures had
already reached "critical proportions" and urged the commission to

reject any calls for more restrictions. What was needed, he said, was a reestablishment of trust between state officials and the press.[11]

The editor of the *Rand Daily Mail*, Allister Sparks, said the government was looking for some basis on which it could take further action against the press without looking too crude. He said he believed the government was already resolved to increase its restrictions on the press. "I am satisfied that this was the Government's motive in appointing this commission—it hopes it will find something in the commission's report that it can use as an apparant judicial justification for introducing new restrictive legislation," Sparks told the commission.[12]

These views were echoed by Joel Mervis, former editor of the *Sunday Times* and observer for the International Press Institute, who argued that the proposed register of journalists was sinister and dangerous. "I repeat my warning that the government sees in this register a subtle means to subdue the press" and, if it is implemented, could effectively control press freedom in South Africa, he said. Such measures were a logical consequence of apartheid, Mervis said, and should be seen as part and parcel of the government's denial of human rights to millions in the country and of such practices as detention without trial. The basic problem of press freedom, Mervis said, was that the government wanted the more than twenty-one million Africans to read and hear only what it deemed fit. "When you have a majority with no democratic or political rights and not represented in the decision-making of the country, then it is the duty of any honorable newspaper to act as the voice of those unrepresented millions," Mervis said.[13]

The Newspaper Press Union (NPU), which represented the proprietors of both the English and Afrikaans daily and Sunday newspapers, made the press's most comprehensive presentation. The fact that South Africa was a country under stress, the NPU argued, did not mean the nation should dispense with freedoms painstakingly acquired over three centuries. "For it is in times like these—wherever they occur in the world—that those in authority tend to increase their power, and in so doing, upset the delicate balance in communication between the rulers and people." The NPU statement urged that the enormous range of laws restricting publication of news and information in the media be reviewed and amended or eliminated from the statute books where possible. "The principle should be the encouragement of a free flow of information wherever possible," the NPU memorandum stated.[14]

Although often at odds with their NPU bosses, the Southern Africa Society of Journalists (SASJ), mainly English-speaking journalists, agreed on the dangers of a register of journalists. The SASJ submission rejected any moves to "professionalize" journalism and establish a statutory body similar to the medical council. The effect of such a move was termed "beyond contemplation," and the SASJ predicted journalism would be irreparably altered.[15]

If these views from the opposition English Press were somewhat predictable, the opinions of leading Afrikaans newspaper editors were not. Editor Harold Pakendorf, whose newspaper, *Die Vaderland*, supported the National party, called for fewer, not more, curbs on press freedom, including a constitutional guarantee of free speech, similar to the First Amendment of the U.S. Constitution. Further curbs on press freedom, Pakendorf said, could turn the country into one in which "civilized, democratic people" would not want to live.[16]

Dr. Willem de Klerk, editor of *Die Transvaler*, said the state must be very careful not to restrict the freedom of the press by any further legislation.[17] Ton Vosloo, editor of the influential *Beeld*, said the Steyn Commission should be the medium to recommend to authorities a revision of existing statutory restraints on the press.[18] Although wide differences between Afrikaans and English editors still remained over the permissible limits on press freedom, all spokesmen for newspapers before the commission opposed any further restrictions.

On February 1, 1982, the Steyn Commission of Inquiry into the Mass Media presented its lengthy report to Parliament at Cape Town some eighteen months after it had started work. Despite accurate forecasts as to its contents and general recommendations, publication of the bulky report still set off a storm of protest in the South African press. For if the report's recommendations were to be carried out, the press faced still stricter controls.

The most far-reaching recommendation was for a legally enforced "professionalization" of journalism under a vague code of conduct to

be enforced by a central general council of journalists.[19] If Parliament
adopted the proposed Journalists Bill, all journalists would be listed
on a "roll of journalists." They would all need certain qualifications
and be required to pass certain examinations before being allowed to
practice. In addition, no one who had been convicted of "any subversive activity" would be allowed to work as a journalist. This could
have disqualified several respected journalists who, at one time or
another, had fallen afoul of the severe security laws. Black journalists
would have been particularly vulnerable although the "chilling
effect" of such a licensing system would have affected any journalist
or publication trying to report the political realities of South Africa.

The proposed general council, which would have powers to discipline journalists who contravened the "code of conduct," would be
initially appointed by the government. In time, its membership
would be partly elected members and partly government appointees,
but press critics expected the council would always have a majority of
government supporters.

The council would enforce a code of conduct that basically called
for objectivity and fairness; however, as outlined, the code was so
vague that its requirements were likely to be whatever the general
council said they were. Two clauses in the proposed code were
particularly troubling to working journalists: One would require that
"due care and responsibility shall be exercised as to subjects that may
cause enmity or give offense in racial, ethnic, religious, or cultural
matters in the republic or incite persons to contravene the law." The
other would require that care and responsibility should be exercised
on "matters that may detrimentally affect the peace and good order,
the safety and defense of the republic and its people, the economy and
the country's international position."[20] If enforced, either clause
could severely inhibit the reporting of the most significant news story
in South Africa: the political confrontation between blacks and the
dominant whites.

The Steyn Commission's other major recommendation proposed
forcing major shareholders in the press to sell off large parts of their
interests in order to obtain as wide a spread of shareholders as possible. Steyn recommended that no one be allowed to own more than one
per cent of a newspaper publishing company if it is a public company

or more than 10 per cent if it is a privately held company. Obvious targets were the Argus company and SAAN, owners of the opposition press, which had large cross-holdings in each other's enterprises. The report said that a monopoly situation posed the "biggest single threat" to a truly free press.

The response by the press in early 1982 to the published Steyn report was immediate and blunt. The *Rand Daily Mail* editorialized: "Let there be no illusions about it: if implemented, the Steyn Commission proposals for a statutory press council will be a massive, perhaps fatal, assault on your right to be kept informed of what is happening in your own country. It does not matter that the Commission believes it is protecting press freedom. The harsh reality is that it is opening the way to destroying it. It is putting in the hands of the Government an ultimate deterrent in dealing with newspapers." *The Star* said, "The latest proposal for control and discipline and licensing of journalists is not merely another straw for the Press's back. It is a hammerblow to standards and to freedom of information. This is our conviction . . . Far from advancing the profession of journalism in this country, the Steyn Commission proposals are likely to drive the best, most qualified reporters out of the business."[21] The *Cape Times* called the proposals "a blueprint for government press controls." If pushed through Parliament, the paper said, "there will no longer be a free press in South Africa."[22] This view was echoed by all the English-language papers, including the right-wing *Citizen*.

The Afrikaans papers generally reacted with bland editorials. But some of the most influential and outspoken editors, including Vosloo of *Beeld* and de Klerk of *Die Transvaler*, expressed strong opposition to the establishment of a statutory press council.[23]

During the outcry that followed the publication of the proposed Journalists' Act, the government hesitated to push the bill through the Parliament. The NPU, backed by its Afrikaans newspaper members, mobilized its forces and held a series of meetings with the key official involved, Interior Minister Chris Heunis. Finally, after five months of bargaining, the Botha government backed off from its plans to license reporters and thus tighten controls over the press.

Instead, the NPU newspapers agreed to set up a new media council of their own design, with powers to reprimand and fine newspapers but not to strike journalists from a register. Further, the government was to "recognize" the new media council formally. Editors expressed concern that this might open the way for an indirect system of government control of the press. But editors felt that they had won a victory of sorts and that this compromise was far less ominous than the register of journalists advocated by the Steyn Commission.

Several factors influenced the Botha government's decision to back off. David Dalling, media spokesman for the opposition Progressive Federal party, believed that the Reagan administration's influence was a major consideration. "This is difficult to quantify," Dalling said, "but I know the Americans have made a prominent issue of press freedom, and the government is reluctant to do anything that will cool its relationship with the Reagan administration."[24]

Another important influence was opposition by the progovernment Afrikaans newspapers which stood solidly with the English papers. Peter McLean, chairman of the NPU, said the support shown by Afrikaans publishers was decisive.

Consequently, after Interior Minister Heunis failed to shake the publishers' unity, a compromise draft law was worked out. The press acquiesced to the minister's demands that it improve its system of "self-discipline" by replacing the old press council with a new one. At the last minute, however, Heunis suddenly introduced another press law on June 11, 1982, to make the new media council a statutory body and force all newspapers to submit to it by joining the Newspaper Press Union.

This partial resurrection of the earlier plan for a statutory council was seen as an effort to control two small right-wing newspapers—*Die Afrikaner* and *Die Patriot*—which do not belong to the NPU and are supported by Afrikaner factions that have broken away from the National party. Botha and his colleagues obviously feared their influence among "*verkrampte*" Afrikaners. In the face of strong opposition, Heunis withdrew the clause making the body a statutory one. The final compromise law, passed in the last hours of the parliamentary session in July 1982, was the Registration of Newspapers Amendment Act, No. 84 of 1982. Key provisions were that the minister of internal affairs could cancel the registration of newspapers if the publishers did not subject themselves for disciplinary purposes to the

NPU's new media council. Thus, the renegade *Die Patriot* and *Die Afrikaner* would be brought under the jurisdiction of the NPU and thus subject to at least indirect government coercion. Further, the act provided for recognition of the new media council by the minister. The media council was to be "an independent and voluntary body (none of whose members shall be appointed by the government)." The clause on government recognition caused a good deal of concern among publishers.

In sum, the Steyn Commission recommendations for licensing of journalists were not adopted by the government. But the inquiry had added an important new chapter to the continuing struggle for control of the printed word in South Africa. The 1,400-page report with its somewhat paranoid and extremist perception of the "total onslaught" was ridiculed by many South Africans and became in time something of an embarrassment to the Botha government. It was too much of a polemic for any but right-wing extremists to take seriously.

Nevertheless, the eighteen-month run of Judge Steyn's commission, well publicized from initial hearing to final published report, illustrated the continuing pattern in press-government relations: the government savagely criticizes the press and then threatens new crippling press controls, but when the NPU agrees to "put its house in order"—i.e., censor itself—the government once again backs down. Until the next time.

Visions of Total Onslaught
with Press Complicity

In addition to the discussion and recommendations directly relating to the press, another extensive section of the Steyn Commission report—all of volume 2 or some 587 pages, plus 45 pages of the introduction—was given over to "the southern African conflict and threat situation." Although this long, rambling, ideological mélange has little to do directly with an inquiry into press performance, it does reveal much about right-wing Afrikaner thinking.

The aims of the external "onslaught" were summarized on page 109:

The external onslaught has as its aim nothing less than the
political and moral subversion of the White man, his replace-
ment by a black majority government in a unitary state with,
depending on who wins, guidelines for a Marxist, radical-
socialist or liberal-democratic welfare-capitalist, socio-political
system. The UN is the main protagonist in the external propaganda onslaught against the Republic. It is eagerly assisted by
the Third World and some Commonwealth Countries and the
Soviet Bloc. The first aim is to isolate the Republic by mobilizing international opinion against it; the second aim is the destruction of the present government in South Africa by, inter
alia, supporting terrorist movements, directly aided by nongovernmental organizations such as the World Council of
Churches. In this process, Soviet strategic objectives are promoted. The Republic has been singled out for a bitter,
ongoing, biased and relentless onslaught.

Various elements of the total onslaught are presumably all working
to the same end, so that even the *New York Times* and *Washington Post*
as well as the South African English press are aiding and abetting
Soviet strategic aims. But even so, there are certain identifiable enemies: Soviet Communism, Western liberalism, black theology and
black nationalism, and the Black Consciousness movement itself.
The main thrust of the onslaught comes from Moscow:

The Soviet Union has launched a fierce, multi-dimensional
and rapidly intensifying onslaught upon the RSA. The Soviet
power structure has an unstoppable momentum for revolution
and war, with the largest military force, and the most sophisticated terror machine in the world, the KGB, with the ultimate
objective of world domination. Soviet imperialism intends to
establish regimes sympathetic to it in strategically important
theaters outside Europe, and this includes South Africa as a
"target state." It operates preferably by the process of using
proxy forces, such as the S.A. Communist Party, ANC and
PAC to conduct the revolutionary war in order to neutralize
Western Europe by denying it access to strategic minerals and

oil, before finally attacking the USA. In this process, the political will and morale of the "target countries" [i.e., South Africa] must be snapped and subverted.[25]

Western liberal democracies (and their media) are said to assist Soviet world domination out of naiveté or stubbornness.

The Western politico-cultural inability or unwillingness to grasp the agonizing reality of Soviet Communism is probably the main reason for the failure of the Western news media to alert their reading and viewing public to the real gravity of the Soviet threat. In this respect, (with some rare exceptions) the Western media have largely misled the public over the past 30 years as to the dread significance of the Soviet and Warsaw Pact military buildup.

Our evaluation satisfied us that the media contribute to the extending of the ambit and the intensity of the conflict situation and they often encourage revolutionary forces. The media apparently do not appreciate (or if they do, they act with preconceived intent) that normal, first world journalistic approaches and practices designed for a homogeneous democratic country are not applicable in their undiluted form in a heterogeneous country with a first and third world population mix, with a massive difference in levels of sophistication, where first world "advocacy journalism" has a much greater impact upon the unsophisticated half-literate mind than in a homogeneous and sophisticated first-world community.

Whilst we do not suggest collusion, the similarity between the selective anti–South African propaganda conducted by the United Nations on the one hand, and the *New York Times* and the *Washington Post* on the other hand, is striking and we suggest, symptomatic of the worldwide propaganda South Africa must *nolens volens* suffer in the face of an inadequate information counteraction.[26]

The report goes on to say:

The anti–South African bias of the liberal Western media is emphasized by the extraordinary selectivity that distinguishes

their reporting. The media also give disproportionate weight to
the evils, as compared to the benefits, of white rule in South
Africa as against civil rights violations in the rest of Africa . . .
American newspapers are by no means all hostile to South Africa. Conservative journals like the *National Review*, *U.S.*
News and World Report, and *Washington Star* generally take a
moderately pro–South African position. But even conservative
journalists usually look on South Africa through the mirror of
the South African English language press, the only vigorous
opposition press to be found on the African continent and one
which is hostile to the Afrikaner government.

In any case, the wider impact of an occasional pro–South
African article in the United States nowise compares with that
of great liberal dailies such as the *New York Times* or the
Washington Post, periodicals like the *New Republic*, or of magazines like *Time*, *Look*, or *Saturday Evening Post*, all critical of
South Africa. . . . The image of South Africa projected in the
international and internal areas is deliberately distorted and
calculated to present a one-sided and grotesquely negative picture of the government of the day and of the White population
as a whole.[27]

Although the Steyn Commission was assigned specifically to inquire into the media, it still paid a good deal of attention to black
nationalism and the organizations that support black political aspirations. The amorphous third world was considered part of the conspiracy, and the report stated that "the main instruments used by the
Third World in its multi-dimensional onslaught against South Africa
are the United Nations and the Organization of African Unity. The
main campaign is aimed at the subversion of the white population of
South Africa."[28]

Religious organizations, particularly the World Council of
Churches and the South African Council of Churches, were singled
out for scathing attack in the report's 242-page digression on black
theology. The report said, "The World Council of Churches is staffed
by professional ecumenists and conference-going 'intellectuals' who
exhibit all the symptoms of the sickness which is common in the

West. Consumed by postimperial and postcolonial 'guilt,' they are convinced that the West can only expiate its 'crimes' by humbling itself before its former 'victims,' the third world, and its future destroyer, communism. Politics are for them, in effect, an elaborate form of suicide for which Christianity affords a moral justification." The South African Council of Churches was accused of "trying to provoke internal socio-economic upheaval by means of destructive political action." And the general secretary of the SACC, Anglican Bishop Desmond M. Tutu, was accused of "open, strong, and oft-repeated support for the armed 'liberation struggle.' " (Bishop Tutu, in fact, had never endorsed violence.) The Black Consciousness movement was accorded attention as well: "Black Consciousness has a pronounced effect on black journalism and, therefore, on the South African media operations because MWASA [Media Workers Association of South Africa] is one of its 'front organizations.' " The black journalists union was said to be "in the process of radicalizing black journalists for the purpose of using them as 'political shock troops.' " The concern about black religious and secular organizations reflected the government's concern about the effects of news and information that reached the great nonwhite majority. The *Sowetan*, the black-oriented successor to the previously banned *World* and *Post* newspapers, was said to be "vociferously anti-establishment" and to be involved in "negative climate-setting."[29]

In a perceptive analysis of the published report, Laurence Gandar, former editor of the *Rand Daily Mail*, wrote:

> The key passage in the Commission's report seems to me to be the following:
> "If black nationalisms are not prepared to allow the co-existence of Afrikaner nationalism, it is likely that the Afrikaner will curb the press for as long as he has political power and for as long as he anticipates that curbing the Press or manipulating it is to his advantage; it will be an instrument to maintain power."
> This, in a blinding flash of frankness, is the essence of the Steyn Commission report. Like the Government, it sees a total onslaught against South Africa and especially against the Afri-

kaner political establishment by Soviet Russia, its allies and
proxies—including, in their view, the main black nationalist
movements. The Afrikaner will fight back with all the means
at his disposal—including control of the press. There you
have it.[30]

A recurrent theme running through the bulky report was the view
that the opposition press of South Africa should cease aiding the cause
of black nationalism and join the "total strategy" of the Botha government to repel the total onslaught. Similar views had been reached by
an earlier commission, also headed by Judge Steyn, the 1980 Commission of Inquiry into the Reporting of Security News from the South
African Defense Force and Police. A key proposal in the 1980 report
called for the formulation of a "national communication policy,"
which in turn would be "determined and controlled by the national
strategy." One significant paragraph read: "The State and the media
need each other . . . because the State is one of the media's chief
sources of information and conversely, because the State is largely
dependent on the media to inform the population. In the case of
conflict between State and media interests, State interests in respect of
national security are paramount."[31]

Professor Les Switzer believes that this first Steyn commission
clearly regarded the flow of news as hierarchical—from the state to the
people—and legitimate news as deriving essentially from official
sources provided by the state. Furthermore, nonofficial sources of
information, ideas, and attitudes—particularly those concerned with
the grievances and aspirations of individuals and institutions deemed
prejudicial to the security of the state—are regarded as potentially (if
not actually) illegitimate sources of news. Switzer thinks that the real
message of the first Steyn commission, which reflected official thinking, was that "the press—in particular, the surviving opposition
newspapers—is to be co-opted into Total Strategy."[32] Publications
failing to promote the interests of the state (and it is abundantly clear
that the National party will continue to define those interests) will be
silenced. The clear intention of the first Steyn commission, then, was
to convert the press from a passive chronicler to an active participant,
even partner, in the government's response to the "total onslaught."

Similarities between the two commissions' reports are due in part to the presence of Steyn, Das Herbst, and Klaus von Lieres on both bodies.

The first Steyn commissioners, concerned over the role of the foreign press, favored greater control over and more effective monitoring of their activities and recommended the registration of foreign journalists. Although the commissioners disclaimed any desire to convert the press into a propaganda medium for the state or for the National party, the effect of their recommendations would have accomplished that end. Switzer aptly summed up the role envisaged for the press by Steyn Commission 1: The press would have to assume three additional functions if it was to survive as a "free" and "independent" medium of mass communication:

1. The press must censor itself in reporting the activities of the state's internal and external enemies as *defined* by the state. (This implies a shift in emphasis in the press's watchdog role from the state to the "enemies of the state.")

2. The press must sustain and promote a positive image of the state's security and defense agencies.

3. Above all, the press must mobilize public opinion in pursuance of the campaign for "total strategy."

In Switzer's view, such cooptation of the press meant elimination of the last vestiges of opposition to government policy. This, perhaps, was the ultimate rationale behind the deliberations of both Steyn commissions.

The apocalyptic, slightly paranoid vision of the "total onslaught," as expressed in the reports of the two Steyn commissions, is not accepted by significant portions of the South African public and is largely rejected by the opposition press and by blacks. However, this perception of a global conspiracy against white South Africa is widely accepted by those who control the bureaucracy, Parliament, the military, and police and security forces. And opposing newspapers, whether foreign or domestic, in that view, are clearly part of the growing peril.

At the root of the conflict between the Afrikaner government and the opposition press lie fundamentally different concepts of the role of the press in society. The continuing debate since 1950 over the Press

Council, as well as the two Steyn commission reports, illuminates three distinct concepts of the press that coexist uneasily in South Africa: the English concept, the Afrikaner concept, and, to a lesser extent, the African concept. National party leaders have different and conflicting views on the proper role and function of the press from those held by journalists, especially English speakers and blacks. Ironically, the view taken by the Afrikaners closely resembles that of third world leaders, who have been highly critical of Western coverage of international news and have been advocating a "new world information order." Afrikaners have long been unhappy with the press because they believe newspapers should present, interpret, and support the policies of the ruling National party. By contrast, the opposition papers see their role as that of an adversary—a watchdog and critic of government.

Afrikaner Concept of the Press

The Afrikaner view of the press is most consonant with National party or Afrikaner ideology. Historically, the Afrikaans newspapers came into being as tools of politics—instrumentalities to bring the Afrikaners to political domination, especially after their defeat by the British in the Boer War. (See Chap. 8 for a full discussion of the changing Afrikaans press.) Since 1948, the Afrikaans press has helped the National party maintain itself in power.

Throughout the twentieth century, the links between Afrikaner politicians and Afrikaans newspapers have been close. A number of prominent National party leaders, including Prime Minister Hendrik Verwoerd, have been editors or have served on the boards of the Afrikaans papers. Out of this political press tradition has evolved the view that the duty of the press is both to support government policies and to report news in a "positive" way, avoiding dispatches that would give aid and comfort to the enemies of South Africa, as defined by the Nationalists. That is what Afrikaans papers have done, and other publications, especially those in English, are expected to do the same.

The Afrikaner view of the press has developed out of the cohesive, close-knit Afrikaner "tribe" or community. All must work together for the common (Afrikaner) good, because of the common peril (earlier the British and now "total onslaught"); dissent or even questioning of the policies of the elders has no place. Further, Afrikaners consider it unseemly to "wash their dirty linen in public." The Afrikaner community has been an *exclusive* one, reluctant to assimilate outsiders or "Uitlanders." Hence, little merit is attached to the Anglo-American values of diversity and tolerance of unpopular ideas. Dissent from the orthodox establishment view is suspect as likely to be subversive.

In the Afrikaner view, the press must support the *"volk"* and, by extension, the ruling elders of the National party. In the final analysis, the press serves the people by giving loyal and steadfast service to the ruling Afrikaner elite. Hence, the press becomes an instrument or extension of political power.

This view has fostered a paternalistic and secretive attitude toward the release of news and public information. Afrikaner journalists that subscribe to it concede that "government knows best" as to whether or not certain kinds of news should be released to the public. Any information that may somehow reflect badly on the ruling Nationalists or their public servants (including police and security agents), or may just be politically embarrassing, may be properly withheld because its release might help the "other side." By the same token, legitimate news stories, such as one about a strike by black unionists or an act of sabotage in downtown Johannesburg, can be considered "subversive" because of the encouragement these reports may give to "terrorists," "Communists," or others involved in the "total onslaught."

This Afrikaner concept is not without its ironies. Though similar to the party press in Western Europe, it also is close to the Soviet Communist theory of the press. Nor do Afrikaners show much sympathy or understanding when the blacks try to use the press in the same way Afrikaners have—as a tool to attain political power. It is precisely when the black press begins to "talk politics" that official repression becomes most swift and ruthless. For historically the Afrikaner concept of the press has fostered deep intolerance and impatience with any other approach to journalism, though as Chapter 8 shows, changes have been occurring in the Afrikaans newspapers themselves.

English Concept of the Press

The people of British stock who immigrated to South Africa imported many of the values and institutions of Britain. Among them were the English concept of freedom of the press which had slowly evolved out of the long, three-way struggle between king, Parliament, and the courts. English-speaking South Africans have maintained close cultural ties to Britain, and South African English-speaking journalists have traditionally shared the values and professional standards of their journalistic colleagues in Britain and America. In earlier years, many of the editors were British nationals. English-language newspapers have long carried a good deal of news from Britain, and both Argus and SAAN maintain large bureaus in London.

This approach is directly at odds with the Afrikaner notion just as it is with the African or black view. The long Anglo-American struggle for press freedom was to gain independence *from* government. The primary allegiance of the press is not to the political leadership but to the people in whom sovereignty (at least for whites) is lodged. The English press ethic was summed up by an editor of the *Times* of London over a hundred years ago: "The first duty of the press is to obtain the earliest and most correct intelligence of the events of the time, and instantly, by disclosing them, to make them the common property of the nation. The duty of the journalist is to present to his readers not such things as statecraft would wish them to know but the truth as near as he can attain it."[33]

In the English view, the people of South Africa, all the people, have the right to know what is happening inside their government, especially in jails and prisons, and what is happening on the borders of South Africa where a low-level guerrilla war has been going on for years. This claim of allegiance to the public, rather than government, has put the English press at odds with successive Nationalist governments.

The English press, then, differs from the Afrikaner over what constitutes "responsibility." The English journalistic viewpoint that its responsibility is to the people of South Africa to report fully and without bias the news they have a right to know collides with the Afrikaner concept that responsibility is to the ruling government, to the leaders of the nation. It becomes "irresponsible" then—or worse—to report news that weakens or undermines the government in place.

English journalists (at least, some of them) believe, too, that they have an obligation to provide, as best they can, news and information to the disenfranchised and politically powerless nonwhite majority, lacking as it does adequate newspapers of its own. The commercial motives of bringing news and advertising to blacks are a consideration as well. As the Steyn report showed, the Nationalist government is particularly concerned about the *kind* of news blacks are getting from the opposition newspapers.

The English press, firmly anchored in private enterprise and with historical financial ties to the giant mining enterprises, must turn a profit in order to survive and maintain its independence from government. The Afrikaner press, historically supported by political loyalties and financial contributions from party members, recently has moved closer to the private enterprise model, but the two big press groups, Perskor and Nasionale Pers, still enjoy indirect government subsidies through lucrative printing contracts.

The English-language press is a partisan party press and, in recent years, has generally supported the moderate Progressive Federal party, the official opposition in Parliament. Thirty-five-plus years of being in opposition has left the English with an adversarial concept of their role, much like that of American journalism. English newsmen have developed a suspicion of and cynicism about politicians that brings to mind H. L. Mencken's dictum that "the only way for a newspaperman to look on a politician is down." More important, perhaps, the English press sees itself as a watchdog checking on abuses of official power and trust. Only the English press, and probably only its liberal minority (*Rand Daily Mail*, etc.), could have uncovered the scandal of the Information Department called Muldergate. But it is also true perhaps that the English press is far too tolerant and uncritical of the political leaders and policies it does support, namely those of the Progressive Federal party. This adversarial approach to journalism may well disappear altogether in South Africa as a result of the current confrontation between the press and government.

Radical Critique of the Opposition Press

The English view of the press is held mainly by professional journalists and political liberals and moderates. As the Steyn Commission testimony showed, this perception is not shared by right-wing Afrikaners and others who see the English-language papers as aiding and encouraging black revolution. But neither is the English concept accepted by radical critics of South African society. Among this latter group, the opposition papers are considered to be very much a part of the white capitalist establishment. Owned and controlled by mining and other financial groups, the papers essentially serve the narrow class interests of the dominant whites. In this view, the capitalist press will serve only the monied interests and certainly not the poor and politically powerless who are denied access to publishing.

These radicals, both black and white, see the English newspapers as providing "opposition" only in such limited areas as parliamentary politics and matters of nonfundamental change such as the easing of petty apartheid. Press opposition, they say, tends to be vigorous only within relatively safe limits; major patterns of power, especially economic power, are rarely challenged. English journalism espouses a press independent of government controls but not, critics say, independent of the conservative financial interests that own and direct the newspapers.

Further, the English press by its lively opposition to the National party serves only to legitimize the apartheid regime and improve its image overseas as a democracy. The English papers and those who own them, it is argued, do not believe in one man, one vote or real political power sharing, much less economic democracy. Instead they believe in ameliorating the harsher aspects of apartheid and in trying to defuse an explosive situation. The radicals say that in the final showdown, the interests that unify the five million whites will prove more crucial that those issues that have divided them. The only differences between Afrikaans and English journalism are over means (or tactics), not ends.

These widely differing perceptions of the English press are further indicators of the deep polarization within South African society and the weakening of moderate approaches. Further, this radical critique of the liberal press is a significant underpinning of the recently emerging African press concept.

The African (or Black) Concept of the Press

Perhaps more than anywhere else on the continent, the indigenous Africans of South Africa historically have published newspapers to serve their own communities. So have the other "nonwhite" groups, the Coloureds and the Asians. But with the implementation of apartheid and the suppression of black political expression of even the mildest sort, most of these papers have disappeared. Nevertheless, a distinct African concept of the press has been emerging in recent years.

The beleaguered black journalists have closely identified with what many call "the struggle," that loosely defined but persistent and determined effort to end white hegemony over South Africa. The purpose, the raison d'être of the printed word, in this context, is to bring about political and economic change in South Africa.

African journalism is marked as well by a strong separatist element. The urban black journalist, sophisticated and angry, has been influenced by the Black Consciousness ideology of Steve Biko and so rejects help from liberal white colleagues. On the English newspapers employing them, blacks have become increasingly alienated from their white editors and colleagues.

Abandoning the long-standing alliance of sympathetic white liberals and black activists, the black journalist says in effect, "This is our fight, our struggle, and we must do it on our own." Among militant blacks, the white liberal (and his press) is increasingly perceived as irrelevant.

At the same time, these African journalists have jettisoned the Anglo-American press standards of objectivity and fairness as well as the idea of a free and independent press since, in their view, blacks have had little freedom or independence to express their own views. So, to them, truth is only what advances "the cause." English press approaches to journalism, the reasoning goes, have not advanced the cause, and the black journalist feels he is restrained by timid white editors who refuse to let him report the "truth" about white oppression for fear of legal problems or official retaliation.

Black journalists are further radicalized by the harassment and harsh treatment they encounter when dealing with police, security, and other elements of the white establishment. Far more than his white colleague, the black journalist must live with the immediate possibility of losing his personal liberty through banning or detention without trial.

Utilizing the press to help bring about political change and to gain power is, of course, precisely the way the Afrikaners, defeated in the Boer War, used *their* newspapers (as well as churches, schools, broadcasting, etc.) in their long struggle to win political control of South Africa from the hated British. Perhaps it is because they employed the approach with success themselves that the Afrikaner elites especially fear black nationalism and are so determined to restrict black expression.

To the right-wing Afrikaner, the black approach is clearly subversive and "Communist" and a threat to the "continuance of Western civilization at the southern end of Africa." While the English press may be tolerated by the government, the African press is too threatening.

Throughout the hearings of the Steyn Commission, the testimony reflected English and Afrikaner press attitudes. But because black journalists, following the lead of their professional organization, Media Workers Association of South Africa (MWASA), refused to testify, there was little articulation of the African attitude. Such a stance was clearly consistent with that attitude. Chapter 6 provides a basis for a fuller understanding of the blacks' approach to journalism.

In sum, the major result of the Steyn Commission was the creation of the South African Media Council, which replaced the Press Council in November 1983. The Media Council retains virtually unchanged the Press Council's mode of conduct and its power to impose penalties ranging from a reprimand to a fine of up to R 10,000. But there are some important differences. For the first time the council includes working journalists and members of the general public. And it is intended to include members of all race groups. The new council also has the right to sit in judgment on media, including broadcasting and magazines, that are not members of the NPU or voluntary subscribers to the council. This provision is included largely to meet the government's demand that the council have jurisdiction over two small right-wing newspapers, *Die Afrikaner* and *Die Patriot*, which do not belong to the NPU and support Afrikaner factions that have broken away from the National Party.

The new council was the result of negotiations between the government, the NPU, the Conference of Editors (representing editors of the major English and Afrikaans papers), and to a limited extent, the SASJ.[34] It represents the newspaper industry's answer to the Steyn Commission's proposals for a statutory press council and for a register of journalists. A key feature of the council was the appointment of a conciliator, whose job it is to mediate between complainants and editors. Only if the conciliator fails to settle the complaint will the matter be referred to the council for a hearing. Here too the proceedings will be less formal than in the past. The parties can no longer be represented at hearings by legal counsel; except in exceptional circumstances they must speak for themselves. An adviser may accompany a person to a hearing but may not address the council or question witnesses.[35]

In this, as in other respects, the new Media Council reflects the influence of the British Press Council. Like the British council, the Media Council has equal numbers of media and public representatives. Its 30 members include a chairman, alternate chairman, 14 media representatives and 14 public representatives. Six of the media representatives are nominated by the Conference of Editors, six by the NPU. The SASJ and the Media Workers Association of South Africa may nominate one member each. The 14 public representatives are chosen by former judges from a panel of candidates submitted by the NPU, which advertised for nominations. The chairman and alternate chairman are appointed by the full council, which also appoints the conciliator and a registrar.

Complaints that are not successfully mediated by the conciliator are heard by a panel of seven members of the council, chosen annually by a selection committee comprising the chairman and one media and one public representative. The panel comprises the chairman, three media representatives, and three public representatives. Decisions are taken by majority vote.

As in the case of the British Council, the Media Council is also meant to promote freedom of expression and higher professional standards. Apart from adjudicating on complaints, it is expected to keep under review developments likely to restrict the supply of information, to report on tendencies towards greater concentration or monopoly in the media, and on matters concerning the good conduct and repute of the media. Inquiries can be initiated by the council without having to wait for a complaint to be levied against any newspaper or broadcast organization.

The SASJ adopted a cautious attitude toward the new council. It pointed out that media representation on the council would be dominated by editors and nominees of the NPU, rather than working journalists, and that the public representatives "revealed a bias towards business and white-dominated organizations."[36] More important, the SASJ cautioned that the government could use a critical Media Council report as justification for banning a newspaper, or individual journalists.

5 | Legal Restraints on Newspapers

"South Africa has the freest press in Africa." Sometimes uttered as a boast by progovernment supporters and sometimes as a grudging admission by government critics, that statement is heard again and again inside and outside South Africa. Visitors to the country are invariably impressed with its outspoken and lively newspapers, particularly the English-language ones, especially when they are criticizing or jousting with the National party government.

This is testimony to the dedication of its practitioners, for the South African press is fettered by over a hundred laws that severely limit access to news of major public importance; further, editors and journalists are subjected to harassment by police and to intimidation and threats from the highest levels of government. Moreover, South African journalists and legal experts say that press freedom is in rapid decline and may soon disappear altogether.

The traditional prior restraint forms of censorship are not the issue here. The thirty-one or so daily and Sunday newspapers of South Africa, as members of the Newspaper Press Union, are exempt from the Publications Act of 1974 which provides the legal basis for censorship of books, motion pictures, periodicals and small ephemeral publications, theatrical productions, student and university newspapers, calendars, etc. (See Chap. 7 for an analysis of this more usual kind of censorship law.) However, censorship of general newspapers exists in other numerous forms, designed in many cases to maintain the political power of the Nationalist government and its apartheid apparatus. A sampling of the powers that government holds and has exercised indicates the scope of the restraints on freedom of the press:

1. The government has unlimited power to close down newspapers as it did in 1977 with the *World* and *Weekend World* and, in effect, did again in January 1981 with those black newspapers' successors, the *Post* and *Sunday Post*.

2. A more insidious power, because its exercise is not widely understood, is the requirement that a new newspaper must register and deposit R 40,000 (about $32,000) as a kind of guarantee of "good behavior" which may be forfeited if the publication errs in the opinion of the relevant government official. An untold number of small papers, reflecting black and dissident opinion, have in effect been smothered in their cribs by this extreme form of the registration power.

3. Authorities can achieve a measure of press control by banning the journalists themselves—those whose stories, associations, or activities displease government officials. This power has been exercised with great frequency in the 1980s, particularly against black journalists associated with MWASA, the black journalists' trade union. Banned persons cannot attend meetings, whether political, social, or business, and in effect are subject to a kind of house arrest. The banning of a journalist, black or white, is a harsh action, denying as it does his or her job and livelihood plus severely restricting personal freedom. Further, it has a chilling effect on press freedom in general.

4. Even harsher than banning is detention, especially if the dreaded Section 6 of the Terrorism Act is invoked. Detention provisions are devoid of due process—they include arbitrary arrest and incarceration without charges or trial for indefinite periods of time. Journalists can and do disappear for days or weeks as a number of black reporters did while covering the Soweto uprising in June 1976.

5. Further, journalists are subject to prosecution under sweeping laws such as the Official Secrets Act, Terrorism Act, and the Prisons, Defense, and Police Acts. These are particularly onerous to the press because reporters must in effect get ministerial permission to publish any story in these important areas.[1]

The severity of these laws and other governmental powers is exacerbated by the fact that they may be applied in an arbitrary and capricious manner. The progovernment SABC can and did report, inadvertantly, the words of a banned person and nothing happened. Such inadvertent infractions by English-language papers usually result in legal action.

When a newspaper is banned or a journalist detained or banned under various security laws the responsible official is not legally required to account to anyone for his action. The arrested persons are entitled neither to a statement of charges against them nor an opportunity to appear before an independent body to make their case. The law has been framed to deny the right of procedural justice; in the eye of the law the minister's word is law.

Working journalists, especially black reporters, are subjected to a good deal of harassment and beatings, if not arbitrary arrest, while covering sensitive news stories such as riots, demonstrations, strikes, and protests. Police are rarely brought to account for such illegal actions.

Such governmental powers to restrain newspapers are far in excess of those found in the U.S. and British legal systems. Certainly, numerous aspects of South African press laws would be clearly in violation of the First Amendment in the American Constitution. Nevertheless, South African papers are lively, outspoken, full of political criticism. This gives them the appearance of being free, an appearance that is misleading and illusory.

First, what freedom exists is essentially for whites only; blacks have no real freedom to publish their own politically relevant newspapers. The limits of the whites-only freedom are circumscribed as well. Most whites, as reflected in the National party's parliamentary majorities, support the status quo—white supremacy—and do not feel that their freedoms are threatened by actions against critics of apartheid. However, a growing and significant number of whites, including numerous Afrikaners, favor amelioration of the more inhumane but less basic aspects of apartheid. Few whites advocate one man, one vote or real power sharing with blacks; those that do risk banning or jail, as has happened to a number of white dissidents since 1948. Therefore, whites enjoy a good deal of apparent freedom of expression and action as long as they do not directly challenge by word or deed the prevailing political ideology. Since few do so, few believe their freedoms are circumscribed.

Second, the freedom enjoyed by the white-controlled newspapers is essentially a freedom of *comment*. Very little freedom of *access* exists because so many areas of significant public information are closed off by law to both press and public.

Third, the freedom of comment is mainly tied to party politics and parliamentary proceedings. The thrust and parry of legislative debate, while often quite heated and acrimonious, is largely tolerated by the ruling Afrikaners, in part, because the National party has long enjoyed such lopsided parliamentary majorities. National party leaders often seem to enjoy these exchanges which help maintain the facade of democracy in South Africa.

The English press, then, enjoys its freedom because it operates within what can be called an entirely white framework. As one English-speaking editor put it: "We are a projection of the all-white electorate and the all-white Parliament which rule South Africa. By far the greater part of our political news and comment falls within the ambit of what is normally discussed in Parliament. The English press therefore acquires an air of respectability because it is to a great degree an extension of what I may call 'white politics.' We may be critical of the government, and sometimes even hostile, but by and large we are playing the game according to the rules, or within the rules; and as long as we continue to do that, even our hostility will presumably be tolerated."[2]

Liberal English journalists then face a dilemma: by going along under present conditions, they give a certain legitimacy to the Nationalist government, but they are providing *some* opposition—virtually the only mass circulation opposition—and are helping to record what is happening in South Africa. For despite the press restraints, many journalists feel they can oppose apartheid more effectively by staying on their jobs rather than emigrating as many liberal whites have done.

Finally, any remaining remnants of freedom of the press—which we define as the right to report and criticize government without recriminations or retaliation from that government—have become weakened and vulnerable, without meaningful protection either in law, custom, or white public opinion. The South African government today has the legal tools, properly provided by Parliament, to close down any newspaper and to place in detention without trial any journalist in the Republic and to keep from public and press scrutiny *any* information it so desires.

Much of the law restricting the press and journalists is related to the vast legal and bureaucratic structure that maintains the apartheid apparatus. For if twenty-five million Africans, Asians, and Coloureds, the majority of the population, are controlled and manipulated against their wills, there will inevitably be restrictions on any protests or even news reports about such political repression and on any advocacy to change or ameliorate those conditions. It must be concluded then that censorship and arbitrary restraints on expression will not significantly lessen until apartheid itself is dismantled.

Understanding press controls in South Africa requires first an understanding of the political system by which the country is governed.[3] Legislative power was, until 1984, vested in a central parliament consisting of a lower house (House of Assembly), the President's Council, and a state president. (In 1981, the upper house, the Senate, was replaced by the President's Council.) Political power was concentrated in the House of Assembly of 165 white members, elected by white voters only in single-member constituencies. The state president is a constitutional, ceremonial figurehead with powers similar to the queen of England or the governor general of Canada. He appointed as prime minister the leader of the dominant party in the House of Assembly who then named a cabinet which formed the executive branch of government.

However, on September 9, 1983, the Nationalists under P. W. Botha pushed through Parliament a new constitutional structure that will dramatically reshape the Westminster parliamentary system. Under the new system, segregated chambers will be set up in Parliament for Coloureds and Asians, thus giving nonwhites a role in the national government for the first time in the country's history. At the same time, South Africa would switch to a presidential form of government, modelled vaguely on the Gaullist system of France, with the crucial difference that the President would be chosen by Parliament under a system of weighted votes designed to keep the office and the government under the control of the majority party in the white chamber.

These constitutional changes provided no role for the twenty-two million blacks, and their exclusion from even this token power sharing was regarded by some as a fatal flaw that failed to deal with a basic political problem. This was power sharing, but never in a way that would threaten white control. Proponents said the new constitution bypassed white right-wing opposition to Nationalist policies by detouring around Parliament. Only the president—and P. W. Botha was expected to be the first president—could introduce legislation, and if Parliament refused to pass it, the president could rule by decree. If that sounded despotic, said Botha's supporters, only a despot can force change on unwilling whites.

Proponents talked of the "De Gaulle option," an authoritarian system dominated by a strong executive who can impose needed change despite the adamant opposition of a determined white minority. The authoritarian, if not totalitarian, implications of the proposals were apparent. Botha and his followers were saying in effect, "If you want to ease the problems, then you must put up with continued repression for some time to come."

Critics said blacks and their leaders would never accept this approach. The trade-off of a strong man for the possibility of some future reforms might not impress the rest of the world either. Opposition leader Frederick van Zyl Slabbert said, "If this goes through, the claim of the ruling whites to the shred of democratic legitimacy that is left to them may be lost. This constitution makes racial discrimination a cornerstone of its operation."

Such radical changes in the whites' constitution will drastically alter the parliamentary system and consolidate power within the Afrikaner elites who dominate the National party. On November 2, 1983, Botha won a mandate from a national referendum of white voters to go ahead with his ambiguous and limited political liberalization. By a margin of 66 percent, the voters approved the new constitutional reforms, thus giving the Nationalists a much larger margin than expected. Right-wing Afrikaner opposition proved less formidable than expected.

Despite these changes, parliamentary supremacy was still basic to the constitutional structure of the Republic of South Africa. Parliament can and does make any law it pleases, and no court may inquire into its validity except for a law affecting equal language rights.

Before 1984, the nonwhite majority (Africans, Coloureds, and Asians) had not been represented in this central Parliament or in the Provincial Councils which have limited legislative powers over the four provinces (Transvaal, Natal, Orange Free State, and Cape). John Dugard said it very well: "South Africa cannot be described as a democracy. It is more aptly described as a pigmentocracy in which all political power is vested in a white oligarchy, which in turn is controlled by an Afrikaner elite."[4] Despite the 1983 constitutional changes, that description still fits.

Supremacy of Parliament is central to understanding restraints on the press and other expression as well as deprivation of human rights. The outward resemblance to the Westminster system of Britain was deceiving. In Britain, supremacy of Parliament protects the British people against abuses of their rights by the executive. When Parliament in Britain passes laws and legislates, the rights and interests of the people are taken into consideration and protected, and, in fact, the constitutionality of each new law is determined at the time it is passed. South Africa's Westminster-style Parliament did not provide for specific statutory restrictions on the powers of the executive authorities. In fact, the South African Parliament has evolved into an ally and servant of the executive branch, providing the executive with wide arbitrary powers vested in one segment (the minority white community) at the expense of the others (Africans, Asians, and Coloureds).

Since 1948, no effective opposition party in Parliament has existed, and the ruling National party can enact almost any legislation it proposes. As a result, as Dugard has written, the Nationalists have transformed the largely social and economic system of racial segregation that existed before 1948 into the aggressive, ideological policy of apartheid. The erstwhile opposition, the United party, supported some policies of the National party but differed on others. Largely of British stock, most UP supporters didn't want to be ruled by Afrikaners.

In the absence of a viable, meaningful political opposition party, the fifteen to twenty English-language newspapers became the de facto opposition. When new legislation was proposed in Parliament, it was usually the *Cape Times* or the *Rand Daily Mail* or *The Star*, among others, who criticized or attacked it, not the United party. The government, in turn, directed its main counterattacks at the English press, not the opposition party. In 1977, the United party was replaced as the official opposition by the Progressive Federal party, which is a real opposition party, differing with the National party on some basic issues. The PFP enjoys more support from the liberal English newspapers than did the United party.

In the general election of April 29, 1981, the National party registered its ninth successive victory, scoring the second biggest electoral margin since 1910. The party was returned to power with a majority of 97 seats, winning 131 of the Assembly's 165 directly elected seats. The Progressive Federal party won 26 seats and continued as the official opposition, and the New Republic party, the successor of the defunct United party, won but 8 seats.

Without a bill of rights or judicial review, as in the U.S. constitutional system, no checks on Parliament other than public opinion, expressed largely through the newspapers, exist upon the legislative tyranny of Parliament. In contrast to what we find in Britain, where parliamentary supremacy is controlled by political tradition, convention, and the rule of law, "in South Africa, few holds are barred as far as Parliament is concerned: Parliamentary sovereignty has been taken to its logical and brutal conclusion at the expense of human rights."[5]

All of this means that the prime minister and his ruling National party are unimpeded by any effective political restraints. However, real political debate does exist *within* the National party, in recent years between P. W. Botha's *verligtes* or "enlightened" faction and the right-wing, hard-line *verkramptes* (literally, "cramped") elements of the party. Because Afrikaners for good historical reasons fear that a split within Nationalist ranks could lead to the demise of Afrikaner political dominance, the right-wingers hold a potential veto power over the proposed reforms of the *verligtes*-minded cabinet and Afrikaans press. It has been said that P. W. Botha must worry about the Afrikaner right wing outside the National party, the right wing within the National party, and the right wing within himself. This threat from the far right, mainly through the Herstigte Nasionale party and the new Conservative party, was the main reason for Botha's strong-president design in his constitutional reform legislation.

More than three decades of National party rule has resulted in a certain arrogance and deceit among the prime ministers and their cabinet ministers. Professor F. D. van der Vyver has cited examples of deception in high places.[6] (1) In 1975, while South African troops were heavily involved in the Angolan civil war and had almost reached the outskirts of Luanda, P. W. Botha, then minister of defense, insisted that South African troops were only protecting the interests of Ovambo, Kavango, and Caprivi near the Namibian border. (2) On July 13, 1977, Louis Le Grange, then deputy minister of information, said in London that in May of the previous year the government had accepted a high-level report on the abolition of racial discrimination in South Africa and that the program was being implemented by the government step by step. It later turned out that no such blueprint existed. (3) Following the death in detention of Steve Biko in September 1977, Minister of Justice Jimmy Kruger, in addition to making callous remarks about Biko, published several misleading statements regarding the cause and circumstances of Biko's death. (4) After the banning of the *World* and *Weekend World* in 1977, the same Kruger said in a television interview that Communist propaganda was ascribed to the papers on the grounds of an article on the Russian Revolution in a series of student history notes. A passage which Kruger read out during the interview had never appeared in the *World*.

But the public deception that most upset van der Vyver was the blatant lie told in Parliament by Dr. Connie Mulder as minister of information regarding the secret government financing of *The Citizen*. Van der Vyver wrote, "It must be appreciated that question time in parliament is one of the most fundamental libertarian corner stones of the Westminster system of government and is in fact the only safe-guard embodied in that system against the abuse of executive power. Telling a lie in question time in parliament is therefore the most despicable offence that can possibly be committed by a member of the parliament."[7]

In Parliament, Mulder denied that *The Citizen* had been secretly funded by the government, when the opposite was true. Mulder later alleged that he had been advised by then Prime Minister Vorster to tell the lie. When Defense Minister John Profumo years earlier had been caught in a lie to the British Commons, it had brought down a government. In South African politics, no such consequences ensued. Prime ministers and top government officials with rare exceptions can lie with impunity. It is somewhat ironic, then, that government spokesmen frequently accuse the press of misleading and inaccurate reporting, and then threaten censorship even though the reporting in most cases was substantially correct.

The long-term effect of the Nationalist government's battering of the press has been a steady diminution of freedom of the press. And despite the assessment of foreign observers that South Africa has the freest press in Africa, the true state is probably closer to historian Leonard Thompson's evaluation: "The liberal Press has been reduced to insecurity and near impotence and the great English dailies are impeded from discovering and reporting the worst evils of apartheid and are under great pressures to refrain from fundamental criticisms of the Government."[8]

Anthony Mathews has raised the question of why the rather tame press of South Africa remains such a thorn in the side of the government. First, he says, the direction of the law over the past thirty years has ensured that to the extent that South Africa remains a democracy, it is a progressively less accountable one. "When absolute power is vested in the political authorities, a carping press is bound to stand out as an anomaly," he writes. "When the press seeks to present fundamental alternatives, its role becomes subversive in the minds of men who are not accustomed to having their judgment qualified or seriously called into question by others." Second, Mathews says, "the press tends to focus on the moral shortcomings of Government policy and actions. It is a kind of moral mirror in which the Government see its own image and the sight is frequently not a pretty one. This explains the irrational outbursts against the newspapers. They produce a discomfort of conscience which is irrationally countered by transforming the Press into a traitorous enemy ranking with, if not beyond, the Communists, the ANC, etc."[9]

Elaine Potter has analyzed the press's role in more political terms:

In the Nationalist government's campaign against the independent press, the Government had two primary objectives: first,
it sought to safeguard its political principles; and second, to ensure its ideology not merely as the policy of a political party
which chanced to be in office, but as a fundamental "truth"
against which only the blasphemous spoke. The importance of
this for the press was the growing tendency to identify all
opposition to apartheid with subversion and criticism of its de-
fenders with treason. Thus in seeking to secure itself in office
and to eliminate all serious opposition to its apartheid ideology,
the Nationalist Government arrogated to itself very extensive
powers. There can be little argument that the government has
provided itself with the machinery to limit the freedom of its
institutional opponents.[10]

If press freedom in South Africa is finally and completely extinguished, it will not be through the passage of just one law. Rather, it
will be merely the end of a long process in which this freedom was
eroded by many laws. The formula is to introduce piecemeal legislation in the guise of measures needed for public safety or state
security.

The multitude of wide-ranging laws enacted over the past thirty-
five years create very immediate and practical problems for the reporters and editors attempting to gather and publish the news. For
example, page 3 of the stylebook of the *Rand Daily Mail* contains this
strong admonition:

WATCH OUT!
1. Nothing said by a banned person, whether living in South
Africa or abroad, can generally be quoted without permission.
Card indexes of banned persons are kept in the News Editor's
office and the Library. Check whether the person concerned
can be quoted.
2. Nothing dealing with South Africa's defence can be published without permission, except in certain circumstances.
Care must be taken in reporting on the activities of the police,

especially the Security Police, BOSS (Bureau of State Security) and action on the borders. In all cases, check on the circumstances.

3. Nothing dealing with South Africa's uranium can be published without permission.

4. No picture of prisoners or prisons, including police vans and any vehicle used to convey prisoners, can be published without permission from the Commissioner of Prisons.

5. Great care must be exercised in all reports dealing with South African jail conditions.

6. The laws of incitement provide that it is an offence to create racial hostility between White and Black.

7. Great care must be taken to avoid defamation in reports.

IN ALL CASES OF DOUBT REFER THE REPORT IMMEDIATELY TO THE NEWS EDITOR, CHIEF SUB-EDITOR OR NIGHT EDITOR.

As any journalist would recognize, only the last admonition—to avoid defamation—would usually be found in a style guide for an American or British newspaper. The other six warnings are capsulized reminders of the legal mine field that South African newspapermen (and their lawyers) must step through daily in putting out the news.

The main purpose of the laws referred to indirectly in the *Mail's* style guide is to close off from public scrutiny and criticism the widespread imposition of official control over the black population and the increasing activities of the police and military forces to counter their perceived internal "enemies" as well as the growing external threat. These laws are an institutionalized reflection of the Afrikaners' fears and concerns—the laager mentality—about the dangers that lurk all around. This array of legislation seriously hampers professional journalists in their day-to-day efforts to report the news, especially in such traditional news areas as police, judicial processes, and political activities.

Here, then, are some of the major laws that South African newspapers have had to deal with:

1. Internal Security Act. Enacted in 1950 as the Suppression of Communism Act, this was among the first laws making inroads into

personal freedom. The act makes it an offense to advocate, advise, defend, or encourage the achievement of any objective of Communism. The definition of Communism is so wide that in effect the government itself decides who is a Communist, and the act has been used extensively against Communists, non-Communists, and anti-Communists.

Furthermore, the act provides that any newspaper deemed to be "furthering" the objectives of Communism can be banned. During the 1950s and 1960s a number of left-wing newspapers with largely black readerships were banned. Soon after the act was passed, the Cape Town, Johannesburg, and Durban offices of the left-wing weekly, the *Guardian* were raided by police, and the paper was subsequently banned in 1952. The paper soon reappeared as the *Advance*, but like its predecessor it too was banned, in 1954. Next the paper appeared as the *New Age* but was again banned in 1962. To prevent banned publications from reappearing under new names, the government amended the Suppression of Communism Act empowering the minister of the interior to require a deposit of R 20,000 when a new paper was started if there was a possibility the publication might later be banned. (The required deposit was doubled to R 40,000 in April 1982 when Parliament revised the Internal Security Act.) If banning does take place the deposit is forfeited. Any effort to start a new publication of political comment is strongly inhibited, and Professor Mathews has said he could cite fourteen efforts to start new papers that did not work out because of such potential monetary loss.[11]

The Internal Security Act makes it an offense to publish anything said or written by a person banned under the act or whose name appears on any list of officeholders of declared unlawful organizations or who has been prohibited from attending gatherings. (The number of persons under banning orders at any one time may range from two hundred to six hundred.) Also, the statements of banned persons, even if made prior to banning or if the persons are living outside the country, cannot be printed without permission. Thus, an important spectrum of opinion is denied to the press. Newspapers, as a result, must keep index card files on banned persons to avoid inadvertently quoting one of them. Also, of course, numerous journalists themselves have been banned and thus barred from writing.

2. Sabotage Act. In addition to being treated by the Official Secrets Act, sabotage is dealt with under the General Law Amendment Act of 1962 which requires that care must be taken to ensure that a news report, article, or story cannot be construed as incitement, instigation, or aid to endanger, among other things, the maintenance of public law and order. The very real question for newspapers is at what point does the mere reporting of events stray into those dangerous areas?

Journalist Benjamin Pogrund points out that even potential witnesses in court cases (which can include journalists) can be detained incommunicado for up to 180 days, and this can be extended indefinitely. Habeas corpus is specifically rendered impossible. Understandably, newspapers shrink from the possibility that overzealous reporters might be arrested under the incitement provisions of this law; hence, newspapers at times censor themselves. There is also provision for a 14-day detention, renewable indefinitely, for "interrogation." Under this provision, the police must place an affidavit before a judge to justify the detention, but the detainee is not entitled to know the allegations presented to the judge. Again, habeas corpus is excluded.[12]

3. Terrorism Act. Perhaps the most feared law is the Terrorism Act which allows for indefinite, incommunicado detention without habeas corpus. Though designed to deal with terrorism, the act places an unusually wide interpretation on the meaning of terrorism which could include press comment and reporting. Essentially, the act regards terrorism as any action which would endanger the maintenance of law and order or would have the effect of encouraging forcible resistence to the government; causing a general disturbance; furthering any political aim (including social or economic change) by forcible means or with the aid of any foreign government or body; causing feelings of hostility between whites and blacks; promoting the achievement of any objective by intimidation; prejudicing the operation of industry and commerce. Even advocating a boycott or interfering with traffic can bring a charge of terrorism.

To establish that the accused intended to endanger law and order, the state simply has to show that the accused's action was likely to have any one of these results. Thus the onus shifts to the accused to prove that he or she did not have that intention. A finding of guilty on any charge under the Terrorism Act means a compulsory minimum five years' imprisonment; the maximum penalty is death.[13]

As the late Kelsey Stuart, a leading expert on press law, pointed out, the impact of the Terrorism Act on the reporting of news and publishing of comments is immediately apparent. Letters to the editor, advertisements, political columns, editorials, and news stories may all contain matter which may be construed as conspiring, procuring, inciting, instigating, commending, aiding, advising, or encouraging such results as those indicated in the act. Like so many others, this law intended to bolster the apartheid apparatus also poses great dangers for journalists merely trying to *report* what is happening.[14]

4. Unlawful Organizations Act. The Unlawful Organizations Act was enacted in 1960 to ban the two activist opposition organizations, the African National Congress and the Pan-Africanist Congress, both now operating in exile. This act proscribes newspapers from publishing ANC or PAC views whether spoken abroad or printed in underground pamphlets.

This law repeats many provisions of the Suppression of Communism Act. The state president is empowered to declare any body, organization, or group of persons, etc., an unlawful organization. The policies or utterances of any such listed persons may not be published. Its provisions even make it impossible for a newspaper legally to publish anything that Lenin ever said or wrote, even when the quotation is the basis for a critical story on Communism. Related to this legislation is the Affected Organizations Act of 1974 making it an offense to ask for or canvass foreign money for or on behalf of organizations declared "affected." Newspapers keep lists of such organizations as protection against unwittingly associating themselves with such appeals for funds.

5. Riotous Assemblies Act. This 1956 act deals with the tricky area of "promoting hostility" between the races, first treated in the Bantu Administration Act of 1927 which made it an offense for anyone to

promote hostility between whites and blacks. The Riotous Assemblies Act has a similar provision but broadens it considerably. Such laws, however, have the drawback of preventing the press from reporting many legitimate grievances of blacks struggling to gain political rights. For example, according to Pogrund, if a meeting is prohibited under the Riotous Assemblies Act, it is an offense to publicize it or encourage it. Second, if a person is prohibited from attending a meeting, nothing he says or writes, whether it be in the past, present, or future, can be reported. Third, a newspaper can be banned if in the government's opinion any cartoon, picture, article, or advertisement calculated to engender hostility between whites and blacks is published. Fourth, it is an offense to publish anything that could have the consequence of inciting others to violence. It is no defense to plead that a newspaper did not intend to incite.[15]

The problems that such laws pose for press reporting are exacerbated by the fact that what constitutes "promoting hostility" is subject to the government's ad hoc interpretation. By reporting plans for an illegal strike or commenting sympathetically on a speech later deemed inflammatory, a paper runs the risk of being charged with incitement. The penalty for the editor includes jailing for up to five years and/or a whipping of up to ten strokes. Again, the chilling effect is obvious: when in doubt, leave it out.

6. Official Secrets Act. This act proscribes the communication of anything relating to munitions of war or any military, police, or security matter to any persons or for any purpose prejudicial to the safety or interests of the Republic. Penalties are severe—up to fifteen years' imprisonment. The words "any military, police, or security matter" pose the most difficulty for the press since no one can be certain what they mean. In practice, they serve to place severe restraints on reporting anything to do with security.

This act, in conjunction with the Defense Act of 1957, drops a curtain of secrecy over all military and naval movements in South Africa, a curtain that cannot be drawn without the permission of the minister of defense or some authorized deputy. The Defense Act restricts reportage of military matters including reprinting of reports appearing in foreign newspapers. Newspapers also cannot publish stories which might "alarm or depress" the public. Consequently, press coverage of the long-standing war with nationalist guerrillas in Namibia (South West Africa) and Angola is almost completely dependent on official press releases. The Defense Act was rigorously applied during the 1975 Angolan War, creating the bizarre situation that South Africans knew less about their own involvement than people elsewhere in the world. Even though foreign radio broadcasts could be heard and foreign newspapers were on sale in South Africa, the South African press was permitted to publish very little about the extensive involvement of the South African Defense Force in that conflict.

7. Prisons Act of 1959 and 1965. The key section of this law affecting the press prohibits publication of any false information about the experiences in prison of any prisoner or ex-prisoner or the administration of any prison "knowing this to be false" or without taking reasonable steps to verify such information. The burden of proving that reasonable steps were taken is on the accused. What constitutes "reasonable steps" is not spelled out.

The *Rand Daily Mail* in 1965 ran a major series of reports on jail conditions based on sworn statements from ex-prisoners. In a series of court trials over four years and costing some R 250,000 in legal fees, the *Mail* and its informants were found guilty of contravening the Prisons Act. The paper was judged not to have taken "reasonable steps," but it was never clear what steps should have been taken. Benjamin Pogrund, a defendant in the case, wrote that it would seem to mean that a newspaper receiving accusations about the Prisons Department must go to the Prisons Department and can then publish only if the department confirms the truth of the accusations.[16]

Harassment was an added dimension to this important trial, an action brought against an outspoken critic of the government with the apparent purpose of discrediting both the *Rand Daily Mail* and its editor, Laurence Gandar.

The Prisons Act and conviction of the *Mail* have successfully inhibited press coverage of events taking place behind prison walls in South Africa, a nation with one of the highest per capita prison populations in the world. The deterrent effect of the trial was severe; no serious, in-depth reporting of conditions in the South African jails has appeared since then.[17] Editor Allister Sparks reiterated this point:

"Very frequently we have information which we suppress, in order to err on the side of caution, because we are not quite sure how these vague laws are going to put into effect. The Prisons Act is a case in point. There is no newspaper in South Africa today that will publish any information about conditions in prison unless it comes from the Department itself."[18]

Recent Laws

8. Police Amendment Act. After P. W. Botha became prime minister in 1979, legislation restricting the press continued to come out of Parliament. Most oppressive was the Second Police Amendment Act of 1979 which extends the criteria of the Prisons Act to the reporting of police affairs. It makes it an offense to publish "any untrue matter" about the police "without having reasonable grounds . . . for believing that the statement is true." Again, the onus of proof is on the newspaper, and maximum penalties can include a R 10,000 fine or up to five years' imprisonment. Journalists believe this law places crippling restraints on press reporting of police irregularities, and one Johannesburg lawyer called it "the worst and most ominous piece of legislation in recent years; there are now no restraints on the excesses of the government."[19]

In July 1983, police formally warned Rex Gibson, editor of the *Rand Daily Mail*, that they were investigating charges against his paper for publishing a report of public statements by Archbishop Denis Hurley alleging atrocities by security forces in South West Africa (Namibia). Police cited the police act which makes it illegal to make statements about the police without reasonable grounds for believing them to be true. *Die Burger*, *The Citizen*, and the *Sowetan* were also under investigation. The inhibiting effect on reporting was obvious.

A particular problem is coverage of alleged police maltreatment of detainees, a very real issue as the Steve Biko affair demonstrated. Any act committed in connection with detainees is unlikely to have been observed by anybody other than policemen, and it is inherently unlikely that police will admit to maltreatment. Allegations of such mistreatment can be published only if a newspaper has reasonable grounds for believing what it has been told by a detainee—who conceivably may have a good reason for misleading the newspaper. Because policemen, just as prison warders, can and do deny press allegations in court, the press is increasingly cut off from reporting what happens to a person in police custody. One legal expert said that the Police Amendment Act and the Prisons Act are likely to spawn distrust because of the immunity from public scrutiny and criticism they provide. The Prisons Act affects a relatively small community, but the Police Amendment Act affects a very much larger proportion of the population.[20]

Further, the act clearly can be interpreted to mean that the media are now prohibited, without the consent of the minister or commissioner, from publishing any information (including, therefore, even the name) about any person against whom any action (including arrest and detention) is taken for the prevention or combating of terroristic activities—in the broad Terrorism Act sense. South African law has reached the point where people—like Steve Biko and Joseph Mavi—may simply disappear without the public's being informed in any way.[21]

9. Advocate General Act. This 1979 law created the office of advocate general—a person appointed to investigate corruption involving state funds. A direct result of the Muldergate scandal (see Chap. 10), the bill in its original form was the most contentious measure to come before the Parliament during the 1979 session. The controversial so-called press-gagging clause required written consent of the advocate general before any report could be published concerning alleged maladministration and dishonesty in government. Coming on the heels of the press revelations of widespread misuse of Information Department funds, this provision was strenuously opposed by the entire press, including the Afrikaans papers. After urgent pressures from the law associations, Newspaper Press Union, and the Southern African Society of Journalists, the government withdrew the controversial clause which would have completely emasculated any watchdog role of the press in regard to corruption in government. Ordinarily public opinion has little deterrent effect on proposed legislation in Parliament, and the defeat of the *sub judice* clause of the

act was a rare example of the prime minister's giving in to public pressures.

However, there remained much in the act which concerned the press. For example, no person may, without the permission of the advocate general, disclose to any other person (this includes journalists) the contents of any document in the possession of the advocate general or the record of any evidence given before the advocate general. The act also empowers the state president to make regulations providing for the preservation of secrecy in connection with matters being dealt with by the advocate general.

The statute does not prohibit reporting of governmental corruption that has not been submitted to the advocate general. However, after it has, the restrictive provisions of the statute become operative. The act does not interfere with the traditional freedom of parliamentary debate and subsequent reporting of such debate. However, in practice government members of Parliament may, when confronted with alleged corruption, merely refer the accuser to the advocate general; this, in effect, replaces the opposition's role as a watchdog over corruption with investigations by the advocate general.[22]

10. Protection of Information Act. In June 1982, Parliament passed the Protection of Information Act of 1982, which provided for several wide restrictions on the public's right to information. The new law, meant to replace and tighten up the Official Secrets Act, sought to restrict newspaper reporting of Terrorism Act cases and other detentions without official clearance, unless the news of the detention was widely known. It provides jail sentences of up to ten years for the unauthorized disclosure of information relating to a "security matter or the prevention or combating of terrorism." The onus is on the editor to prove that any facts he publishes could not be construed as prejudicial to state interests. Consequently, the new law seriously restricts the ability of the press to report security arrests, and such reports were virtually the only assurance that an arrested person had that the security police might eventually have to account for that arrest.

The government's first application of the new law involved the news reports that South Africa's secret service was involved in the aborted attempt to overthrow the Seychelles government in 1981. The government had denied this. After a lengthy trial, three leading journalists were found guilty in March 1983. They were editor Rex Gibson and reporter Eugene Hugo of the *Rand Daily Mail* and Tertius Mybergh, editor of the *Sunday Times*. Each was fined, but the fines were suspended. The articles in question had been written before the Protection of Information Act had been passed by Parliament.

11. National Key Points Act. The National Key Points Act is a recent law permitting the government to designate certain crisis areas, such as the scene of a terrorist bombing, as off limits to the press. Even officials seem unclear about the guidelines for applying it: reporters could be covering a riot in the middle of a city, for instance, and then be told on the spot by police that this locale was a "key point," prohibiting reportage. The intent of the act seemed to be to subject news of an act of sabotage at any "key" installation (such as Sasol, the coal gasification project) to approval by military authorities before publication.

The 1980 act was greeted with considerable outrage by both the press and legal authorities. Dugard said the bill was in keeping with the present legislative policy of suppressing information about hostile acts directed at the state and strategic installations. "The danger of such legislation is that it will conceal information which should be available to the public so that it can form an opinion," Dugard said. If government policy led to hostile acts, he said, it was essential that the public be told "so that it can take such information into account in forming its own attitude toward the need for change."[23]

12. Petroleum Products Amendment Act. This 1978 act was another Botha administration law restricting press coverage. Journalists faced maximum fines of R 7,000 and seven years' imprisonment for publishing without ministerial permission information about the source, manufacture, or storage of any petroleum products acquired for or in South Africa. Petroleum is, of course, the Achilles' heel of the economy in South Africa which has no oil deposits of its own. It was an open secret that South Africa, despite boycotts, had been importing and storing a good deal of petroleum purchased from the spot market in recent years to supplement that produced from coal by the

Sasol plants. Oil tankers flying various foreign flags steamed into Durban or Cape Town regularly and openly, but the press was barred from taking any official notice of their presence. In October 1983, Harvey Tyson, editor of *The Star*, was prosecuted for having allowed a report to be published 11 months earlier concerning fuel supplies in Zimbabwe. Reports on the same subject were published in Britain at the time. Tyson and the paper were both fined for contravening the Petroleum Products Act.

James McMillan, editor of the *Natal Mercury*, said his paper was unable to report a major petroleum swindle because of the Petroleum Act. An oil tanker offloaded its oil cargo in Durban and then was scuttled at sea off Senegal with the claim that the oil was lost at sea. The British press reported the story in full, but Durban papers could not publish a word even though the tanker was seen unloading in Durban harbor. As a result, McMillan said, the public was becoming increasingly apathetic about defense news and other news being withheld from them.[24]

Similar restrictions concerning the stockpiling of strategic commodities are imposed under the National Supplies Procurement Amendment Act of 1979. This act empowers a rather obscure government official, the minister of industries, commerce, and consumer affairs, whenever he deems it necessary or expedient for the security of the Republic, to publish a notice in the Government Gazette prohibiting the disclosure of any information regarding *any goods and services*. If, for example, the United Nations applied extensive trading boycotts against South Africa, this law could be used to repress this important economic news within South Africa, news the rest of the world would know.

Here briefly are several other laws that inhibit reporters from getting at the news:

12. The Atomic Energy Act of 1967 imposed severe penalties for unauthorized publication of information about uranium or thorium, nuclear research, and many activities of the Atomic Energy Board.

13. The Hazardous Substances Act of 1973 makes it an offense for anyone, including a journalist, to refuse to give information about such material to an inspector who demands the information or an explanation. Broadly speaking, a hazardous substance is one which

has toxic, corrosive, irritant, radioactive, or flammable properties or is an electronic product.

14. Finally, the Radio Act of 1952 makes it an offense to intercept and publish radio communication which a person is not authorized to receive. In many Western nations, news reporters monitor ambulance, police, and fire department signals to pick up news tips. This is not permitted in South Africa.

In addition to these major laws, there are others, totaling over a hundred, that restrict press reporting. All are detailed in *The Newspaperman's Guide to the Law* (3d Edition) by Kelsey Stuart, who as a board member of SAAN and practising attorney worked closely with the editors of SAAN papers in dealing with the perils of trying to edit a newspaper amid such legal restrictions. Unquestionably, a good deal of time and effort is consumed in newspaper offices on checking out with lawyers the legal implications of borderline stories. Most editors are well versed in the law and must constantly look over the shoulders of reporters and subeditors, especially during riots or civil unrest, to ensure the legality of what is about to be published. One editor of the *Rand Daily Mail* estimated that lawyers might be consulted ten or twelve times in one day.

In addition to these specific laws, press coverage is inhibited in other more indirect but effective ways. One such is the British-style ban on reporting *sub judice* matters. Once a case comes before a judge, the press cannot comment on it. After the death of Steve Biko in police custody, inquests were ruled to be also *sub judice*.

The removal or denial of a passport, often arbitrarily and without any given reason, serves to intimidate journalists and also may prevent the coverage of a story outside South Africa. Critical white journalists are often "punished" by this method, but Africans suffer additionally because at the best of times it is extremely difficult for them to obtain passports; they must post substantial deposits, produce certificates of good character, and often must be interviewed by the Security Police. For an African, the process of obtaining a passport could take months.[25]

The apartheid laws severely restrict freedom of movement, especially among blacks but among whites as well, and this has a decided effect on the ability of newspapers to collect information. Africans, of course, have the greatest difficulty because their right to live and work anywhere is entirely controlled by the "pass" laws. An African journalist, for instance, who has the right to live in Johannesburg, cannot legally remain in any other city for more than seventy-two hours at a time unless he or she has official permission. By law (often ignored) whites are absolutely prohibited from entering any African areas, without permission, in the city or rural districts. From time to time, entry to specific African rural areas is restricted so that both whites and nonlocal Africans need permission to go there. This situation requires newspapers to cover some stories with a team of reporters—one black and one white—in order to deal with the problems of movement and access. Furthermore, in polarized South Africa, some white news sources will not talk with a black reporter, and some black news sources will refuse to speak with a white reporter.

Another kind of restriction on journalists' movements occurs when the police will suddenly ban reporters and photographers from an area of strife. One such example, mentioned in Chapter 1, occurred on June 20, 1980, when police declared the whole of Uitenhage, an industrial suburb of Port Elizabeth, an "operational area" as unrest flared among striking workers who had brought the motor industry to a standstill. Although thousands of people within Uitenhage itself could see and hear what was happening, the press was barred from reporting it to the rest of the nation. Such official actions could only help create rumors and add to the confusion, thereby contributing to serious credibility problems for the government as well.

A final example of restriction of movement involves South Africa's immigration policies. Since the late 1960s, according to McMillan, the government generally has not allowed journalists, academics, or clergymen to immigrate to South Africa. McMillan said he had been trying for years to arrange for a certain journalist from Rhodesia (now Zimbabwe) to join his Durban paper, but the government would not let the man immigrate.[26]

All the various laws in combination with the government/National party enmity toward the opposition press have engendered continuing harassment, both legal and illegal, of reporters and editors by police, government prosecutors, and security officials. The threat of law enforcement is often used as a bludgeon to induce self-censorship by the press.

Gerald Shaw, chief assistant editor of the *Cape Times*, has characterized the intimidation and harassment of reporters and photographers during coverage of stories of unrest (riots, boycotts, demonstrations, etc.) as the biggest problem in news gathering. Police provide no protection to the press in such situations and instead often harass reporters and seize photographers' cameras and film.[27]

Journalists on English-language newspapers or on black publications continually and in considerable numbers have been beaten, detained, arrested, subpoenaed, threatened, spied upon, or just subjected to verbal abuse by public officials assigned to maintain law and order in the Republic.

A few examples illustrate the kind of treatment journalists and editors have been and are subjected to:

• David Evans, reporter on the Port Elizabeth *Evening Post*, was sentenced to five years in prison for sabotage in 1964.

• Brian Bunting, editor of the *Guardian* and *New Age*, was jailed for five months without trial in the 1960 state of emergency. In 1962, he was placed under house arrest which prevented him from practicing his profession.

• Laurence Gandar, editor in chief of the *Rand Daily Mail*, was sentenced to a R 200 fine or three months' imprisonment in 1969 for exposing conditions in South African prisons. The board of directors of the South African Associated Newspapers were intimidated enough after the lengthy and costly trial to relieve Gandar of editorial control of the *Mail*. However, Gandar was permitted to pick his own successor, Raymond Louw, who proved just as defiant a foe of apartheid.

• Margaret Smith, reporter on the *Sunday Times*, was detained under the ninety-day no-trial act in 1964 and was held in solitary confinement for thirty-one days.

• Owen Vanga, a reporter for the *Daily Dispatch*, spent several hundred days in detention under the Terrorism Act and after two trials was acquitted. Afterward he was served with banning orders which barred him from practicing journalism.

• Arnold Geyer, a reporter for the *Rand Daily Mail*, was arrested by security police in October 1980 while covering the annual conference of the Methodist church in Welkom. Geyer vanished while on this assignment, and his paper had no idea where he was. It was inadvertently learned that he was being detained under the General Laws Amendment Act which permits a person to be held incommunicado for fourteen days.

• Deon du Plessis, an assistant editor of the *Sunday Tribune*, endured long and harrowing harassment from the authorities. His home was raided, he was jailed in the middle of the night, and he was tried in total secrecy. (While researching a book on the Rhodesia war, he had received some classified information.) Harvey Tyson, *Star* editor, commented: "Those of us who knew the circumstances of his unaccountable harassment knew all along how trivial the offense was. Yet the heaviest machinery of the State was brought to bear on a reporter and a vague atmosphere of spies, treachery and all sorts of images was created through the concealment of facts under the Official Secrets Act."[28] Du Plessis was finally freed on appeal in 1981.

At any given time in South Africa today there are numerous journalists who have possible jail sentences hanging over their heads. In December 1980, the *Journalist* pointed out that forty journalists faced the new year with charges ranging from public disturbances to violations of the Internal Security Act.[29]

What are the effects of all these laws and the arbitrary and vindictive ways they are sometimes applied? Obviously, some newspapers and some journalists are intimidated and do indeed censor themselves. Some news stories go unreported because of possible legal complications that could result. Some editors insist, however, that despite the laws and the official attitudes, a surprising amount of important information does get published. And there is no question that a good number of reporters and editors, black and white, demonstrate on almost a daily basis a good deal of courage, defiance, and professional skill in telling their readers (and the world) the continuing story of racial conflict and crisis in South Africa. The full, no-holds-barred coverage of the Soweto riots and of the "Muldergate" Information Department scandal of 1978–79 were clear evidence that when the opposition English press is good, it is very good indeed. In the latter situation, reporters like Mervyn Rees and Kitt Katzin as well as editors like Rex Gibson of the *Sunday Express* and Allister Sparks of the *Rand Daily Mail* showed that the press can be an effective, probing watchdog on a government becoming increasingly secretive and unresponsive to public concerns.

But on the other hand, persons within the press as well as perceptive outside observers are convinced that the opposition press has indeed been intimidated and does not do what it could—even within the present confines of law and official intimidation—to publish the news that it should.

Professor Mathews says, "I think there is much self-censorship by the white press. Editors will sit on stories that reporters dig up; stories that may not be illegal but are too hot politically to publish. Proprietors and stockholders fear the financial loss that occurs when papers (such as *Post* or *World*) are banned and really don't care that much for press independence. The press generally is too fearful. The *Rand Daily Mail* is one of the few courageous ones."[30]

Editor Shaw agreed in part: "No doubt certain stories are not covered, and a certain amount of restraint and self-censorship is occurring. Fear of lawsuits and costly trials certainly inhibits the press."[31]

Journalism professor Les Switzer says, "The opposition English press is intimidated, scared, and practices too much self-censorship. It runs stories that are irrelevant or that are ten or twenty years old—things that people have known for a long time. The press must break some laws to bring about some change but is unwilling to do so."[32]

John Grogan, a former staff member of the *East Province Herald*, agrees there is some self-censorship and says there are a variety of reasons for it. Most papers, he pointed out, lack staff and resources to cover adequately black news, and, further, many blacks do not trust the opposition press and won't cooperate with it. Liberal editors, he said, are reluctant to publish inflammatory material, and the commercial and advertising aspects inhibit them as well. Grogan said the English press takes a soft line on big business, and, for example, during the Port Elizabeth strikes against Ford and Volkswagen in 1980, the papers urged the black strikers to settle. Many of the charges of self-censorship, he feels, arise out of the tensions between editors and reporters which can be fierce at times.[33]

Whatever the causes, and there seem to be several, the Nationalist government appears to be achieving its goal of taming the press. Among journalists around the world who believe in and really do practice the Anglo-American tenets of freedom of the press, few are as harassed, vilified, and legally hamstrung by their elected government as are the newspapermen and women, white and black, who work in South Africa. As Anthony Mathews put it, "In a nutshell, laws directly and indirectly controlling information in South Africa constitute a fine-meshed screen through which little material of consequence may pass without the permission of the authorities."[34]

Legal controls over the press are a part of the long, continuing campaign by the Nationalist governments, begun in 1948, to maintain Afrikaner political dominance and to neutralize the white opposition and African newspapers. Under the various governments of Prime Ministers Malan, Verwoerd, Vorster, and Botha, laws restricting the press have been added, revised, or strengthened. The government today has the legal authority to shut down any newspaper and to jail or otherwise silence any reporter or editor in the Republic. The one action it has not taken—yet—is to silence a major newspaper critic such as the *Rand Daily Mail*, the *Sunday Express*, or the *Cape Times*. No doubt the government has the legal powers and the inclination to do so, but so far it has been unwilling to face the great outcry of protest that would surely follow at home and abroad.

Besides, the Nationalists may find it unnecessary to take such a final draconian step because continuing legislation restricting press access to public information—censorship, as it were, at the source—may enable them to achieve the impotent, acquiescent newspapers they have long sought.

6 | Suppression of the Black Press

Black journalists and what is called the black press are at the cutting edge of the confrontation between Afrikaner nationalism and black nationalism. The government's primary motivation for repressing political expression has been to prevent blacks from speaking (or writing) to other blacks about political alternatives or using the printed word to report in any depth their serious affairs and describe their common problems.

Suppression of black perspectives, even in bland and moderate forms, is considered essential to the maintenance and, by extension, the very survival of Afrikaner dominance. Almost any black political viewpoint is viewed as an aspect of African nationalism, something to be resisted and extinguished whenever and wherever it appears.

So, within divided South Africa, where many believe a civil war has already begun, the black journalist plays a curious and perhaps pivotal role. That role, like much else in that troubled land, is contradictory, precarious, and enmeshed in politics.

On the face of it, the black journalist is powerless and ineffectual. He lives with his fellow Africans, Coloureds, and Asians in what for them is an authoritarian police state, and virtually without protection against its excesses and abuses. Because of his complexion, he is subject to the indignities and inequities of the apartheid system.

Black reporters and photographers are often singled out for police harassment, beatings, or detention without trial—hazards rarely faced by their white colleagues, who live in a different, more affluent world and who still retain some semblance of civil rights and protections of law. Journalism is one of the most dangerous occupations for blacks in South Africa today. Furthermore, a black press hardly exists in South Africa. If asked to describe the black press, a Johannesburg black journalist is likely to say, "There is no black press. It's wrong to even talk about it."[1]

Almost all the two hundred or so black journalists active on South African publications work on newspapers owned and controlled by white publishing organizations, mainly SAAN and Argus. There are no newspapers of general circulation owned and controlled by Africans, Coloureds, or Asians, and none that express the real political concerns of the nonwhite majority. If press freedom means, at a minimum, the right to talk politics, then there is no free expression for blacks. Moreover, there is considerably less freedom than forty years ago just as there are fewer black publications today.

However, despite his political and entrepreneurial impotence, the black journalist *is* important in South African journalism and is perhaps becoming more so all the time. Black literates now outnumber white literates and are an increasingly significant factor in newspaper readership. Black readership of some of the English-language papers, such as the *Rand Daily Mail* and the *Daily Dispatch* of East London, is now greater than white.

The readership trends and demographics of population increase clearly point to ever-expanding black newspaper circulation. According to one study, 33 per cent of daily readers in 1962 were African, Coloured, or Asian. By 1977, the figure was 45 per cent.[2] Since 1962, claimed readership of dailies has risen for whites by 30 per cent, for Coloureds by 125 per cent, for Asians by 80 per cent, and for Africans by almost 250 per cent. Urban Africans, their lower wages notwithstanding, are buying more of the consumer products advertised in newspapers and magazines, and the majority of customers in Johannesburg's downtown retail stores are black.

English-language papers have responded to this increasing black readership in two contrasting ways: generalization and specialization. The Argus company specializes, producing separate publications for various ethnic groups—weeklies like *Ilanga* for Zulus and the *Cape Herald* for Coloureds and the daily *Sowetan* for Africans. (Some critics see this as another aspect of apartheid.) Other papers, notably the *Rand Daily Mail* and the *Daily Dispatch* of East London, generalize and aim at a mixed readership. The *Daily Dispatch*, says editor George Farr, who succeeded Donald Woods, is "very conscious of the needs of black readers. Our emphasis is on *all* the news in the area."[3] In recent years, the *Mail* has had twice as many black readers as white; the *Dispatch* four times as many. The growing importance of urban blacks as consumers and users of the mass media is a major reason that the SABC (and the government) moved so quickly to establish a black television service (see Chap. 9).

During the 1970s, newspapers expanded coverage of black news, an area long ignored, and some have been publishing special or "extra" editions for black readers. As a result, English papers in particular have been using more black reporters and are often quite dependent on them. English papers report much more news about blacks than a few years ago, but most of it is in the special or township editions.

Though no true independent black press exists, there are publications edited and produced with nonwhite readers in mind. What is called the black press in the realities of South Africa today can be described this way:

1. The English press has become a "surrogate" press for blacks through the special township editions, with reporting by and edited for blacks, especially of papers like the *Rand Daily Mail, Daily Dispatch, Sunday Times*, and others. Most of the more experienced black journalists work for these papers.

2. There are several weekly black-oriented papers such as *Imvo Zabantsundu* in Xhosa, *Ilanga* in Zulu, and the *Cape Herald*, an Argus-owned paper edited for the large Coloured community in Cape Town. Afrikaans publishing groups put out several black-oriented magazines including the successful "look-read," *Bona*.

3. The *Sowetan*, the Argus company's daily successor to the *World* and the *Post*, is produced by a black staff and edited for Africans.

4. The *Golden City Press*, a new Sunday paper for blacks in Johannesburg, entered the field in April 1982, to fill the void left after the *Sunday Post* stopped publication. The joint owners, SAAN and Jim Bailey, publisher of *Drum* magazine, however, split up in December

1982, and the black-oriented weekly continued under Bailey's control with a new name, the *City Press*, but in a shaky financial condition.

5. Finally there are several marginal publications such as the *Graphic* and the *Leader*, two Asian-owned publications in Durban, and *Muslim News*, a small black-owned paper for Coloureds in Cape Town. Two other black weeklies, the *Nation*, mouthpiece of the Inkatha movement, and the *Voice*, sponsored by church groups, have both ceased publication in recent years.

The "black press," then, can be defined in terms of what Africans, Coloureds, and Asians *read*.

In the precarious state of nonwhite journalism in South Africa today, the black newsperson plays his or her most useful role within the "surrogate press." In the 1976 Soweto uprising, for example, white reporters were sealed off from the upheaval both by police and by black suspicion. "Suddenly, it was black journalists who were bringing out details for the white press from places where they lived and the people they lived among," reported Caryle Murphy of the *Washington Post*. "The black journalists found themselves in a new role. Their sheer guts and professionalism during those days gave notice that the black journalist had matured and has now arrived," said Percy Qoboza, editor of the *World* whose reporters did a good share of that hazardous reporting.[4]

Yet despite this newly acquired recognition and status, black journalists often feel alienated, frustrated, and angry, caught as they are between a harsh, repressive government and a white-dominated profession that doesn't fully accept them. On white newspapers, they consider themselves professionally thwarted, underpaid, and relegated to second-class status. Further, many of them, and especially their union, MWASA, reflect the angry political extremism spawned by the Soweto riots and later so pervasive among younger urban blacks. Considering themselves part of "the struggle" to rid South Africa of white domination, most insist that journalistic objectivity is impossible: "There is only their side and our side."[5]

Increasingly, militant black journalists are rejecting moderation of any sort, including even cooperation and association with sympathetic white colleagues. This black separatism, related to the Black Consciousness movement of Steve Biko, is alienating them from liberal white journalists. Some of the impetus for this separatist stance is the government's policies toward black journalism, which seem at times to be dictated by the most paranoid and ruthless elements of the security forces.

For, in recent years, even the most routine reporting in black newspapers such as the *World* and the *Post* of ordinary political expression and activity that would be easily tolerated in democratic Western nations has been viewed as seditious by the South African government. By silencing black voices of moderation, the government has radicalized nonwhites in South Africa into supporting those advocating violent measures. Thus the possibilities for discussion, conciliation, and compromise over political alternatives have become increasingly remote, if not nonexistent. Urban black journalists, sophisticated and knowledgeable, are keenly aware of black political nuances and currents; they are both actors and spectators in the confrontational politics that characterize their land.

From the beginning, black journalists and their publications have been much more vulnerable than white publications to the legal fetters on free expression detailed in the previous chapter: suppression of publications, deregistration of papers, banning orders against journalists, and detention without trial. But, recently the tempo of repression has accelerated. Between June 1976 and June 1981, about fifty black journalists were detained without trial for periods of up to five hundred days. At least ten were detained more than once. Ten black journalists were banned in that time, and one was tried and was sentenced to a seven-year term on Robben Island. (During the same period, the figures for white journalists were: one detained, one banned, and one tried and jailed for six years. A 1977 manpower survey counted 3,761 white journalists compared with about 220 black journalists.)

Several months after the 1976 Soweto riots, some black reporters were still in detention while others were being arrested in connection with their reporting of those events. Fifteen or more reporters covering Soweto disappeared into custody, including Peter Magubane, Nat Serache, Jan Tugwana, and Willie Nkosi of the *Rand Daily Mail*, Joe Thloloe of *Drum*, and Duma Nklovu of the *World*. Many were arrested under the Terrorism Act and most were finally released without trials or even being charged. Enoch Duma of the *Sunday Times* was tried under the Terrorism Act but found not guilty after he convinced the court that his contacts with black resistance groups had been part of his work, not an attempt to subvert the government.

The hazards of being a black journalist are well illustrated by the career of just one—the distinguished photojournalist Peter Magubane, who began in the 1950s as a photographer for *Drum* magazine and for twenty years after that was a staff photographer for the *Rand Daily Mail*. For five of those years, he was a banned person: he could not go into a building with a printing press, and, confined to his home, he could not practice journalism. In addition, he was imprisoned several times for a total of two years, spending six months in ordinary confinement and 586 days in solitary confinement (a record for a journalist). Yet Magubane has never been convicted of any crime.

While working, Magubane has felt the muzzle of a policeman's machine gun against his temple, been struck in the face with a rifle butt, and had his film and camera confiscated. But Magubane has said his experiences are not unique. Others, he says, could tell tales more shocking. "At least, I've been able to go ahead in life with my profession. I am no martyr. I am no hero. I am a photojournalist."[6] While producing dramatic photos of the Soweto rioting, Magubane was frequently picked up for interrogation and then released again. Then about a month and a half after the riots ended, he disappeared into detention for months.

On October 17, 1977, the black press was again caught up in a cataclysmic event—the nationwide crackdown against a variety of political dissenters, especially those associated with the Black Consciousness movement of Steve Biko who had died in police custody a few months earlier. As mentioned in Chapter 1, the *World* and the *Weekend World*, the largest and most influential newspapers speaking to blacks, were closed down by the government for "contributing to a subversive situation," and their editors, Percy Qoboza and Aggrey Klaaste, were arrested. Justice Minister Jimmy Kruger had warned Qoboza several times to tone down the paper's coverage, but Qoboza ignored the warnings. John Marquard, Argus company manager of the *World*, said later that Kruger had been talking to the wrong man. "Just one call to me would have settled the matter," Marquard said.

Also, the banning of the *World* and *Weekend World* was a blow aimed against the giant Argus company, the largest and most successful newspaper publisher in Africa. The *World*, with its growing circulation (at the time the fastest-growing English-language paper in the country) and increased acceptance by blacks in Soweto and the Reef, was then the single greatest influence in black journalism. The masthead of the *World*, a sensational tabloid edited for urban Africans, proclaimed it was "OUR OWN, OUR ONLY NEWSPAPER." With its white ownership and control, it wasn't quite that but it tried to be, and under Qoboza it was getting better. Although it offered its readers a steady diet of crime, sex, death, and sports, it did identify with the urban African and reflected his or her fears, hopes, and frustrations.

The actions against Qobozo and the *World* were the government's response to Biko's Black Consciousness movement and the national furor that followed his death in police custody. One observer, Professor Les Switzer, has said, "In the *World*, Qoboza had recorded and sympathized with Black Consciousness views but did not advocate them."[7]

Perhaps most police repression of black journalists results not from suspected political activity but from resentment of reporters' *reporting* the news. A typical example was the experience of Zubeida Jaffer, a twenty-three-year-old graduate of the journalism program at Rhodes University. Jaffer was in her first year as a reporter at the *Cape Times* and was involved in reporting the student boycotts and riots in Cape Town in June 1980. Her access to the Coloured community enabled her to interview families of the riot victims and assist in cataloguing deaths, undisclosed by police, but then published in the *Cape Times*. Several times police warned her to "not get involved." On October 27, 1980, she was picked up by police and detained without trial for two months. She was in solitary confinement part of the time, moved to several different places, and subjected to frequent interrogations.

Jaffer's plight was widely publicized in the British press. The *Guardian* and the *Observer* reported her detention in detail and the *New Statesman* wrote, "Her reports from the local black community have been far more detailed and authentic than a white journalist, however well intentioned, could have produced." The *Cape Times*'s editor, Tony Heard, was told by the minister of police that her detention had nothing to do with her journalistic activities. "It was her job to have the right contacts and it was my suspicion that the police want to know about these and close them down," Heard said. For a long period, neither Heard, her family, nor an attorney could see Jaffer, detained as she was under Section 6 of the Terrorism Act which provides that people can be held indefinitely on the order of a senior police officer and restricts to officials access to detainees. Finally, she was charged with the possession of three books banned under the Publications Act. One was *The Wretched of the Earth* by Frantz Fanon. Jaffer said later she didn't even own the books, and when her case was brought before a judge, it was promptly dismissed. This case, typical but less harsh than many (she apparently was not physically abused), illustrates the difficulty experienced by a non-white reporter in handling news that the government considers "sensitive."[8]

The void left by the banning of the *World* was quickly filled when the Argus company brought its weekly, the *Natal Post*, up from Durban to Johannesburg and began publishing it daily as the *Post* (Transvaal) with Qoboza as editor after his release from custody several months later. His staff included most of his colleagues from the *World*. But in January 1981, the *Post* was closed in turn, causing widespread disbelief, confusion, and condemnation of the Botha government. Even some supporters of Botha and the National party felt that the actions were self-wounding and unnecessary particularly in light of the new prime minister's promise to South Africa and the world that many aspects of apartheid, especially certain "petty apartheid" laws, would be rescinded. The South African government had been obviously trying to improve its image in the world. But actions against the *Post* and black journalists did much to dispel the optimism that accompanied Botha's promises to ease up on controls of black activities and somehow present apartheid in a more humane light.

It is apparent from hindsight that the real targets were not the *Post* papers but a handful of black journalists, those organized into MWASA—Media Workers Association of South Africa—the successor of two previous unions for black journalists, the Union of Black Journalists (UBJ) and the Writers Association of South Africa (WASA). The two English press groups, Argus and SAAN, are bitterly resented by the National party leadership, but it strains credulity to believe that the conservative proprietors of Argus, who hire and fire the editors on their black-oriented publications like the *Post*, *Ilanga*, and the *Cape Herald*, were covert supporters of the Black Consciousness movement.

The obvious move for the government would have been to go after the "subversive" journalists themselves—not the papers that employ them—but the South African security officials who make such decisions are not noted for their logic. Their victims sometimes report that the security forces and police are ruthlessly efficient, yet often they can be clumsy and even ludicrous—like bureaucrats anywhere. (A well-circulated jibe, even among loyal Afrikaners, has it that in Pretoria there are two secret agencies, the Department of Bad Timing and the Department of Dumb Mistakes; although supersecret, the two work very closely together.)

In the October 1977 press crackdown, the 150-member Union of Black Journalists was among the numerous organizations banned. Twenty-six black journalists were later fined for taking part in a protest march against this action. The government obviously perceived the UBJ as a part of Biko's broadly based movement and therefore subversive. Two of the reporters detained after the Soweto riots were Joe Thloloe and Harry Mashabela, the sitting and past presidents, respectively, of the UBJ.

The Union of Black Journalists evolved out of a series of meetings convened by Mashabela in 1973 to discuss discrimination against black journalists. At the time, the major journalists' union in the country, the white-controlled South African Society of Journalists (SASJ), which under South African laws could not bargain for wages if blacks were among its members, had only recently been opened to blacks. Mashabela, then a reporter on *The Star*, and others decided to reject SASJ membership and go ahead with their blacks-only union which was inaugurated on February 12, 1973, with Mashabela as president.[9] This began a period of union activity much influenced by the Black Consciousness movement. Significantly, the UBJ was founded during the wave of labor unrest and sporadic strikes in 1972–73.

A year after UBJ was banned in 1977, WASA was formed. Whites
were officially and explicitly excluded, leading to accusations by white
journalists of "racism" and denials from WASA. The union claimed
that black journalists had unique and separate problems and that
liberal or sympathetic white colleagues knew little about the realities
of life for blacks and so could not effectively contribute to their
"struggle."[10]

This militant separatism was well illustrated by a resolution attacking Donald Woods, editor of the *Daily Dispatch*, and passed at a
WASA congress at Durban in 1978. The resolution called him
"irrelevant to the Black struggle and to black journalism" and condemned Woods as an opportunist in exploiting the name of Steve Biko
and as a hypocrite who did nothing to improve the condition of black
journalists on his paper. Woods's reply from Britain could not be
quoted in the South African press as he was a banned person. However, white colleagues came to his defense, including *Dispatch* editor
George Farr, who said, "Journalists here are treated according to
their merit. I know of no writer in this country who campaigned
harder and more eloquently for the cause of non-racialism than
Donald Woods."[11]

In October 1980, WASA decided to open its membership to "workers in the communications media"—journalists, typists, messengers,
drivers, etc.—and the name was changed to Media Workers Association of South Africa. Unquestionably, MWASA attracted the
membership and loyalty of the majority of urban black journalists,
including some of the best. But a generation gap exists within black
journalism. Younger journalists are more angry and identify with
MWASA. Peter Magubane, who in a lengthy career has stood up to
police repression longer than most, was ridiculed by some younger
colleagues for belonging to SASJ and taking a more professional
approach to his work. Another veteran, "Doc" Sipho Bibitsha, has
said, "They take us old journalists as softies, as moderates. They say
we have been under the system for so long that we don't see things as
they are. It does hurt."[12]

MWASA represented about 90 per cent of all black journalists and
apparently a good number of noneditorial workers as well. National

executive at the time was Zwelakhe Sisulu, a *Rand Daily Mail* reporter and son of Walter Sisulu, secretary general of the ANC. The father is serving a life sentence with ANC leader Nelson Mandela on Robben Island.

Then, two weeks after MWASA was formally constituted, the members on the *Cape Herald* struck for better pay and working conditions. Several weeks earlier, workers on the *Post* and *Sunday Post* won all their wage demands after a seven-day strike. The *Herald* walkout in Cape Town sparked a nationwide sympathy strike by MWASA members at most of the Argus and SAAN papers around the country. (They did not strike at the Afrikaans papers where, it was believed, they would have been promptly fired, or at the church-supported *Voice* which had an all-black staff.)

The demands by MWASA were: better pay and working conditions on the *Cape Herald*; no loss of pay during the walkout or sympathy strike; and recognition of MWASA as the negotiating body for black media workers. At the *Herald* the strikers' demands were met, and the Argus and SAAN employers did recognize MWASA. But the issue of payment for time on strike prolonged the work action and exacerbated the differences and growing animosities between black journalists and their liberal white colleagues as well as their often not-so-liberal employers.

Furthermore, the strike added an important new dimension to the escalating conflict in South Africa, in that it was a direct confrontation between blacks and the English press, that bastion of English institutions which had been leading the assault on the racism and injustices of the political and economic establishment. Moreover, most of the English papers affected by the strike were also in the forefront of attacks on the government and industrial management for their mishandling of labor unrest, particularly for failing to understand the real grievances of black workers.[13]

The confrontation showed dramatically then that blacks basically made no distinctions between the actions of the racist Afrikaners and the liberal English. The dispute, one press observer, Hennie Serfontein, wrote, had "laid the liberal English press wide open to black accusations of 'double standards,' 'hypocrisy,' and 'dishonesty.' "[14]

The strike also illuminated the growing differences between black journalists and the majority of white journalists and editors on these English newspapers. Liberal journalists denounced MWASA in tones of hostility previously reserved for the government. "The dormant white radical resentment of Black Consciousness became open," another commentator, Denis Beckett, wrote. "MWASA's name was punned into 'Mediocre Workers Association.' The white journalists had grown so used to the official Black Consciousness line that liberals were irrelevant, getting in the way of black self expression, hypocritical, and so on, that many had come to believe that this was just morale-boosting beating of ritual drums. Now it suddenly seemed that maybe the blacks meant it after all."[15]

For their part, newspaper executives were deeply embittered and disillusioned by the actions of their black journalists. Raymond Louw, general manager of SAAN, considered the strike a political power play by Sisulu, whom he regarded as politically ambitious. "MWASA didn't really want to settle on bread and butter issues. We were ready to settle on the first day, but we couldn't get the national leadership to even show up to discuss the issues," Louw has said.[16] Benjamin Pogrund, deputy editor of the *Rand Daily Mail*, reflected the bitterness of other news executives: "They even tried to close down the *Mail* and told news sources not to talk with us. MWASA wouldn't even talk with the newspapers while the strike was on. But worse, I was appalled by the racism of it all."[17]

English newspaper executives generally shared Louw's feeling that MWASA was not really interested in issues of pay and working conditions but, as primarily a political organization, was trying to make a political statement. Obviously, the government saw MWASA in the same light, but as subversive in addition.

The two-month strike ended two days before Christmas 1980, with recognition of MWASA by the Argus and SAAN papers. The strikers lost on the issue of full pay for time lost on strike, but won full pension and medical contributions for the period.

A week later, the government started to act against the MWASA leadership. On December 29, 1980, both MWASA president Sisulu, who was then news editor of the *Sunday Post*, and Marimuthu Subramoney, thirty-five, a BBC correspondent and national vice-chairman of MWASA, were banned for three years and placed under partial house arrest under the Internal Security Act. Sisulu was later detained and held for 251 days in solitary confinement. He was released in February 1982. Shortly thereafter banning orders were also served on Mathata Tsedu, general secretary of the union's northern Transvaal region and a *Post* reporter, and two other MWASA officers, Phil Mtimkulu and Joe Thloloe. In another crackdown on MWASA on June 24, 1982, Thloloe and Tsedu were placed in detention. Then in May 1983, Thloloe drew an unusually heavy prison sentence of two and a half years for possession of a single banned book. In this case, Thloloe was charged with being an activist for the outlawed Pan-Africanist Congress. Then came the closing of the *Post* newspapers.

Despite the decimation of its leadership, MWASA managed to hang on. Membership in early 1981 was reported to be about 288, of whom 210 were journalists. But after the strike and the bannings, the alienation between white and black journalists working on the white man's newspapers became even more apparent.

Peta Thornycroft of the *Sunday Express* believes that there is little closeness left between working white journalists and black journalists. "Polarization today means that, even in journalism, whites are getting whiter and the blacks are getting banned," she said.[18] On the English papers, she said that black and white journalists just don't talk with each other. There is only mutual hostility. To blacks, Thornycroft said, liberal journalists and papers like the *Rand Daily Mail* are considered irrelevant. She considered the antiwhite anger of the black journalists far worse than in the years just after the Soweto riots.

Black journalists too recognize this "element of mistrust" between black and white journalists. On white papers, a moderate story by black standards is considered radical by white editors, some black journalists have complained. Moreover, they feel that major stories are assigned usually to the white reporters. "Even on a story about one of the Homelands, where a black reporter would know the language and the culture, a black reporter would go along as an interpreter for a white reporter. This is much resented," one black said.[19] And because they don't get good assignments (most blacks are general assignment reporters), they don't get the promotions. This was a major grievance of the thirty-five MWASA journalists working at SAAN on the *Rand Daily Mail, Sunday Times, Financial Mail,* or the *Sunday Express.* If they had their own papers, the blacks said there would be a psychological difference but conceded they would be subject to greater government repression.

The extra or special editions, edited for black readers and distinct from the regular editions, were almost unanimously resented by these black journalists who still conceded that in the immediate future there was no alternative to them. "Extra editions carry stories about influx controls and pass raids and blacks know all about these things. It's the whites who should know about them but these stories are not reported in the white editions," one reporter said. In their view, if the South African press had started much earlier to become fully integrated newspapers, things would not be so bad today.[20]

Black reporters resent the way their stories are handled and often rewritten by white subeditors, who frequently tone down or sharply edit black-written or reported items—often to conform to the harsh and complex laws restricting what the press can report. However, blacks claim that white editors are overly timid and often censor themselves unnecessarily. If there were more black subeditors, they believe, more of "their news" would get into the papers.

The status of many black journalists is another sore spot. A disproportionate number work as "stringers" on modest retainers supplemented by payment for what gets into the papers. Salaries for full-time black journalists still lag behind those of white reporters, in part because they are in the lower positions. Such a subordinate role for the black journalist is particularly galling in light of the impressive history of black journalism in South Africa.

Brief History of the Black Press

The black press of South Africa has had a long history quite separate from the white or European newspapers. Les Switzer, a leading authority on the subject, points out that the South African press in general has been a sectional press throughout its history, and *race—*

not language, religion, or culture—has proved to be its dominant characteristic.[21] In the past, as in the present, the black press is defined in terms of readership—what Africans, Coloureds, and Asians have read.

The "separateness" of the African press was of course a result of South Africa's racial compartmentalization, which long predated the National party dominance. White newspapers quite simply ignored the non-European majority. Allister Sparks, editor of the *Rand Daily Mail*, said in a 1979 speech:

> A look through newspaper files of the prewar years, and indeed through the 40's, is a revealing exercise. A visitor from another planet, going through these pages, day after day, year after year, would get the impression that South Africa was a country populated almost exclusively by 3,000,000 whites. There is almost no reference at all to black people—except occasionally in the odd crime report, or in some general allusion to "the Native Problem." As individuals, or as a community, they simply didn't exist. Black names just don't appear in the news columns. And the newspapers certainly didn't regard them as a political factor. There are no reports on ANC meetings—even though the ANC was formed in 1912. Those early newspapers were reflecting the norm of South African society in those days. It was a white man's country. Blacks didn't exist, except as nameless units of labor force and as constituting a vague and amorphous Native problem.[22]

Under such circumstances, separate publications to serve the African, Coloured, and Asian communities were a necessity. As a result, between 1836 and 1977, there were more than eight hundred publications written by or aimed at blacks in South Africa. Some were small, ephemeral newsletters of only two to four pages; others were full magazines or newspapers with circulations of up to 170,000. Nowhere else in Africa was the indigenous, non-European press as diverse, widespread, and sophisticated as in South Africa. During its early years, the African press had no immediate political importance (that was to come later), but it was an indication of the growing westernization and articulateness of its readers, and an important means of developing a sense of cohesion that surmounted tribal distinctions.[23]

Tim J. Couzens of the University of the Witwatersrand, an authority on black literature, writes that one of the main functions of black newspapers in South Africa has been to create a reading public. "The black newspapers have created the skills and the taste for reading literature to the extent that those skills and tastes exist among black people today. Furthermore, until very recently, the black newspapers provided the major, if not the sole, outlet for literary production and creativity. Almost all our early black writers were connected with newspapers as editors, reporters, or contributors: John Dube, Sol Plaatje, the Dhlomo brothers, Stanley Silwana, Peter Abrahams, Walter Nhlappo, Can Themba, Ezekiel Mphahlele, etc."[24]

Missionaries were a significant component of the history of the black press. In the early nineteenth century, the missionaries taught the local people how to read and write and how to operate the printing presses they had brought from Europe. The black press was born at mission stations in the remote areas of the eastern and northwestern Cape and Basutoland (now Lesotho), and from these stations emerged a new black intelligentsia comprising such people as Sol Plaatje, John Tengo Jabavu, John Dube, Selope Thema, Rolfes Dhlomo, Pixley Seme, and many others.[25] These men became leaders of the black community and also were the earliest creative writers as well as journalists.

These missionary-owned and controlled publications, according to Switzer, represented the first of four phases in the history of the black press: (1) the missionary period; (2) the independent period; (3) the white-owned period; and currently (4) the multiracial period. Each earlier phase lasted about fifty years while the fourth is still evolving.

Missionary Period

Umshumayeli Wendaba [Publisher of the News], printed by the Wesleyan Mission Society in Grahamstown from 1837 to April 1841, is considered the first serial publication aimed at a black audience in southern Africa. It was published in Xhosa.

Shortly thereafter, the Presbyterian Glasgow Missionary Society at

Lovedale in the eastern Cape became the center of black learning and publishing in southern Africa. From 1862 to 1865, it printed the first English-language black newspaper, *Indaba*.[26] In 1870, Lovedale began the *Christian Express* which continues to this day as *South African Outlook* and is the oldest continuous black publication.

Independent Period

An independent but struggling press, controlled for the most part by blacks, emerged from the 1880s to the 1920s. In November 1884, John Tengo Jabavu, only twenty-five years old, and then editor of the missionary newspaper *Isigidimi*, established the first independent black newspaper, *Imvo Zabantsundu*, in King William's Town. This paper quickly became the most influential organ of African opinion in the Cape Colony, and Jabavu became the most widely known mission-educated African until 1910.[27] Published in Xhosa and English, *Imvo* continues today as a publication of Perskor, the Afrikaner newspaper group.

Other papers followed. John Dube founded *Ilanga lase Natal* in 1904. Both Dube and Jabavu and their papers established traditions of forthright discussion which were followed by other shorter-lived papers. Among the most vigorous and interesting was *Abantu-Batho* [the People], the organ of the Native National Congress, founded in 1912 and the forerunner of the continuing African National Congress (ANC).

Other early publications of political parties were Abdul Abdurraham's (Coloured) African People's Organization's *APO* and the Natal Indian organization's *Indian Views*. The Indian newspapers were the most intensely political and community oriented of the nonwhite press because of their greater independence from European capital. Mahatma Gandhi founded the first Indian newspaper in South Africa—*Indian Opinion*—in 1903, and it was edited by his son, Manilal Gandhi, until his death in 1956. *Indian Views* was started in 1914. Both papers were weeklies published in Durban and served their community well.

Switzer points out that these independent papers survived on shaky economic foundations. Lacking capital, newsprint, equipment, skilled tradesmen, and distribution agents, the newspaper entrepreneurs had to appeal to a public that was largely illiterate and poor. White business and financial interests, however, began to take an interest in the black press, and an indicator of things to come was the launching, by the Chamber of Mines, of the *Umteteli wa Bantu* in May 1920, which soon employed some of the more talented black journalists of the day. This set the stage for the white takeover of the black press by the early 1930s.

White-Owned Period

Key publisher for the white-owned period was Bertram F. G. Paver, an ex-farmer and itinerant salesman who founded the Bantu Press, Ltd., and inaugurated its national newspaper, *Bantu World*, in April 1932. Paver was a liberal who was motivated by both commercial gain and the desire "to provide the Native people with a platform for fair comment and presentation of their needs and aspirations." Fourteen months later the Bantu Press was taken over by the Argus company, which controlled it as the major stockholder from 1933 to 1952. During this period, Bantu Press acquired seven subsidiary companies with newspapers, and by 1945 Bantu owned ten weekly newspapers and printed, distributed, and handled the advertising for twelve other publications in eleven different languages.[28]

Bantu Press, the first monopoly in the black press, had newspapers and magazines throughout southern Africa, including the Rhodesias, High Commission Territories, and Nyasaland (now Malawi). In March 1948, circulation of their publications came to 113,000. *Bantu World*, with 24,000 copies per issue, was the leading paper in black journalism, and each copy was read by at least five adult wage earners who in turn read aloud to illiterate friends and family members.[29] Thus, with white chain ownership and corporate control, the black press was transformed into a contemporary medium of mass communication. Bantu Press was a significant training ground for young blacks in the Western norms of journalism with its stress on objectivity, separation of news and comment, and an event-related concept of news.

Black journalism and black writing underwent a major change in the 1950s when Jim Bailey, wealthy son of legendary mining magnate Abe Bailey, launched the *African Drum* in May 1951 and then the *Golden City Post* in March 1955. Bailey has been called the William Randolph Hearst of South African journalism. Switzer writes that Bailey's version of "gee whiz" journalism, based on the sex-crime-sports formula, overwhelmed the traditional reluctance of the elite black press to deal in entertainment news and bridged the final gap in forging a mass, popular press. In October 1951, the magazine, by then called simply *Drum*, was moved from Cape Town to Johannesburg and under its British editor, Anthony Sampson, began to produce both sound reporting and short stories.

Its sensationalism was tempered by good writing and major innovations in graphics. Two successive expatriate editors, Sampson and Tom Hopkinson, made major contributions to the success of *Drum*, bringing the journalistic techniques of Fleet Street to Johannesburg. Hopkinson, who followed Sampson, had been editor of Britain's *Picture Post* and described his *Drum* experiences in *In the Fiery Continent* (1962). Sampson, also a distinguished journalist, wrote about his tenure in *Drum: A Venture into the New Africa* (1956).

Journalism scholar Graeme Addison has written that *Drum* became a mouthpiece of the township masses, expressing as never before their social and political grievances—directly with great stylistic verve, in a new africanized English that was punchy and colorful.[30] More than any other publication in South Africa, *Drum* was relevant to the frustrations and aspirations of urban blacks; its reporting of South African prisons and the dramatic pictures of the Sharpeville massacre in 1960 shocked the world as well as South Africa. *Drum*'s extraordinary success began with Sampson's realization that people of the cities wanted to read about jazz, soccer, women, and issues close to them—not about tribal homelands.

And a success it was. West African and East African editions of *Drum* were launched, eventually attaining a greater combined circulation than the South African edition. In 1969, *Drum*'s three editions had a weekly circulation of 470,000. The *Golden City Post*, which followed the same formula of sex, sin, and soccer—plus relevant reporting—had a weekly circulation in 1968 of 224,000 with an estimated 1,158,000 African, Coloured, and Indian readers.

In addition, *Drum* had a lasting impact on black journalism and creative writing. Several of its great names are still around: Ezekiel Mphahlele, now a professor of literature at the University of the Witwatersrand, photographer Peter Magubane, and Juby Mayet, a banned former staff member of *Voice*. Many others are not. Nat Nkasa committed suicide in New York. Can Themba drank himself to death in Switzerland. Bloke Modisane, Lewis Nkosi, James Mathews, Alex La Guma, and Alfred Hutchison were among those who fled the country about the time of Sharpeville or soon afterward. Perhaps the best-remembered fiction writer is the late Casey "The Kid" Motsisi; a collection of Motsisi's columns was published by Ravan Press in 1979. Most black writers in South Africa today acknowledge their debt to *Drum*.

Not only its talented staff but *Drum* itself became a casualty of the 1960s when the banning of the various black nationalist movements and their newspapers killed off most significant black journalism. *Drum* was not banned but was withdrawn by its publisher in 1965. It reappeared later in a far milder guise and has since steered clear of the aggressive reporting of political issues that had earlier produced news and photos of meaning to the urban blacks.

In 1962, Argus gained full control over Bantu Press and the *World*, now a daily, adopted Bailey's sensationalism and became a tabloid modeled after the *Daily Mirror* of London. From then until its banning in 1977, the *World* became the most significant voice in black journalism. Although leery of actively supporting black political aims, it did report the concerns and problems of the urban blacks, especially those in the townships of Soweto. A few months after the 1976 Soweto uprising, Percy Qoboza was appointed sole editor in charge of both the *World* and *Weekend World*, the first African in almost a generation who was free of white editorial supervision. About a year later, these papers and their editor were silenced.

Starting in the 1950s, the South African government sought to reach the black reading public which was expanding as African literacy rose. To promote apartheid policies, Hendrik Verwoerd, then minister of native affairs, helped launch *Bantu* in 1954. Later the same year, the Native Affairs Department published *Bantu Education Journal* for the African schools. By the late 1970s, the Department of

Information was publishing thirteen serial publications in nine languages for blacks. The Afrikaans publishers, which put out multilingual picture magazines, worked alongside the government and sometimes in cooperation with it and soon gained a monopoly over that market. These "look-read" magazines, really photo comic books, were highly successful and apolitical (*Bona* founded in March 1956, had a 1983 circulation of 290,000, the second highest of any magazine in South Africa) and proved lucrative for both Nasionale Pers and Perskor.

The white press, which first long ignored the black population and then controlled its publications, found itself increasingly dependent on the cultivation of its own black readers. During the 1960s, blacks assumed an increasing share of newspaper readership, which led by the mid 1970s to the still-developing fourth phase in the history of the black press.

The Multiracial Period

Several factors have contributed to the multiracial period, the latest stage. White newspapers had reached the saturation point with white readership—in 1976 there were ten newspapers vying for two million white readers in the Johannesburg-Pretoria area alone. Only the *World* newspapers were expanding and attracting new readers. Increased production costs and incipient competition from television were cutting deeply into profits.

Moreover, the newly introduced regular black "township" editions of the English and Afrikaans papers were successfully drawing new readers to the white newspapers. Also, of course, those black readers were spending money in downtown Johannesburg and Pretoria. The "extra" editions of the *Sunday Times* (with split runs for Africans in the Transvaal, for Asians in Natal, and for Coloureds in Cape Town) had a combined circulation of 100,000 in 1977.[31]

Black journalists, originally hired for the township editions or as stringers, began to move onto the regular news staffs, albeit in lower positions. A few papers with high black readerships, such as the *Rand Daily Mail* and *Daily Dispatch*, have taken the lead in integrating more black news into all parts of the papers—general news, sports, women's features, society, etc. Although this trend has not helped the financially troubled *Mail*, it may in time lessen the long-standing practice of news based on race. In any case, since the mid 1970s, the white press, especially the English papers, have become in varying degrees a surrogate for the black press.

The Coloured community, mainly centered in Cape Town, had no general newspapers of its own (until the the Argus-owned *Cape Herald* was founded in 1965), except for a few minor publications produced by religious groups. The Indian community, centered in Durban and independent of white financial control, has the most commercially viable of the nonwhite publications. The two main Indian newspapers, the *Leader*, founded in 1941, and the *Graphic*, in 1950, continue as community newspapers but lack general appeal.

In their struggle to survive professionally, black journalists recognized that basic education and journalistic training were pressing needs. There is not an adequate corps of black journalists able to articulate the aspirations, strengths, weaknesses, problems of the black community. A 1977 manpower study found there was one white journalist per 1,171 white people but only one black journalist for every 51,961 blacks.[32]

Blacks aspiring to journalism are handicapped at the outset by the deficient nature of their education. Graduates of the segregated African schools generally tend to fare badly when compared with their white (and Coloured and Indian) counterparts. Their competence in written English is usually low, and they lack the broad background needed for journalism. Working black journalists have varying levels of competence, but generally, according to their editors, their standard of work leaves much to be desired. Black journalists recognize their shortcomings and are eager to overcome them.

A real need exists for organized training for black newspersons, both on the job or as a preparation for journalism. Recently, a few efforts have been made to help those now on the job, such as short courses organized or supported by the Thomson Foundation and the South African Catholic Bishops' Conference.

For some years, the chief regular training programs have been the cadet courses run each year by Argus and SAAN. SAAN conducts two six-week training courses a year; Argus holds two five-month courses. Together these training programs, which operate independently of each other, produce forty to forty-five journalists a year. Only a handful of these are black. The problem is that black candidates, because of their general level of education, can seldom compete with the white, Coloured, and Indian candidates.

The universities have been little help in dealing with this problem. Blacks are effectively barred from white universities, with some exceptions, and the black universities offer no adequate preparation for careers in journalism or mass communication. Rhodes University's Department of Journalism has the only professional journalism program at the university level in English but has been prevented by apartheid-related restrictions from training nearly as many black journalists as it would like.

Certainly black journalists will become increasingly important in South African journalism in the years ahead; this seems inevitable in light of the growing black population with its increasing urbanization, literacy, and affluence. The education and training of these mass communicators of the future will have to be done by the black community itself or groups outside the governmental structure since the training of more black journalists is obviously not a high-priority concern of the Nationalist government.

The multiracial phase of black journalism will perhaps continue for some time because of the persistent twin barriers of government repression of black expression and the lack of capital to support black newspaper enterprises. The black journalist therefore must continue to seek professional realization on the white-owned and controlled surrogate and sectionalized press, an unsatisfactory situation for the black practitioner.

The vacuum created by the demise of the *Post* was quickly filled. On February 2, 1981, the Argus group substantially transformed its free sheet or throwaway for the African market, the *Sowetan*, into a daily tabloid (price fifteen cents) to replace the *Post*. (Since the publication's name was already registered, Argus did not have to pay the heavy registration fee.) The new paper employed thirty-two of the fifty former *Post* and *Sunday Post* journalists.

According to the *Sowetan*'s new editor, former *Post* deputy editor Joe Latekgomo, "The fact that we will be serving the same market makes it imperative that we reflect the same concerns and aspirations as were reflected by *The World, Weekend World, Post* and *Sunday Post,* . . . and that we continue to fight for a just society for all."[33] Only time will tell whether Argus, twice burned by government bannings, will permit the smaller-staffed and more modestly funded *Sowetan* to take up where the *Post* left off.

The demise of the *Post* newspapers and the decapitation of MWASA's leadership affected the morale of black journalists and the black community. Though more sophisticated blacks have been turning increasingly to the "white" newspapers for a wider view of the world and other blacks have found the special or township editions relevant, the black-oriented papers such as the *World* and *Post* undoubtedly played a special role because, despite white ownership and management, the editorial staff from the editor downward was mostly black. This forged a psychological bond between newspaper and reader that is not easily duplicated. In addition, the *World* and *Post* consciously articulated the interests and concerns of the black community in a manner closed to newspapers serving a wider, multiracial circle of readers. Those papers were much closer to the historical traditions of the black press.

Pushed underground, the thoughts and aspirations of black communities have more recently been finding expression in various community and trade union newspapers, student magazines, and other "alternative" publications—all outside the general press. Examples of such ephemeral papers are *Grassroots, Staffrider, Graphic, Muslim News,* and *SASPU National,* a student publication which circulates to both black and white campuses.

Also an essential but often forgotten function of the black press is as an important conduit to whites of black thoughts and perspectives. In a divided society like South Africa, the press could play a critical role in providing effective communication between blacks and whites. But government policy clearly prohibits this from happening. As a result, whites know little about blacks and blacks know little about whites, exacerbating an already tragic and violence-prone situation. Dissatisfied blacks are becoming more insistent that their voices be heard, as is evidenced in the increasing amount of urban violence, disturbances, bombings, strikes, demonstrations of varying kinds, and the number of young blacks who have left the country for military training since 1976. These acts, too, are a form of communication, a way of making political statements.

The government has the choice of continuing to choke off the avenues to two-way communication, with its inevitable violent consequences, or of opening up the clogged channels of communication to encourage blunt and candid communications that might ultimately avoid cataclysmic confrontation. The latter course would mean freeing the black press from its fetters and letting the authentic voices of black South Africa be expressed.

7 | Censorship under the Publications Acts

The censorship of literature, films, and various forms of creative expression has long been an integral part of the maintenance first of white domination and then apartheid and of the failing attempt to promulgate the morality of the Afrikaner brand of Christianity. Novelist Nadine Gordimer has written: "We shall not be rid of censorship until we are rid of apartheid. Censorship is the arm of mind control and as necessary to maintain a racist regime as that other arm of internal repression, the secret police."[1] A student of censorship, Dorothy Driver, writes: "Censorship in South Africa is part of apartheid; it is an authoritarian strategy that imposes on the public an ideology that is Calvinist, capitalist, racist and increasingly militaristic."[2] According to South Africa's best-known Afrikaans writer, André Brink, "the history of censorship in South Africa upholds the belief that it is primarily a political weapon."[3]

On the other hand, many Afrikaners and other whites regard censorship as essential to keep out the "corrupting" and "obscene" influences of permissive Western societies as well as the subversive influences of the political and social ideas of both Communism and egalitarian democracy. Among right-wing Afrikaners, there is little inclination to ease censorship. Dr. Andries Treurnicht, who broke from the National party in the early 1980s, told the Dutch Reformed church's public morals congress in Pretoria in 1970 that people who wanted to relax censorship hoped to "make a Sodom and Gomorrah out of South Africa." He said, "Should the accomplices of those who want to corrupt South Africa with filthy literature succeed, they

would be handing South Africa to the communists. It is unthinkable
that censorship should be relaxed or abolished."[4]

South Africans, white and black, have long lived with official
controls over what they read, view, or hear. Censorship in the narrow
(and traditional) sense of prior restraint or prior government approval
before publication or exhibition of books, motion pictures, plays and
live performances, and various publications (as well as postpublica-
tion censorship) has in recent years been authorized by two stat-
utes—the Publications and Entertainments Act of 1963 and its revision, the Publications Act of 1974—and applied by an elaborate
bureaucracy.

The daily and Sunday newspapers and other periodicals that belong
to the Newspaper Press Union have been explicitly exempted from
these laws, so ostensibly are free of censorship. But as Chapter 5 has
shown, newspapers and publications in general have long been subjected to censorship in the broad sense through numerous laws,
particularly the Internal Security Act of 1950, which was designed to
control political writings but has also been used to suppress a good
deal of creative writing and to censor by banning both publications
and writers.

Here, the focus is on the publications control acts of 1963 and 1974,
and the particular concern is with books, motion pictures, and various
publications, such as university student newspapers, which are outside the NPU. Black expression, whether literary or political, has
been particularly circumscribed by such censorship.

During the past fifteen years and especially since the 1974 revision,
official controls on ideas and expression have been undergoing a good
deal of change and modification. In the bookstores, especially in the
affluent sections of Johannesburg, Cape Town, and Durban, for
instance, a much wider range and variety of books and magazines are
available than before, including numerous publications from abroad
and even some critical of government abuses of power. Books by
distinguished South African writers with international reputations—
such as Nadine Gordimer, André Brink, J. M. Coetzee, Wessel
Ebersohn, Alan Paton, and others who have been outspokenly critical
of apartheid, police brutality, and totalitarian methods of the

Nationalist regime—have become available to the South African public. Not all such books but a surprising number can be purchased.

Motion pictures from abroad are subjected to less cutting or outright suppression than in earlier years. Subject to the idiosyncrasies of the individual censor, the typical R-rated American film usually passes largely intact, especially if primarily intended for a white audience. Explicit language or erotic scenes in popular foreign movies are more tolerated than before. The wide acceptance of mass culture from America and Britain apparently has affected even the censors, whose concern about alleged obscenity and blasphemy seems to have subsided.

However, these changes in censorship do not bespeak greater freedom. Although more tolerant, the censors have not been consistent and fail to follow their own precedents in passing or censoring a book or "object." While established writers like Gordimer and Brink were getting published, unknown black writers and those writing only in Afrikaans were still being suppressed and finding it difficult to reach *any* reading public.

Furthermore, though erotic realism may be tolerated, strong evidence indicates an increasing intolerance of dissident political expression especially as it may relate to black nationalism or any expression of black political aims. Two recognized experts on censorship, John Dugard and Anthony Mathews, both respected law professors, have noted a clear trend of increasing political censorship. Unquestionably, the apparatus of censorship is still very much intact, and the ruling Afrikaner elite would not hesitate to suppress any ideas deemed threatening to its continued dominance.

Dugard's cogent explanation of the Afrikaners' reasons for censorship still applies:

Political expression is limited in the cause of white supremacy. Literary and artistic expression, where it is politically uncolored, is restricted to protect the ruling Afrikaner oligarchy from the permissiveness of the second half of the twentieth century. A common theme running through statements is that permissiveness leads to communism but as no communist soci-

ety is renowned for its permissiveness, such claims cannot be
taken seriously. The real objection to the social and cultural
freedom of the twentieth century is that, if exported to South
Africa, it might release the average Afrikaner from the tena-
cious grasp of those institutions which at present control both
his mind and his voting habits: the Dutch Reformed Church,
Afrikaner cultural organizations, the Afrikaans language press
and the National Party. In order to ensure isolation from the
views and lifestyles of the modern world there is a comprehensive system of censorship covering both literary works and
entertainment.[5]

In other words, the purpose of censorship is to retard social change
and to maintain the status quo, but the gradual secularization or
detribalization of the Afrikaner has, to some extent, led to an easing of
these controls.

Writing in 1980, Dugard pointed out that since 1978 there had been
a dramatic increase in the number of works declared "undesirable" on
political grounds under the 1974 revision. Newspapers, particularly
student newspapers, were increasingly being banned, as were other
publications, local and foreign. "In this way," Dugard said, "South
Africans are being denied access to the writings of persons propagat-
ing views radically opposed to the status quo. Without such information, however, there can be no real debate in South Africa, and no
effective planning for the future."[6]

Mathews has discerned an ominous trend growing out of the 1974
censorship revision:

There has been a decided expansion of censorship from its
more traditional concerns (obscenity, heresy, blasphemy) into
the social and political arena. The Publications Act makes no
distinction between the censorship of facts and opinions, and a
publication may be declared undesirable even if it is essentially
factual in nature . . . The Publications Act is broader than
other measures in one important sense. The other laws, such as
those relating to official secrets, defence, prisons, and police,
refer in the main (but not exclusively) to *official* information—
information, that is, held by or emanating from an official

source. An enormous extension of the censorship of information has been achieved by the Publications Act since, under its provisions, the dissemination of privately generated information as well as official information can be prohibited. The source of the information is irrelevant under the Publications Act; it may be banned whatever its origin. By extending control to private information, the authorities have closed the net entirely and all factual information is potentially subject to control."[7]

Censorship before 1963

Controls on literary and artistic works predates Nationalist political domination, though the process accelerated after 1948. Before the 1963 law pulled it all together, censorship powers were vested in several laws. Imported books and publications could be barred by the Customs Act when considered to be "indecent or obscene or on any ground whatsoever objectionable." Motion pictures, imported and domestic, required approval by a board of censors established by the Entertainments (Censorship) Act of 1931, passed well before the National party took office. According to Dugard, little effort was made in those years to ban locally produced publications, since that involved legal proceedings. But foreign publications were ruthlessly banned under the customs law. Among the thousands of banned items from abroad, mainly allegedly pornographic magazines, were the works of such writers as John O'Hara, John Steinbeck, Erskine Caldwell, Christopher Isherwood, and Vladimir Nabokov. By 1956, some five thousand items had been banned, and by 1963 the total had risen to nine thousand.[8] These works have remained banned, as succeeding censorship arrangements have usually inherited the banned works of their predecessors. However, a banned book may be unbanned later as happened with D. H. Lawrence's *Lady Chatterley's Lover*.

Publications and Entertainments Act of 1963

In order to systemize the existing haphazard arrangement, the Publications Control Board was established in 1963 with the passage of the

Publications and Entertainments Act. The board was mandated to determine the acceptability of publications (except NPU newspapers), films, objects, and public entertainments according to standards of decency and obscenity provided in the act. The act included a right of appeal to the courts except for motion pictures where the only appeal was to the minister of the interior.

During its ten years of existence, the board prohibited 8,768 publications, not counting those barred before 1963 under other laws.[9] Some of the best-known Western contemporary writing was kept out of South Africa, including Mary McCarthy's *The Group*, Philip Roth's *Portnoy's Complaint*, John Updike's *Couples*, Jean-Paul Sartre's *Age of Reason*, John Steinbeck's *The Wayward Bus*, and Erica Jong's *Fear of Flying*. Among movies barred were *Bonnie and Clyde*, *Belle de Jour*, *Guess Who's Coming to Dinner*, and *Easy Rider*. Movies admitted after considerable cuts were *The Graduate* and *M.A.S.H.* Books including revolt, socialism, or "black" in their titles were among the thousands kept out. The second volume of the two-volume *Oxford History of South Africa* (1877–1966) was available in South Africa only in a special edition, with fifty-three blank pages substituting for a chapter entitled "African Nationalism in South Africa, 1910–1965" by Leo Kuper. The problem seemed to be that it contained policy statements by African leaders. The former chairman of the Censorship Board, J. J. "Jannie" Kruger, claimed there was no truth in the legend that censors had banned Anna Sewell's children's story about a horse, *Black Beauty*, because of its title.[10]

During this period, many works by South African writers were censored as well, of course. Wilbur Smith's *When the Lion Feeds*, published in England, was banned, an action upheld by the appeals courts in a famous split decision. The courts also upheld the banning of an early novel by André Brink, *Kennis van die Aand* [Knowledge of the Night], which dealt with interracial sex and police brutality.[11] Brink's work had won an award for the best Afrikaans novel of 1973 and had become a best-seller in South Africa before the censors acted. Afrikaners take pride in their own writers because they feel strongly about supporting Afrikaans literature; therefore, some organizations that normally supported censorship policies protested this particular banning. The Afrikaans newspapers and other groups, for example, suggested that the views of writers and the public be considered before the board banned a book. There was, however, considerable support for the banning of Brink's novel, including that of the moderator of the Dutch Reformed church, Dr. Jacobus Vorster, who said that if Brink's novel was art, "then a whore house is a Sunday school."[12]

Publications Act 42 of 1974

By the time of the Brink affair in 1974, the Censorship Board had been under attack from a number of quarters, including even some government sectors. To liberal critics, the censorship apparatus had failed—choked by its own blue pencils and red tape. A series of blunders, coupled with a narrow-mindedness that was clearly out of step with the changing moral standards of culturally diverse South Africa, had made the whole system look ridiculous and in full public view at that.

Time after time publications banned by Jannie Kruger's censors had won a reprive in the courts. Typical was the case of the country's best-selling magazine, *Scope*, which was banned no fewer than nine times, then unbanned nine times by the courts. According to editors of *Scope*, the bannings began when the magazine ran a series of articles on the evolution of man, which suggested that the biblical story of Adam and Eve may not be the literal truth.

The censorship apparatus had become an obvious embarrassment to the government. Therefore, after a commission of inquiry considered the problem, a new publications act was introduced which completely revised the structure and procedure of censorship machinery. The new law sought to improve the image of the censors in three ways: (1) The right of appeal to the courts was removed, thus sparing the censors the embarassment of having their decisions reversed; (2) The most outspoken critics (English-speaking intellectuals) were wooed by trying to bring them on the review committees (this did not succeed); and finally (3) Insulting or belittling the new appeal board was made an offense—thereby muting public criticism.

The 1974 act provided for a directorate of publications, headed by a director of publications, responsible for carrying out the law. This body in turn appoints committees which operate around the country and are charged with deciding whether any books, films, objects, public entertainments, etc., are "undesirable" under the terms of the act. These committees are anonymous and take no evidence; many censorious acts begin and end with them. Some 250 volunteers serve on these committees, and as would be expected, they are not a cross-section of South African society and are heavily weighted with Afrikaners. In 1981, there were only 12 Coloureds, 10 Asians, and no Africans on the committees.[13]

The key standard of the act is "undesirable," and in terms of Section 47 (2), something can be undesirable if it

1. is indecent or obscene or is offensive or harmful to public morals;

2. is blasphemous or is offensive to the religious convictions or feelings of any section of the inhabitants of the Republic;

3. brings any section of the inhabitants of the Republic into ridicule or contempt;

4. is harmful to relations between any sections of the inhabitants of the Republic;

5. is prejudicial to the safety of the state, the general welfare, or the peace and good order.

In applying the act, the committees and the Publications Appeal Board are to be guided by, in the words of the act's preamble, "the constant endeavor of the population of the Republic of South Africa to uphold a Christian view of life." (The opposition in Parliament wanted to add a phrase to this—"with due observance to the individual's freedom of conscience and religion"—but the government refused to accept the addendum.)

Moreover, in judging a work, the motive of the author or the distributor is irrelevant, and a work may be found to be "undesirable" if "any part of it" is undesirable. A prime example of this provision was the banning of Gore Vidal's novel *Kalki*, on the ground that one passage compared the Holy Trinity to male genitalia. Publications and objects are thus banned if any isolated part is undesirable, while motion pictures may be passed after certain excisions are made. The SABC banned the playing of Beatles records for years after John Lennon was quoted as saying that the musical group was more popular than Christ.

Under the law, producing or distributing works declared undesirable is a criminal offense. In any judicial prosecution involving the act, the court is bound by the committee's determination of undesirability and may not make an independent inquiry into the question of undesirability. Therefore, if a published book is adjudged undesirable months after publication, the author may be prosecuted for writing and publishing a book which at the time was not so labeled.[14]

There is no set period during which the censorship review of a creative work must take place. A book may be declared undesirable at the time of publication or months later if a complaint is registered. A book could be banned while it is being written if authorities have reason to believe that it will be deemed undesirable. Some writing, therefore, takes place with the author looking over his shoulder for police. Wessel Ebersohn says he was harassed while writing *Store Up the Anger*: "We received hundreds of anonymous phone calls, friends were visited by men who said they were police and seemed interested in what I was doing, rumours about impending raids on our home were allowed to reach us, recordings of pieces of our telephone conversations were played back to us, we were followed by car, my wife was followed on foot. I fled my home to finish the manuscript in hiding."[15] After the book was published, it was banned but later unbanned.

In certain cases, a work may be judged "radically undesirable," making mere possession a criminal offense. For example, in 1978, Clive Emdon, a journalist on the *Rand Daily Mail*, was found guilty of being in possession of "undesirable publications" and sentenced to R 400 or 180 days in jail by a Johannesburg court. (He finally paid a R 200 fine.) The books were *The War of the Flea* and a church pamphlet, *South Africa: Time for Change*; both had been declared undesirable for possession. Because Emdon was a journalist on an opposition newspaper, there was more than a hint of harassment in this case.

The Publications Appeal Board must have at least three members including the chairman, who is appointed by the state president for five years. There is no appeal to a court of law from the Appeal Board decisions, but a decision may be reviewed by three judges.

In certain cases, the Appeal Board may be advised by a committee of experts, that is, persons with a special knowledge of art, literature, and so on, and willing to be censors. This committee of experts was introduced in 1978 following the outcry over the banning of Etienne Le Roux's novel *Magersfontein, O Magersfontein*, which was later unbanned. A number of Afrikaner academics and writers who had agreed to serve on the literary committee later resigned because of pressures from persons opposed to censorship.

An appeal against the decision of a committee may be brought before the Publications Appeal Board by the directorate itself, as happened with Nadine Gordimer's novel *Burger's Daughter*, which was banned and then later unbanned.[16] Or an appeal may be brought by any person with a financial interest in the banned work such as an author, publisher, or distributor. Both the directorate and the minister of the interior may demand reconsideration by the PAB of a committee's finding that a work is not undesirable.

The censorship bureaucracy certainly keeps busy protecting the morals of South Africans from what it considers corrupting influences from abroad. As far as conservative Afrikaners are concerned, censorship is an essential part of governance, and there is little inclination to abolish it. In one typical year, 1979, the Department of the Interior reported the following statistics for the Directorate of Publications and the Publications Appeal Board: Some 2,138 publications or objects were submitted for examination. Most were submitted by customs officers (822) and police (903), but 120 came from the public and 204 items from publishers, who sought approval before distribution began.

Books published in Britain or America are submitted to the Publications Directorate before many copies are imported; otherwise, they face confiscation at considerable financial loss to the publisher. Books published in South Africa are carefully checked before printing by lawyers, at some expense, to head off potential problems. Months after a book is published within South Africa, any member of the public who personally finds it offensive can complain to the censors; if the book is then declared undesirable, no further copies can be sold. However, there are no problems with the copies already sold, unless the book is also banned for possession.

Of the 2,138 items reviewed in 1979, 1,207 were found "undesirable." Among films examined, 34 were rejected (undesirable), 322 were approved unconditionally, and 288 approved subject to excisions and/or age restrictions. Among public entertainments, 12 were approved unconditionally, 11 approved conditionally, and only one rejected in toto. Periodicals of which every edition was declared undesirable came to 21. And publications and objects which were prohibited for possession totaled 420. The Publications Appeal Board generally upheld the decisions of its committees when appeals were made.

In recent years, similar patterns of censorship have persisted. In 1981, more than half of the publications submitted to the censorship committees were declared undesirable. The committees reviewed a total of 1,021 publications during the first six months, and of those, about 55 per cent (565) were undesirable under the Publications Act and the rest (453) were approved. According to the *Survey of Race Relations in South Africa, 1982*, the committees also prohibited the possession of 258 publications, most of them concerning "state security."[17]

The Publications Appeal Board upheld bannings of publications in eighteen cases and set aside ten. Among bannings affirmed were *Mozambique Sowing the Seeds of Revolution* by President Samora Machel, *Male Sexuality* by Shere Hite, *Asking for Trouble* by Donald Woods, and *Mao Tse-tung's Selected Works*.

Each week, the *Government Gazette* in Cape Town publishes the latest list of undesirable items—books, ephemeral publications, calendars, T-shirts and buttons with some message inscribed, serious novels, political tracts, and so on. According to the United Nations Unit on Apartheid, over twenty thousand such items are currently banned. This situation, of course, is a bookseller's nightmare, and the local guide through this labyrinth is *Jacobsen's Index of Objectionable Literature . . . Containing a Complete List of All Publications . . . Prohibited from Importation into the Republic of South Africa*. This essential publication, found in all bookstores and libraries, is updated weekly with looseleaf pages listing the latest bannings from the *Gazette*.

As of 1980, K. J. K. Jacobsen had more than thirteen thousand items in his *Index*. In addition to books, the *Index* includes musical records or their covers, such as *Hair* and the songs of Pete Seeger.

Some items are crude postcards, or novelty stickers ("Tennis players have hairy balls"), or printed T-shirts (including the feminist slogan "A woman needs a man like a fish needs a bicycle," or "Of all my relations, I like sex best"). T-shirts must be considered particularly dangerous because even those with the peace symbol and the motto "Black is beautiful" are forbidden. Also, such various and sundry items as double entendre greeting cards, jigsaw puzzles, an "Adam and Eve salt and pepper set," and various kinds of "sexual aids" are listed.[18]

But the great majority of banned items are books, and the range is awesome (and, at times, inexplicable): *Kinflicks* by Lisa Alther, *Jaws* by Peter Benchley, *The Joy of Sex* by Alex Comfort, *A Book of Common Prayer* by Joan Didion, *Something Happened* by Joseph Heller, *Black Money* by Ross MacDonald, *The Last Picture Show* by Larry McMurtry, *Gravity's Rainbow* by Thomas Pynchon, *Goodbye, Columbus* by Philip Roth, *An American Dream* by Norman Mailer, and at least one work by the following authors: Kingsley Amis, Daniel Defoe, James T. Farrell, William Faulkner, Nathanael West, James Jones, Tennessee Williams, Ken Kesey, Tom Wicker, Richard Wright, Herbert Gold, John Irving, and on and on.

Scholarly works are banned as well, sometimes for the mere suggestiveness of their titles, such as John Hope Franklin's *From Slavery to Freedom*. High-priority targets are any books dealing with Communism and Marxism, even including such works of a critical cast as Sidney Hook's *From Hegel to Marx*, and those of British historian Robert Conquest. Since such authors as Marx, Lenin, Trotsky, Marcuse, Mao Tse-tung, and others are proscribed, serious scholarly study of Marxism is made difficult. Even collected works in German and esoteric journals in which academic Marxists argue with each other are prohibited.

Government supporters claim that these measures are both necessary and justifiable on moral and security grounds, arguing that children and the less educated must be protected. Allowances are made, it is claimed, for the genuine student or scholar, who will always have access to works necessary for his or her studies. The problem is that banned books and books by banned authors, however academic and significant, are mostly no longer purchased by libraries, so that even if permission to read them is obtained, the books are simply not available.

Dr. André du Toit, of the Political Philosophy Department at Stellenbosch University, has warned that academic study in his discipline could become virtually impossible. The politically safe Stellenbosch University, however, does have an institute for the study of Marxism. Banned books are usually kept under lock and key in university libraries. They can be consulted by students who have letters from their professors saying that the reading is essential for the student's research.

Dr. David Welsh at the University of Cape Town had five books seized, and when he asked for permission to consult them, he was required to supply a statement from his dean certifying that they were absolutely necessary for his research. The permit was given but the books were to be kept for personal study only and had to be kept under lock and key and not loaned out to anyone.[19]

Censorship of Motion Pictures

For many years, films have been extensively scrutinized in South Africa, and many of the motion pictures most widely acclaimed in Europe and America have been either totally banned or severely abridged by the censor's scissors. A film or videotape intended only for private noncommercial use is not subject to prior censorship, but mere possession of a "blue" film such as *Deep Throat* can lead to a criminal conviction under the Indecent or Obscene Photographic Matter Act 37 of 1967, which is also utilized to bar such magazines as *Playboy*, *Penthouse*, etc. Even though showing any "obscene" film is a criminal offense, a considerable market exists for pirated X-rated or erotic movies smuggled in from abroad for home viewing.

All films intended for public exhibition require the prior approval of a publication committee which evaluates the film according to the same criteria of undesirability applied to books. The censors have wide powers to ban a film, order excisions, and make the exhibition of a film conditional upon certain restrictions. In such a system, the personal preferences of an individual censor or committee can be crucial. Recently, after a new and more "enlightened" censor took over, all but three of the previously excised twenty-seven minutes of the movie *Apocalypse Now* were restored. In this case, the censor said she did not like to watch chopped-up movies.

Without question, the Directorate of Publications has become more tolerant of imported motion pictures—as long as they are devoid of "undesirable" political messages and are intended primarily for white audiences. In June 1983, the director of publications announced that the directorate had rejected 84 of the 979 films submitted to it during the previous year. Another 366 were approved subject to age restrictions, cuts, or both. Slightly more than half of all films submitted were approved unconditionally. In what *The Star*, on May 30, 1983, called a "major censorship breakthrough," four films—*Looking for Mr. Goodbar*, *Percy*, *Carry on Emmannuelle*, and Fellini's *Satyricon*—were passed by the censors. A few years earlier, all four would have been prohibited.

Political Censorship

Censorship trends, charted by Professor Dugard and Louise Silver at the Centre for Applied Legal Studies at the University of the Witwatersrand, show that the censorship board has become more liberal in regard to literature and obscenity, especially when dealing with serious writing. However, Dugard reports, that new tolerance does not extend to magazines, calendars, and public entertainments with greater mass appeal. Also, Dugard has detected an increased tolerance for satire and criticism, especially that directed at the Afrikaner community.[20]

However, blasphemy, although it has largely disappeared from U.S. law, is still a serious matter for South African censors. John Miles's Afrikaans novel *Donderdag of Woensdag*, for instance, was banned because God was portrayed in one passage as a woman, and Gore Vidal's *Kalki*, as mentioned before, was censored for a single passage in which the Trinity was judged to have been blasphemed.

Nevertheless, Dugard detects some subtle and significant changes in matters relating to race relations and the safety of the state. Historically, the state has not hestiated to crack down on literary works sharply critical of police and security forces or the whole apartheid apparatus or that contained any sympathetic portrayals of black nationalism or black activists. Also, the censors earlier rejected sympathetic accounts of interracial sex. A notable example was the suppression of Jack Cope's *The Dawn Comes Twice*, which was critical of apartheid and showed understanding both of sex between the races and a black revolutionary movement. In a number of such decisions, the board accused publishers of failing to provide a "balanced" picture of South African life.[21]

However, by the late 1970s, the board began to take a noticeably different tack with literary works dealing with such politically sensitive (and officially embarrassing) issues. Acting on the advice of the newly constituted literary committee, Dugard says, the Appeal Board has displayed a sensitivity not shown before. This changed attitude was first apparent in the cases of André Brink's novels *Rumors of Rain* and *Dry, White Season*, and Nadine Gordimer's *Burger's Daughter*. During 1979, the earlier bannings of the three books were overturned on appeals; furthermore, the Appeal Board indicated in its decisions that harsh political criticism formed part of South African political life and that the reasonable reader was aware of this and would read the books in that light. This reasoning was a significant departure from the earlier stance demanding "balanced" comment presenting "both sides" of the picture. Some critics of censorship were surprised by these words from the Appeal Board in the *Burger's Daughter* decision: "When considering a political novel such as the present, the adjudicator must bear in mind that strong derogatory language is a typical feature of the South African scene. Political criticism is often one sided and would probably in most cases, not fall within the bounds of good taste or be in accord with the opinion of a substantial number of South Africans. However, this is not enough to find a book undesirable."[22]

Although South African censors are not noted for following their own precedents, they are permitting books of literary merit which would be published abroad anyway—works sharply and even savagely critical of contemporary South Africa. (Apparently, the state does not believe that serious books have much influence because of their comparatively small sales.) This new tolerance, however, seems to apply mainly to internationally known writers—not to the struggling and as yet unpublished black writer or one writing only in Afrikaans.

Political censorship, on the other hand, is clearly on the increase. Before the 1974 revision, the law directed attention mainly to obscenity, and in any event the publications board lacked powers to prohibit the possession of banned works. During the first year of the new act, 1975, only 191 publications of a total of 938 were banned on "political grounds" as opposed to obscenity or blasphemy, and no political works were banned in respect of possession. By 1978, 474 works of a total of 1,185 banned were declared undesirable on political grounds and 321 of 438 were prohibited in respect of possession on political grounds.[23] However, Silver later reported that a balance of sorts had been restored for the year 1981 when 385 obscene works were banned, compared with 379 politically undesirable publications.

Suppression of Student Newspapers

Based on the number of bannings, student publications at the five English-language universities (Cape Town, Rhodes, Natal [Durban], Witwatersrand, and Port Elizabeth) have been one of the major casualties of the 1974 censorship law. Between 1975 and 1979, 235 student publications were banned, 134 of them during 1979. And during the first ten months of 1980, 55 student newspapers and magazines were suppressed.

Student newspapers are subject to the Publications Act because they are not members of the NPU. Owing to their association with universities, they are exempt from the R 40,000 registration fee. Action against a student publication can take three forms: individual issues can be declared undesirable and distribution prohibited; a paper can be found "strongly objectionable" and people forbidden to possess the paper (about a third of the papers banned have been found illegal for possession); and third, a paper can be banned permanently, a step known euphemistically as "banning for all future editions." In May 1979, this drastic measure was imposed on two official student publications—*Varsity*, the student paper at the University of Cape Town, and *National Student*, an intercampus paper of the National Union of South African Students.

Not only the papers but the student journalists themselves have come into serious conflict with authorities. In April 1982, two students and the national publication they edited were banned. Clive van Heerden and Keith Coleman of the University of the Witwatersrand were banned for two years shortly after their release from months in detention without trial. This was five days after their paper, the *National*, published by the South African Students' Press Union, was banned. The paper, with a circulation of eighty thousand, had been launched two years earlier by students who argued that the full spectrum of events and opinion in South Africa was not adequately recorded in the commercial press.[24] By September 1983, six of its first twenty issues had been banned for being prejudicial to the safety of the state.

This view is shared by other student journalists, many of whom belong to that minority of university students who strongly oppose government policies. Most university students are apolitical and shun such controversy. Norman Manoim, a former editor of *Wits Student*, which has also run afoul of the Publications Act, said in an interview with journalist Helen Zille, "The commercial press has always left a gap, a void of facts, information and analysis. In the student press, we have found that when we begin to fill that gap or move into the void of sensitive areas, we have encountered resistence." The student press has taken a leadng role in political debate, Zille reports, and has often defined issues long before they surfaced in the society at large or in the commercial press.[25]

This explains, perhaps, why the government harasses student publications, though the crackdown did not begin with political issues. The campaign started in 1972 when the *Wits Student* published a photograph of a small child peering into a toilet bowl saying, "Excuse me, are you our prime minister?" Following a public outcry and debate in Parliament, the student editor, Mark Douglas-Home, nephew of a former British prime minister, was ordered to leave the country. After passage of the 1974 Publications Act, bannings against student newspapers markedly increased as the young journalists moved into more sensitive political areas.

Black Writers and the Publications Act

Black writers, whether journalists or creative writers, have long been harassed and frustrated in their efforts to communicate their views and feelings through the written word. Quite independently of the publications acts, writings by blacks have been suppressed and the writers themselves banned under various apartheid-related legislation. Over the past thirty years, through the Internal Security Act and the earlier Suppression of Communism Act (see Chap. 5), most leading black writers were banned and their writings prohibited from distribution in South Africa. Among them were Dennis Brutus, Ezekiel Mphahlele, and Alex La Guma, all of whom have been published in America and Britain.

Nonetheless, the Publications Act poses special problems for the black writer. The situation was well described in a memorandum submitted to the Steyn Commission by the Southern Africa Society of Journalists:

> It is almost unfortunate that so much attention was focussed on the banning of *The World*. We believe that what has been of far greater significance in keeping black opinion out of sight and mind of the authorities and the balance of the South African community is the manner in which the provisions of the Publications Act have been used to extinguish so many hundreds of attempts—often humble and simple attempts—to create some form of communication and expression of black ideals, aspirations, and frustrations. With regular but never diminishing harshness, committees set up under the Publications Act ban magazines, journals, reviews, and anthologies which can be described as authentic products of black society. Black people who have the energy and creative ability to strive for communication have in common a bitter resentment of the political dispensation under which they live. To believe otherwise is naive. It is quite inevitable that their bitterness and frustration will be manifested in what they write or create. Yet, time after time, committees set up under the Publications Act hold that such expression of bitterness or frustration must be suppressed in the interests of state security or the maintenance of sound relations between different population groups.[26]

Obviously, if censorship is an integral part of apartheid, then much of what blacks write will ipso facto be considered unlawful.

Their white colleagues recognize the difficult plight of black writers. André Brink describes three fictional case histories based on actual occurrences: "A young black playwright writes and produces a play about the 'confusion' of the black man ensnared in a maze of white man's laws; for some time, while the play is performed in the townships on a fly by night basis, it escapes the attention of the authorities. But the moment it is published, it is banned outright; and soon afterwards the author is arrested and detained without any charge for several months and released only after his health has deteriorated badly, resulting in urgent inquiries from outside." A second writer, Brink points out, may be a young black poet who submits some of his work to the magazine *Staffrider*, published by Ravan Press, and is invited to join PEN, the writers' organization, in Johannesburg. "Immediately afterwards he is picked up by the Security Police, interrogated and insulted, and warned to steer clear of 'bad connections.' " A protest is lodged by PEN and "this results in another swoop on his home: it is searched and left in a shambles; once again he is insulted and humiliated and a final warning is issued: 'if you complain to your writer friends about this, you will be detained indefinitely.' "

Brink's third hypothetical black writer is a leading voice among the younger generation of blacks, who already has a reputation abroad, which means detaining him would attract a measure of attention from overseas. He is awarded a scholarship to America but his application for a passport is turned down three times. For obvious reasons, Brink says, white writers can breathe much more easily because they do not face such harassment.[27]

Black writers generally have difficulty in getting published because of the high probability that their works will be banned; publishers in South Africa are hesitant to take a chance. One remarkable publisher, Ravan Press, is an exception, and under the leadership of its director, Mike Kirkwood, has published an impressive amount of black writing within South Africa. Ravan has published not only books by blacks, under extremely difficult circumstances, but also *Staffrider* magazine in which well over a hundred black writers have appeared since 1978. Kirkwood's strategy is simple: bring out the publication and try to sell as many as possible before it is banned. *Staffrider* was periodically banned and sometimes unbanned but kept appearing again and again.

A locally published "sensitive book" may remain available for only six weeks or so before a ban, and the likelihood of such a banning can reduce to five thousand the initial press run that under normal circumstances might be twenty thousand. Even to move five thousand copies may prove difficult, Kirkwood has written. But the tactic has worked, notably with Miriam Tlali's novel *Amandla* and Mtutuzeli Matshoka's *Call Me Not a Man*. *Amandla* was banned in March 1981, and the action was described by the newly formed African Writers' Association (AWA) as "not only a senseless act against a black Soweto woman but an iron-fisted act against all black South Africans."[28] Tlali's first novel, *Muriel at the Metropolitan*, was banned by the Directorate of Publications in 1979—four years after the book had been published in South Africa.

Kirkwood's activities are hazardous because, under existing legislation, the publisher, author, or printer can be fined or jailed for producing a book which is subsequently banned—although, as of 1983, the state has not been successful in prosecutions in this field. Some of the proscribed Ravan Press books are also banned for possession. Ravan's efforts on behalf of black writers has attracted the support of a number of important white writers. Books on Ravan's list include Nadine Gordimer's *July's People*, copublished with Taurus Press, John Coetzee's *Waiting for the Barbarians*, Wessel Ebersohn's *Store Up the Anger*, and Christopher Hope's *A Separate Development*—all novels critically well received in Britain and America.

The alienation of blacks from liberal whites has also affected the South African literary world. Early in 1981, the nonracial PEN Centre, formerly an affiliate of PEN International, the worldwide writers' organization, formally disbanded after its multiracial executive board agreed that blacks' involvement in a nonracial organization harmed the struggle for black cultural liberation.

Commented Afrikaans writer and critic Ampie Coetzee, "This is all a symptom of apartheid. Everybody's moving into their own little ethnic or ideological group."[29] PEN member Nadine Gordimer said the disbanded PEN center had "been defeated by history" and that nonracialism alone was not an adequate response to the South African situation.[30]

These developments were yet another reminder that white liberals were increasingly being perceived as irrelevant in the contemporary

South African struggle. As one commentator said: "In so many cases, the great liberal cause of nonracial cooperation towards future justice and equality lies in tatters, ripped apart by the swelling roar from harder black men that the future is ours, only we will determine it. In the minds of most politicized blacks, the battle lines are drawn already: hard black men against hard white men, black nationalism versus white nationalism and any whites wandering the stony no man's land in the middle are only going to blunt the struggle, indeed spoil the aim."[31]

The multiracial nature of PEN was viewed as an anomaly, and black PEN members were subjected to growing criticism from within the black community. The parallels with the attitudes of black journalists in MWASA were obvious; in justifying this racial separatism, one MWASA member had said, "The best our white colleagues can do, no matter how well intentioned, is look through a window at our condition. Just because they're white, they cannot be part of us, not at the moment anyway." Black creative writers felt the same way.

Alan Paton, a preeminent liberal white writer, predicted that the breakup of PEN would do no service to black literature. The language of protest will become paramount in black writing and too much of that becomes unreadable, Paton said. White liberals, he felt, were going to have to show considerable stoicism and tolerance in this terrible time South Africa was passing through. "If Blacks don't want me at a certain place, I don't want to be there," Paton said.[32]

The Dilemma for Afrikaans Writers

The Afrikaner community itself has not escaped the deep and acrimonious cleavages and stresses created by the censorship of literary expression. The preservation and enrichment of the Afrikaans language and culture are important to Afrikaners of all political persuasions from a *verkrampte* Transvaal farmer to a *verligte* in Cape Town. And in recent years some outstanding creative writing in Afrikaans has been produced by novelists such as J. M. Coetzee, Wessel Ebersohn, André Brink, John Miles, Etienne Le Roux, and others.

But the problem for the Afrikaner ruling elite is that these are writers of anguished protest highly critical of what has been happening in South Africa. These talented and articulate Afrikaners have been writing about such "taboo" subjects as police brutality against blacks, the inhumanity and injustice of apartheid, and not only interracial sex but sexual and other hanky-panky among upright Afrikaners themselves. This has put the Afrikaans writers, at least the more outspoken ones, in direct conflict with other Afrikaners who control the censorship apparatus. The Afrikaner censors are in a quandary: suppressing these "subversive" books means suppressing some of the finest expression of Afrikaans writing, but yet such writing may contribute to the dismantling of the Afrikaner power structure.

Afrikaner writers, academics, and intellectuals have been deeply split over how to respond to this situation. Law professor Jacobus van Rooyen, second chairman of the Publications Appeal Board, responded by showing a surprising tolerance for serious writing. Under his direction, the Appeal Board has been overturning the banning of such powerful antiestablishment books as Ebersohn's *Store Up the Anger*, an episode in whose plot bears a remarkable similarity to the death in detention of Steve Biko, the Black Consciousness leader. The earlier unbanning of *Dry, White Season* and *Burger's Daughter* indicated that the Afrikaner censors were willing to tolerate such writing, apparently because it does not reach a mass audience and seems to have little impact on blacks, who do not read Brink, Gordimer, Coetzee, et alia. But it also reflects a new sensitivity by censors to the outrage of South Africans, including numerous Afrikaners, over the censorship of serious and significant writing.

An important influence for greater exposure for Afrikaans writing has come from Taurus Press, a modest publishing operation started by three teachers of Afrikaans literature at the University of the Witwatersrand: Professors Ernst Lindenberg, Ampie Coetzee, and John Miles. Their aim is to publish writers, especially those in Afrikaans, who cannot find a publisher. They use mail subscription lists to get their books out and read by a significant number of people before censorship problems arise.

A major problem for all writers—black or white, English or Afrikaans speaking—is whether to boycott the whole censorship apparatus as Gordimer advocates or try to work within the system and appeal any bannings of their books. Despite the modifications and liberalization of censorship in specific areas such as motion pictures and literary works, the structure of thought control that the Publications Act perpetuates is still intact. And if a novel like *Store Up the Anger* is unbanned, it is because the censors themselves decide to make an exception; the power to prevent any other voice from being heard remains firmly in the hands of the Nationalist government. The new *verligte* censors like van Rooyen can easily be replaced because political and artistic expression alike remain at the mercy of the Afrikaner dominant minority that controls both the legislative and executive branches of government. As Dugard has pointed out, the courts with no power of judicial review and "with little inclination to disturb the status quo, can hardly be viewed as a bulwark of free speech." The Publications Act is just one of numerous laws on the books providing legal authority to proscribe overnight all opposition to the government, and what freedom of speech or press there is really exists at the convenience or tolerance of the ruling elite. "In such a climate, free speech is unable to play the vital role of a catalyst of change," Dugard says.[33]

8 | The Afrikaans Press: Freedom within Commitment

For many years Nationalist attempts to muzzle the press were aimed at the English-language opposition newspapers. And it was those papers that virtually single handedly tried to fight off further restrictions. More recently, however, the country's Afrikaans newspapers, once completely subservient to the ruling Nationalist party, have become dynamic political institutions in their own right.

At first, while the National party consolidated its power, the papers did little more than toe the party line. As the party become more firmly entrenched, they increasingly ventured to step over the line. Lately they have begun to suggest where the line should be drawn. The Afrikaans papers often are far ahead of the government in calling for sweeping changes in traditional Nationalist policies. They have urged the dismantling of segregation, the development and consolidation of black homelands, and local autonomy for urban blacks. Their persistent campaign for inclusion of Coloureds and Indians in the white parliamentary system eventually bore fruit. In the process, the Afrikaans papers became an important internal opposition within the National party. Increasingly, Afrikaans editors began to set the pace and determine the goals of the party. They began to adopt a more Western concept of the role of the press. They saw themselves as not merely propagandists for the government, but watchdogs over the implementation of government policy; as a forum for exploring alternatives to apartheid; and as a teacher whose task it was to wean

Afrikaners away from the idea that the country's problems could be solved entirely within the context of white politics.

This growing independence was unwelcome to powerful National- ists who preferred a tame mouthpiece for their views and resented this laundering of the party's dirty linen in public. Legislative and other restraints on the press, then, threatened both the English papers and the Afrikaans journals. In consequence, Afrikaans editors found that to preserve their new independence they had to make common cause with their traditional rivals in fighting off government attempts to curb the press. Freedom of expression, they discovered, was not divisible.

The Afrikaans press was a creation of Afrikaner political aspira- tions, established by the National party to spread its message and strengthen its power base. Unlike virtually all the English papers, not a single Nationalist newspaper began as a commercial venture.[1] They were intended to sell not news so much as a party line. The Nationalist hegemony in South Africa was built on a foundation of language and culture, church and politics. And the press was subservient to the needs of the party, the church, the schools and the cultural organiza- tions that formed this foundation. Even the news columns of the early Afrikaans papers seldom strayed beyond the activities of these institu- tions. The papers, in short, were established to bring the Nationalists to power, and once having achieved that, to keep them there.

This political function of the press was clearly demonstrated in its choice of editors. Senior Afrikaans newsmen were chosen, not for their journalistic experience or expertise, but for their ability to provide political leadership.[2] Their careers demonstrate also the inti- mate links between church, journalism and politics. Most originally trained as Dutch Reformed Church ministers. After a term as editor, they usually moved on to senior political posts—as cabinet members if not prime minister. Few had any intention of making a career of journalism: it was simply a springboard to political advancement. Thus D. F. Malan progressed from being a rural minister, to editor of *Die Burger* and leader of the National party in the Cape, to cabinet minister, and ultimately to the premiership. H. F. Verwoerd was a cleric before becoming editor of *Die Transvaler*, than a cabinet minister, and then premier. More recently A. P. Treurnicht edited *Die Kerkbode*, the journal of the Dutch Reformed Church, before being appointed editor of *Hoofstad* in Pretoria. He resigned to become a member of Parliament, a cabinet member, and head of the National party in the Transvaal.

The newspapers' bonds with the party were strengthened at the management level. They were owned by party members. Their boards of control were top-heavy with politicians. From 1948 until 1967, every Nationalist prime minister had close links with either or both of the major Afrikaans press companies. Although Malan resigned his position with *Die Burger* when he became prime minister, he continued to contribute to the paper. Strydom and Verwoerd served as chairmen of the Perskor papers in the Transvaal virtually ex officio during their terms as prime minister. Vorster resigned his chairmanship of those papers in 1967 because growing ideological rifts and commercial competition between them and the Cape-based Nasionale Pers had made his position untenable. But the boards remained under the firm control of Nationalist cabinet members. In the mid-1970s, for example, the fourteen-member board of the Dagbreek group included six cabinet members and the head of the Senate. Not until 1979, in the uproar over the Information Department scandal, did Prime Minister P. W. Botha feel constrained to forbid cabinet members to hold newspaper directorships. The directorships remained in politically safe hands, however, and continued to be dominated by members of the powerful Broederbond, the secret organization of right-wing Afrikaners.

There were some attempts in the early years to loosen the bonds. *Die Burger*, for example, was asserting a measure of independence as early as 1924—although to the uninformed reader it may not have been apparent. According to A. L. Geyer, Malan's successor as editor, the paper's policy was to support the Herzog government yet remain free to criticize the government or an individual minister if it thought this necessary. *Die Burger*, he wrote, could not support government policy unless it could do so with a clear conscience. Herzog was not impressed and complained to the directors about Geyer's attitude.[3]

The real change began in the late 1950s. By 1958 the Nationalists had been in power for ten years, having won three elections, each with increased support.[4] Although haunted by the historical fact that the Afrikaners, when divided, had been defeated or forced to share political power, some now felt confident enough to permit public discussion of their differences. As Elaine Potter points out, the impetus toward greater independence developed for three main reasons. In the first place the newspapers themselves desired to be treated as an equal of the institutions they promoted. Second, they were increasingly being used by rival factions within the party to take their case directly to the public. And third, the reading public was responding to the avoidance of any coverage of party divisions by turning to the English newspapers that gleefully reported quarrels, real or imagined, in Afrikaner ranks.

The freedom sought by the Nationalist editors was not the same as that which the English editors regarded as their birthright. In Afrikaner political philosophy, the relation of the individual to the state differed from that of the Anglo-American tradition. Restrictions on the freedom of the individual were acceptable if necessary for the greater cause of constitutional freedom for the community and the interests of national security. To the Afrikaner, said the distinguished Afrikaans editor Schalk Pienaar, press freedom was not a watertight concept but part of the various liberties enjoyed by every free and independent state.[5] It was the power of political, or constitutional, freedom that guaranteed press freedom—not the other way around. There could be no thought of elevating press freedom to a position where the stability of the state could be endangered. From this flowed Pienaar's concept of the press as having "freedom within commitment." The National party would be loath to undermine the freedom of an institution to which it owed a great deal, he wrote. But this did not mean it would accept undisciplined excesses that could rock the ship of state. This consciousness of being but a part of a more important whole produced a strong sense of restraint and self-discipline in the Afrikaans newspapers.

The initial intention of the editors, then, was not to assert their independence from the National party. What they wanted was to be recognized as equal partners, not merely ventriloquists' dummies. It was one thing, said Pienaar, if an institution like the Afrikaans press worked with other institutions as a friend and ally, and a very different matter if the other institutions viewed the newspapers as assistants in carrying out their duties.

The cherished Afrikaner ideal of a republic led to the first assertion of the press's independence. The strong showing of the Nationalists in the 1958 election had made the attainment of a republic more likely. There was disagreement within the party, however, as to what kind of republic should be established, and about how best to achieve it. Provincial differences between the Cape and the Transvaal Nationalists, suppressed in earlier years in the interest of party unity, became apparent as the Nationalists' grip on power grew more secure. The Transvaal Nationalists, who with their superior numbers were asserting their leadership, favored a Kruger-type republic with a strong executive president, preferably outside the British Commonwealth. Cape Nationalists thought a president with largely symbolic powers, like the British governor general, and a republic within the Commonwealth would be less alarming to English speakers, and therefore more within the realm of practical politics. *Die Burger* took the lead in expressing this latter view and, in the process, forced a debate on the issue even though Transvaal Nationalists thought it premature and resented *Die Burger*'s successful bid to determine the shape of the new republic.

Establishment of the republic in 1960 was a turning point in the relationship between the National party and its newspapers. Once the Afrikaners' political dominance could not be challenged, their papers began to move from uncritical support of the party line to a more independent position. In the early 1960s, for example, *Die Burger* joined issue with the Transvaal Nationalists, led by Verwoerd, over the political rights of Coloureds. Nationalists at the Cape, where most of the Coloureds lived, had always felt that the "brown Afrikaners" should be treated differently from the blacks. They favored a more liberal implementation of apartheid, believing that segregation and discrimination should not be ends in themselves. This view was anathema to the more doctrinaire Transvaal Nationalists. So when Piet Cillie, editor of *Die Burger*, came out strongly in favor of direct representation of Coloureds in Parliament, Verwoerd was infuriated. A war of words ensued between the Cape wing of the party, using *Die Burger*, and Verwoerd, speaking through *Die Transvaler*. Although many Nationalists supported direct representation for the Coloureds, the party's federal council vetoed the idea. *Die Burger* was unable to make its views prevail—at least not for another twenty years. Cillie, reacting to criticism that his defiance of party leadership would split the ranks, argued that if Nationalist newsmen were to become a lot of parrots and "hurrah-pamphleteers," then "they will go down as certain as the sun sets, followed by the government and the National party and the Afrikaners."[6]

Despite these occasional public disagreements, South Africans— including Afrikaners—not privy to party secrets and who wanted to know what was going on had to turn to the English press, and especially the Sunday papers. Unlike the daily papers, with limited regional circulations, the Sunday papers were distributed nationally. They had by far the largest circulations in the country, built on a shrewd formula of roughly equal parts of sport, scandal, and politics. The *Sunday Times*, with insightful political writers like Stanley Uys, Hans Strydom, and Hennie Serfontein, offered a far more complete picture of developments in the National party—and in the supersecret Broederbond—than could be found in any of the Afrikaans papers.

Rise of *Die Beeld*

An Afrikaans Sunday paper in Johannesburg, *Dagbreek*, founded in 1947 originally as a politically independent newspaper with a bilingual board of directors, had come under Nationalist control in 1953. It had a difficult time building circulation. Blue laws, statutory relics from before the time of Union, prohibited the publication of Sunday newspapers in the Cape and the Free State—although they could be sold there if published elsewhere. The Dutch Reformed Church still preached that buying papers on a Sunday was sinful. Consequently the Sunday field was dominated by successful English papers. Despite this tight market, a competitor to *Dagbreek* apeared in 1965 when Nasionale Pers decided to start a Sunday paper of its own in the Transvaal.

The reason for doing so were both economic and political. The Transvaal accounted for about half the country's newspaper readers, and for the Nasionale Pers to ensure its long-term future, it had to claim a share of that market. As usual, however, political considerations were uppermost. By the mid 1960s, it was no longer possible to conceal the growing rift between the *verligte* or "enlightened" Nationalists, and the *verkrampte* or "conservative" faction, associated mainly with the Transvaal. The Cape Nationalists badly needed a mouthpiece in the north. Nasionale Pers' decision to start a Sunday paper, *Die Beeld*, in Johannesburg met with strong resistance from Transvaal Nationalists, who perceived it as an invasion of their turf and declared a boycott against the paper even before its first issue appeared. Nasionale Pers went ahead. With Schalk Pienaar as its first editor, *Die Beeld* was published in Johannesburg but printed also in Cape Town and Bloemfontein, which gave it national coverage.

The launching of *Die Beeld* was a significant step in the emancipation of the Afrikaans press from slavish obedience to the party. Spurred by its circulation battle with *Dagbreek*, and determined to woo Afrikaans readers away from the English Sunday papers, it became a newspaper such as Nationalist politicians had never before experienced. As Willem Wepener, general manager of Nasionale Pers, remarked later, *Die Beeld* recognized no holy cows.[7] It saw matters concerning the Afrikaner merely as news, nothing more or less. Its editor saw no reason for Afrikaners to have to go to English papers to find out what really was going on in Afrikaner politics. Thus *Die Beeld*'s first leading article dealt with a quarrel in the National party; the second was about a quarrel in the Dutch Reformed Church. The more conservative *Dagbreek* was forced to brighten its own pages to survive. Competition between the two, especially in the coverage of hitherto taboo political matters, brought the Afrikaans reader a very different kind of newspaper from any he had known before.

One effect was to exacerbate the conflict between the *verligtes* and *verkramptes*. *Die Beeld*, representing the *verligtes*, exposed the extent to which *verkramptes* were taking over Afrikaans institutions. Disputes that otherwise would have been swept under the rug now became matters of public debate. The argument concerned the direction the party should take. The conservatives wanted to maintain a narrow Afrikaner exclusiveness, concerned that the Afrikaners could not survive if "foreign" elements, including sympathetic English speakers, were admitted to their ranks. They resented any attempt to liberalize the government's immigration policy, wanting to limit immigration essentially to Protestant Europeans. They feared that the government's new outward-looking foreign policy, which included accepting black ambassadors from neighboring African states and treating them as "honorary" whites, would undermine apartheid at home. The *verligtes* took the opposite view on each of these issues, arguing that the country's survival required reaching an accommodation with black states in the north, and seeking allies domestically to strengthen the Afrikaner power base.

By forcing these issues into the open, *Die Beeld* and other Nasionale Pers group papers created considerable uncertainty and anxiety among the Nationalist rank and file; it was not at all clear just who in the party leadership stood for what. One reaction was for the political leadership to attack the newspapers for rocking the boat. Thus M. C. Botha, a cabinet minister, warned in 1966 that the Afrikaner should be wary of attacks against conservatives from within his own ranks. Unfortunately, said Botha, columnists in Afrikaans newspapers had made attacks on conservatives. The papers were criticized also by the chairman of the South African Broadcasting Corporation (who also was the leader of the Broederbond), Dr. Piet Meyer. Officials of Afrikaner cultural organizations joined in the fray. The ritual attack on English newspapers at Nationalist party congresses every year was expanded to include the "liberal" Afrikaans press, which was accused of spreading heresies; of trying to undermine the party leadership.

The fight also was costing both Sunday newspapers a great deal of money, since the limited readership could not support them both. Pressure built for the two to amalgamate, the assumption being also that once their circulation battles ceased the party could again speak with a single voice. In 1970 they were merged into a new Sunday paper, *Rapport*, with the two publishing houses having equal shares in the venture. News of the merger brought sighs of relief from Transvaal Nationalists. Ben Schoeman, a former cabinet minister and leader of the Transvaal Nationalists, announced in public that the National party now had a paper that would stand by it "through thick

and thin." *Dagbreek*, commenting on the imminent merger, said that
the two giants, having tried to plow each other into the ground, now
were joining forces to challenge the real enemy—the English press.
Die Beeld, however, saw the merger in a very different light. It was
determined the new paper would continue to promote the *verligte*
cause. What is more, it sought audiences larger than the traditional
party faithful. While the new paper, said *Die Beeld*, would address
itself in the first instance to the Afrikaner, "it would very definitely
not address the Afrikaner alone. It would serve South Africa."
Although billed as a merger the deal in fact amounted to a takeover by
Nasionale Pers. Editorial control of *Rapport* remained firmly in the
hands of *Die Beeld*'s staff. Willem Wepener, the first editor and
long-time Nasionale Pers employee, followed what was, in the context
of Afrikaans journalism, a remarkably liberal line. The paper campaigned for multiracial sport, for restaurants and theaters open to all,
for greater political rights for the Coloureds. Were it not for papers
like *Rapport* that cleared the way for such ideas and made them
acceptable to the public, says Wepener, the government's liberalizing
changes would not have been possible.[8]

Rapport, although more moderate in tone than *Die Beeld* at the
height of its competition with *Dagbreek*, continued to upset conservative Nationalists. At the party's Transvaal congress in 1972, it came
under fire from delegates for criticizing party policy. In response, Dr.
Connie Mulder, minister of the interior, said that *Rapport* was not an
official organ of the party. But he appealed to *Rapport*, if it wanted to
serve the Afrikaner cause, to cease promoting ideas that it knew were
not Nationalist policy and so create confusion among Afrikaners.
Mulder was cheered by the congress when he said that it was clear
that, in general, party members were not happy with the newspaper.

Encouraged by the success of *Rapport*, which quickly built the
second largest circulation in South Africa (second only to the *Sunday
Times*, but with more white readers), Nasionale Pers decided in 1973
to launch a daily paper in Johannesburg to serve the Transvaal, Natal,
the Northern Cape and the northern parts of the Free State—those
areas not covered adequately by its existing publications. The
announcement said the move was being made to ensure the survival of
the group's existing papers. The political implications, however, also

were obvious. The decision was taken in the face of bitter opposition
from the Perskor group, which feared an invasion of its territory, and
of the Nationalist hierarchy, which desperately wanted to avoid
another newspaper war between its northern and southern press
supporters. Nasionale Pers went through the motions of consulting
with Perskor before launching the paper, called *Beeld*. The first editor
of the new daily, Schalk Pienaar, wrote that consultation with Perskor
and with the Transvaal leaders of the National party was necessary for
two reasons. One was to see if some kind of accommodation could be
worked out to avoid head-on competition. The second was to try to
avoid "political unpleasantness."[9] No agreement could be reached,
and the Nationalist leaders in the Transvaal, including Prime Minister John Vorster, opposed the new venture.

Nasionale Pers went ahead regardless. Soon *Beeld* was engaged in
cutthroat competition with Perskor's existing Johannesburg dailies,
Die Transvaler and *Die Vaderland*. One Perskor tactic was to liberalize
the image of *Die Transvaler*. It appointed Willem de Klerk editor of
the paper. De Klerk, who previously had taught religion at Potchefstroom University for Christian Higher Education, was an outspoken
verligte—the one in fact who had coined the terms *verlig* and *verkramp*.
He had attacked petty apartheid; he had warned the country to pay
more attention to the views of the outside world; he had criticized the
standard of parliamentary debate. His appointment was made in the
face of opposition from the new leader of the Broederbond, Andries
Treurnicht, who was himself the editor of *Hoofstad*, a Perskor paper
in Pretoria, and was heir apparent to the editorship of the group's
flagship paper. De Klerk transformed *Die Transvaler* from a stodgy
party rag into a far more lively and independent-minded paper.

Die Transvaler, even with direct competition in the Transvaal
morning market from *Beeld* and from *The Citizen* (many of whose
readers had Nationalist leanings but preferred to read an English
newspaper), reported soaring circulation figures. So did its afternoon
stablemate, *Die Vaderland*. Perskor circulation executives attributed
the increases to improved distribution, and to the fact that many
readers were buying both *Die Transvaler* and *Beeld* because of their
exciting competition.

The truth was very different. An exposé in the *Rand Daily Mail* in

1980 revealed that Perskor had been lying to the Audit Bureau of Circulations about the sales of its three main papers, *Die Transvaler*, *Die Vaderland*, and *The Citizen*. An ABC audit showed that Perskor had exaggerated the circulation figures of *Die Transvaler* by about 20,000 copies a day—virtually the entire claimed increase. Figures for *Die Vaderland* and *The Citizen* had been inflated by about 6,500 copies a day each. In September 1983, Perskor pleaded guilty to criminal charges of falsifying the circulation figures for three and a half years from January 1977. The fraud was ascribed in court to "misguided zeal" on the part of some employees who had become engrossed in the fierce competition with *Beeld*. The company was fined R 20,000. Nasionale Pers, publishers of *Beeld*, filed a civil damages suit against Perskor that was settled out of court. Perskor also was abliged to offer reparations to advertisers in the form of a R 1.3 million refund, or advertising space.[10]

The exposé came at a bad time for Perskor. Its papers had never made money and were subsidized by the group's other printing and publishing activities, which included lucrative government contracts. But the political eclipse of its powerful former director, Minister of the Interior Connie Mulder, after the Muldergate scandal (see Chap. 10), forced Perskor to share its government contracts with Nasionale Pers, which supported the Cape wing of the National party, led by Prime Minister Botha. Perskor lost a multimillion rand contract to print the glossy Information Department magazine *Panorama*. And it had to surrender to Nasionale Pers 40 per cent of its profitable contract to print the Post Office's telephone directories. The circulation scandal also shook the confidence of advertisers in Perskor publications, giving *Beeld* a clear advantage over *Die Transvaler*.[11]

Perskor also faced acute political problems. The split in the National party after Muldergate, with the right-wing Nationalists led by Andries Treurnicht and Connie Mulder hiving off to form the National Conservative Party, left Perskor in an awkward position. Its board included several *verkramptes*, or right-wingers, who were anxious to use the Perskor papers to back the conservatives. But the flagship paper, *Die Transvaler*, was taking a strongly *verligte* or enlightened line under editor Willem de Klerk. Since the Nasionale Pers paper *Beeld* was equally liberal, there was no major paper the conservatives could depend on in their fight against Botha's liberalizing reforms. Nor were they getting any help from the pro-Botha SABC. Perskor, losing the battle for *verligte* readers to *Beeld*, apparently decided its future lay with a different readership, and in 1982 summarily fired de Klerk.[12] The political infighting within Perskor continued, however, and the group's managers eventually declared their full support for the National party.[13] De Klerk was appointed editor of the Sunday paper *Rapport* in 1983.

The upshot of the battle for control of the Afrikaans morning market in the Transvaal was a major setback for Perskor. In February 1983, Perskor and Nasionale Pers reached an agreement rationalizing the market and ending the competition that was estimated conservatively to have cost them R 20 million each. *Die Transvaler* was forced to retreat to Pretoria, where it was merged with Perskor's two struggling dailies there, *Oggendblad* and *Hoofstad*. *Beeld* was left in control of the morning market in Johannesburg, with the Perskor paper *Die Vaderland* surviving as an afternoon daily.[14]

Growing Independence

One clear indication of the Afrikaans newspapers' growing independence was the change in their attitude toward government restraints on the press. The Afrikaans editors had stood squarely behind the government in its early attempts to curb newspapers. Their papers, after all, were not those threatened. The editors supported the establishment of the original Press Commission. They backed the Newspaper Press Union in setting up its Press Council. And they made little objection when the government intimidated the NPU into increasing the council's powers. Cries of outrage from the English were seen as a hysterical overreaction to a doom they had brought upon themselves, and an attempt to tarnish the country's image abroad.

There were occasional exceptions. After Vorster announced in September 1973 that legislation would be introduced that would enable the government to ban any newspaper that "persisted in inciting racial hatred," some signs of alarm appeared in the Nationalist press. The Pretoria daily, *Oggendblad* said it was "deeply concerned about the steps being contemplated . . . these will naturally be

aimed at all newspapers. We trust that further thought will take place
before so drastic a step as a ban on newspapers is adopted."[15] The
editor of *Die Transvaler*, de Klerk, wrote that the press could not be
blamed if it reported "irresponsible and provocative" statements by
politicians in the field of race relations. Who is responsible, he asked,
"the clergyman who is guilty of scandalous conduct; the official who is
guilty of corruption; the farmer who meddles in race relations, or the
press that reports these things?"[16] Nevertheless, when the S.A. Society of Journalists organized a symposium on press freedom in Cape
Town in 1974 to warn against further curbs, not a single Afrikaans
newspaper was represented—although all had been invited to
attend—apart from two journalists from *Die Burger*, who were there
not as participants but to report the proceedings. Faced with threats
of government action, the reaction of Afrikaans newsmen and their
employers was always to negotiate, to knuckle under, to accept a more
draconian press council provided it kept the appearance of self-
discipline. Where they did feel their interests were threatened, they
preferred to talk privately with government leaders, rather than take a
confrontational stance in their columns.

This tendency could be seen clearly in the reaction of the Afrikaans
papers to the more stringent press code adopted by the Newspaper
Press Union in 1974 in response to Vorster's threats. The new code
included a provision for fines of up to R 10,000 on newspapers that
contravened its rules. The Afrikaans newspapers generally welcomed
the new code if it would head off direct government control of the
press. The proposed amendments could only benefit the press, said
Die Vaderland, "if they made the government less inclined to introduce censorship."[17] *Die Transvaler* was pleased with the effort of the
NPU to "lay down punitive measures against offenders within its own
circle"—rather than have the government enact legislation.[18] The
strong condemnation of the code by some English editors was seen by
the Afrikaans papers as an attempt to bring about a confrontation
between the press and government. *Die Burger* for example, complained that the English journalists were "puffed up with a spirit of
confrontation" in their resistance to the strengthened council.[19] *Die
Transvaler* wrote that there was a clear motive behind the sustained
campaign by English papers against the code: "The government must

be forced to pass legislation against the press, so that a confrontation
between the press and government can be created. The impression
that freedom of the press is being limited can then be sent around the
world, whereby the stream of distrust against South Africa will gain
further momentum." This, said *Die Transvaler*, bordered on unpatriotic action.[20]

As the papers began liberating themselves from stifling party political control, however, this attitude changed. For one thing, Afrikaans
editors themselves were on the firing line as conservative Nationalists
took aim at them for trying to reeducate their readers to accept
political changes they had long been taught to resist. For another, an
increasing sense of professionalism was developing among Afrikaans
newsmen, a growing proportion of whom were committed to journalism as a career, rather than merely as a stepping stone to political
office. Always well educated (Afrikaans newspapers, unlike their
English counterparts, seldom hired anyone without a university degree), several had also been exposed to journalistic practices abroad,
particularly through programs like the Nieman Fellowships at Harvard.

The first major confrontation between the Afrikaans press and the
government it supported was, however, unexpected. It began with
the publication in March 1977 of the Newspaper Bill. This amounted,
said *Die Vaderland* in a bold headline that would have been unimagin-
able a few years earlier, to "War between the Press and Government."
Until this time Nationalist threats to muzzle the press through
legislation had been largely bluster—though bluster was backed by a
mailed fist. Now for the first time they were actually proposing to
enact a statutory press council with a tough new code of conduct and
the power to impose heavy fines to back it up. All newspapers would
be affected. There would be no appeal to the courts. This was a direct
attack on the Calvinistic concept that institutions should be sovereign
within their own sphere. Control over the press would no longer lie in
the hands of the newspapers themselves.

The tone of outrage in the Afrikaans papers now rivaled that of the
English press. Dirk Richard, editor of *Die Vaderland*, took the unusual step of running a front-page editorial complaining that the new
law would "muzzle the press to the extent that it could not fulfill

its normal function." The paper appealed to the government to amend the bill to "eliminate its authoritarian nature and the danger of censorship through outside control." Until now, it said, South Africa could pride itself on a free press—at least the freest in Africa. But observers abroad "would interpret the new system as the end of press freedom in our country." In a signed column four days later, Richard said the legislation could lead to ever more drastic steps, until "individual freedom was so restricted that South Africa became a spiritual prison." Just this first step, he said, was enough to set the country on the road to a dictatorship. Never before had such language been directed by a Nationalist paper against the party that gave it sustenance.[21]

The influential Sunday paper *Rapport* led its front page with a condemnation of the bill by Ben Schoeman, chairman of the board of the Perskor newspaper group and a former Nationalist cabinet minister. The bill, said Schoeman, was aimed at establishing press censorship. It would cause untold damage to the press in South Africa. Even more serious was the fact that South Africa's already tarnished image abroad would receive a further blow. *Rapport* said in an editorial in the same issue that there could be only losses in a war between the government and the press, and the biggest loser would be the image of South Africa as a free country. South Africa had always been proud of its free press. It was the one fact that the most malevolent critics of the country could not ignore.

For *Die Transvaler*, this "vicious" law was also front-page news. And it editorialized that, although the press had its faults, the price to be paid for them was disproportionately high. The Afrikaans papers pulled out all stops in their effort to block the legislation. They quoted each other's editorials and those from English papers; they reported at length criticism of the bill by the parliamentary opposition. They informed their readers about what influential newspapers in England, Europe, and the United States had to say about the bill. Some carried articles pointing out that even without the bill, newspapers in South Africa were not as free to criticize the government as their counterparts abroad. South African papers, said *Die Vaderland*, could not have exposed such affairs as Watergate or Britain's Profumo scandal—although ironically they were to do so soon after in the Informa-

tion Department scandal. It was ironic also that the main argument
the Afrikaans editors used to protect themselves—the effect the law
would have on the country's image abroad—was one that they had
excoriated the English papers for using for thirty years.

The spectacle of both English and Afrikaans newspapers ganging
up to berate the government was unique in the country's history. And
before long even the more outspoken Afrikaans editors felt it necessary to dissociate themselves from the appearance of too close a
collaboration with their traditional opponents. Dirk Richard wrote
that the unified resistance should not be seen as a new ideological
camaraderie in the South African press. What the papers had in
common, he said, was an objection in principle to government intervention in the affairs of the press. He emphasized that the Afrikaans papers, even the most liberal, rejected the way a section of the
English press handled the racial situation.[22] De Klerk wrote in *Die
Transvaler* that although the impression had arisen that the English
and Afrikaans papers had become allies in the fight against a common
threat, there was in fact no question of a conspiracy. De Klerk
distanced himself from reports in the English press that his criticisms
had implied the government was seeking to establish a dictatorship.
He urged that the bill be referred to a select committee of Parliament,
since in that way the government could show it was receptive to
criticism and appreciated the objections of the press.[23]

The Nationalist government had never been deflected from its
course by criticism in the English press, or in newspapers abroad.
Now, however, faced with a revolt by its own party press as well, it
backed off. Vorster shelved the bill and gave the Newspaper Press
Union a year in which to discipline its own members.

The Afrikaans papers did not follow up on their new adversary
stance. They applauded the reprieve and resumed their supportive
role. When new legislation affecting the press was introduced their
tone was that of a loyal opposition. They voiced their misgivings when
the government introduced its Police Amendment Bill in March 1979
requiring newspapers to clear all reports concerning the police with a
police-press liaison unit before publication—under penalty of five
years in jail or a R 10,000 fine. Thus *Die Transvaler* pointed out that it
had always displayed "appreciation and understanding" of the dif-

ficult task of the police, "but we have yet to be convinced that
censorship affecting police reporting is really necessary at this stage."
Beeld, while also appreciative of the "good work done by the police,"
was worried that "the new practice could smother frankness and
openness in the machinery of the state. And we should have more of
that rather than less."[24]

It took the shock of the Information Department debacle, Muldergate (see Chap. 10), however, to finally convince the Afrikaans papers
that it was the responsibility of the press, if not to act as an adversary
to government, at least to keep a watchful eye on its activities. The
scandal shook Afrikaner confidence in their leadership. It was clear
that without the press—largely the English press at first but eventually the Afrikaans papers as well—the details of corruption in high
places would never have been revealed. In May 1979, in the aftermath
of the scandal, the government introduced in Parliament its Advocate
General Bill that would have banned newspapers from reporting
allegations of bribery and corruption in Parliament. Newspapers
would be required to lay before the advocate general any accusations
of corruption. He would investigate and then report to a parliamentary select committee empowered to decide whether to make the
matter public or bury it. Afrikaans papers, while not as vitriolic in
their reaction as the English press, were unusually outspoken and
embraced the concept of the press as a watchdog over government
rather than merely a mouthpiece for its views. *Hoofstad*, for example,
argued that the bill "cannot be interpreted as anything less than
obstructive to the role of the press as a watchdog over the country's
administration. And there is no denying that the press has a major
function in this respect."[25] *Die Volksblad* likewise argued that the bill
"would deprive the press of its function of exposing things in matters
like corruption and misapplication of funds in state administration.
The press must be permitted to bring such malpractices to light where
these are brought to its attention."[26] *Rapport*, pointing out that the
press had opened "evil sores" and had contributed to clean administration, argued that the proposed measure "is undeniably a drastic
reduction of press freedom which has already been pruned and will
therefore mean a reduction in the freedom of the individual."[27] Faced
again with the united opposition of both English and Afrikaans papers

the government backed down and dropped the most contentious clauses of the bill. The earlier spirit of total trust between the National party and its newspapers had, however, been irreparably damaged. As *Beeld* remarked, "Since the Information scandal the public is assessing state action in terms of new norms. One of these is a greater vigilance in the matter of personal freedom."[28] The strongest affirmation of independence came from *Die Transvaler* when, in an editorial on the Information Department saga, it warned that "this country will in future demand and is in fact already doing so that crudeness and inefficiency of its leaders be exposed. We will never again allow ourselves to be misguided by great visions while the actual task is being incapably carried out."[29] Also growing out of these events was a realization by Afrikaans newsmen that freedom of the press was not divisible, that the Afrikaans papers could not stand aside as the government clamped more restrictions on newspapers, even if they appeared to be aimed at the opposition press.

Commenting on the appointment of the Steyn Commission, with its implied threat of new legislation regulating the press, *Die Burger* complained that critics of the press were not using the existing machinery to seek redress for their grievances. "Is it perhaps because they balk at a bit of extra effort?" *Die Burger* asked. "The public shirks its own responsibilities and duties and then expects the government to make a law. People who reason in this way do not realize that they, by their own carelessness, are eroding the ground of freedom from under their own feet."[30] *Beeld* was even more forthright in its editorial comment. There was, it said, very little understanding of a free press, and the value of criticism. If the press increasingly became the target, "we, and specifically also our Afrikaner community, will in the long run dig a grave for ourselves. No one is immune to the swinging of the pendulum."[31]

This new awareness of the indivisibility of freedom extended also, at least in the case of *Beeld*, to newspapers produced for black readers. Commenting on the banning of two black journalists, both members of the Media Workers Association of South Africa, *Beeld* said MWASA was not so much a journalistic organization as an arm of radical black power. "We don't blame MWASA for it. Indeed we are painfully aware that Afrikaners in similar circumstances did the same to achieve power. The Afrikaner's newspaper was an instrument for mobilizing forces so that victory could be gained at the polls."[32] When the Cillie Commission report on the unrest in black townships in 1976–77 was published in 1980, *Beeld* noted that although black newspapers had been accused at the time of fomenting the riots, and that *World* and *Weekend World* had been banned and some of their staff imprisoned, the commission had exonerated the press of any blame. The report had, in fact, expressed appreciation of the balanced reporting in the Press during the disturbances. Nothing could now be done about the journalists who had been detained, said *Beeld*, but "we think it would be a good gesture to help put things right were the government to lift the ban on *World* and *Weekend World*. We are eager to make this suggestion."[33]

The ban was not lifted, and less than a year later the government had effectively banned *World*'s successors, *Post* and *Sunday Post*. The ban, *Beeld* said, would harden black attitudes, give new ammunition to enemies of the government, and upset the government's friends at home and abroad. The consequences of the ban would "be extremely negative."[34]

The country's newspapers again presented a united front in opposing the government's Newspaper Registration Amendment Bill in June 1982. The bill was intended to rectify what the government perceived as a fatal flaw in the Press Council—the fact that newspapers were not obliged to be members of the Newspaper Press Union and hence were not bound by the union's council and press code. Most papers were members, with three main exceptions. One was *The Citizen*, a right-wing English daily established in Johannesburg with secret funding from the Information department to counter the influence of the liberal English papers, specifically the *Rand Daily Mail*. After the Muldergate scandal broke, *The Citizen* was turned over to a company in the Perskor group. It was strongly supportive of the National party and was quoted with approval by the Steyn Commission of inquiry into the press, which praised it for preaching the way of moderation. *The Citizen* clearly was no threat. A second paper that had refused to join the NPU was *Die Afrikaner*, a weekly political sheet published by the Herstigte (Reconstituted) Nasionale party. The Herstigtes, led by former cabinet minister Albert Herzog, had

broken off from the National party in the late 1960s during the first
verligte/verkrampte rift. The HNP, although active in opposing the
Nationalists in elections, did not attract a strong following, and *Die
Afrikaner* had a limited circulation. Its hard-line approach to racial
segregation struck a responsive chord among many conservative Afrikaners, however, and made the government particularly sensitive
about undertaking liberalizing reforms.

Of far greater concern was a new paper, *Die Patriot*, launched in
1982. *Die Patriot* was established by the newly-formed National
Conservative party that split from the National party over Botha's
intention of sharing the whites-only Parliament with representatives
of the country's 2.7 million Coloureds and 840,000 Indians. The
Conservatives presented a very real threat to the Nationalists, many of
whose followers rejected the concept of a racially mixed government.
The Conservatives enjoyed the support of powerful former Nationalists in the Transvaal, including Connie Mulder, who would have
succeeded Vorster as prime minister had it not been for his leading
role in the Information Department scandal. It was led by Andries
Treurnicht, a former cabinet minister and head of the National party
in the Transvaal until he was expelled from the ranks for challenging
Botha's constitutional changes. *Die Patriot*, said Treurnicht, would
"fight for the right of our Afrikaner people to govern itself through its
own representatives and not be dominated by any other peoples."[35]

Within a month of the announcement that the Conservatives would
launch *Die Patriot*, the government introduced its Newspaper Registration Amendment Bill. It preserved the Newspaper Press Union's
Press Council, but stipulated that all papers would have to submit
themselves to the council's discipline. Those refusing would have
their registration canceled, and in effect be banned. This struck at the
roots of the concept of a voluntary press council, introducing an
element of statutory control that the newspapers had long fought to
avoid. Both English and Afrikaans papers were unanimous in their
denunciation of the bill. The NPU, representing the proprietors, and
the Conference of Editors, comprising editors of both English and
Afrikaans papers, issued a joint statement announcing that they
would establish their own voluntary media council. The council
would refuse to serve as a basis for government decisions on whether

or not the registration of a paper should be withdrawn. Ton Vosloo of
Beeld and Willem de Klerk of *Die Transvaler* expressed strong opposition to the creation of a statutory press council. *Die Burger* noted the
irony that rightist publications might be the first to be affected by the
legislation and it was right-wing quarters that always campaigned
most loudly for legislation to curb the press. But, said *Die Burger*, this
lesson applies to all. Those who campaigned for legislation must bear
in mind what the position would be if one day they found themselves
at the receiving end. It was a lesson papers like *Die Burger* had come to
learn themselves as press freedom was gradually whittled away.

The Afrikaans papers may have become more objective, more
critical, more aligned to the Western concept of the role of a newspaper, but the very substantial changes that have taken place over the
past two decades do not mean that they have ceased their primary
function of serving the National party. While the party's hold on
power appeared unshakable, its press developed the freedom to criticize the application and details of its policies, if not the policies
themselves. More recently the leading Nationalist papers have begun
to criticize the basic tenets of the party's ideology, challenging the
belief that the country's problems could be solved within the limited
context of the white oligarchy. It is unlikely that Botha's plans for
constitutional reform could have won approval of the white electorate
in the referendum of November 1983 without the support of the
Afrikaans papers in preparing public opinion for them. But the
papers are, above all, still purveyors of a political message. This poses
an uncomfortable dilemma. As sociologist Heribert Adam has
pointed out, they are obliged to seek credibility on two levels.[36] As
newspapers they must be perceived as being independent of direct
party control. If they are not, they will lose readers to the English
papers that are more than willing to expose Nationalist shortcomings.
As Nationalist newspapers they must maintain their influence on the
Afrikaner elite. Being too outspokenly critical, or getting too far
ahead of the party ideology, would entail the risk of severing their
links with the establishment that has nurtured them. Thus the sense
of urgent need for reform is often muted in their columns. As Schalk
Pienaar noted, neither side can afford a split. The Afrikaans newspaper must keep a foot in the door of the establishment, otherwise it

becomes powerless. The Afrikaner establishment cannot afford a war against the newspapers. It is too vulnerable, especially within itself.

This partisan commitment to the Nationalist cause was clearly demonstrated in a memorandum circulated to reporters and correspondents of the Nationalist paper in Bloemfontein, *Die Volksblad*, before the general elections of April 1981.[37] "It is surely unnecessary to remind you that *Die Volksblad* works enthusiastically for the cause of the National party and that no mercy must be shown to other parties," the memorandum said. "Regarding the Herstigte Nasionale party and the National Conservative party and other opposition parties, if they think they can say anything positive let them say it in their own little newspapers. *Die Volksblad* will not allow itself to be abused by their propaganda, therefore you must concentrate on their more shocking and far-out statements—the things that will anger Nationalists and that will expose these parties for what they are." When the memorandum was leaked to the English press the editor of *Die Volksblad*, Hennie van Deventer, responded to the outcry in an editorial. The paper stood foursquare behind the National party and would fight all the way to help it achieve the greatest possible victory, he wrote. *Die Volksblad* believed from deep conviction that the National party "must crush, at the polls, the radical opposition of the right and left now and forever."

Dirk Richard spoke for the editors of the mainstream Afrikaans press when he wrote that when it comes to cardinal questions of continued existence "we are stubborn fighters for nationalism. And there are times when we put aside loyal opposition."[38]

9 | Broadcasting: Propaganda Arm of the National Party

The South African Broadcasting Corporation (SABC) provides the most pervasive and technologically advanced radio and television services in all of Africa. Over 9.5 million South Africans listen daily to its radio programs and almost 70 per cent of the country's whites sit before television sets each evening. With its sixteen radio services and three television channels broadcasting a total of 2,269 hours per week in seventeen languages, the SABC clearly has a large, loyal audience among whites, Africans, Coloureds, and Asians.

Yet the SABC is one of the most controversial institutions in South African society—hated and disliked by hundreds of thousands in all racial groups. The reasons are varied. For one thing, the SABC has long been totally controlled by the Afrikaner elites who rule South Africa. Thus the strict Calvinistic morality and cultural values emanating from the Dutch Reformed church have lain heavily on broadcasting. The SABC does not reflect the cultural diversity and pluralism of South African society.

Further, and perhaps more important, the ruling National party has adroitly used the SABC as a tool with which to dominate its political opposition and to reassure its own followers. To its critics, the SABC is, in the context of South African politics, the "propaganda arm of the National party."

News and public affairs programs have been especially controversial. Critics charge that the SABC through its skillful use of selection, placement, and omission deliberately gives the South African public a

distorted and unrealistic picture of daily events—a world view that
conforms to Afrikaner aspirations and fears. In the rough and tumble
of South African politics, and especially during election campaigns,
the views of Nationalist leaders and candidates dominate the airways;
those of the white political opposition are scarcely heard. Black voices
expressing authentic political concerns of the African, Coloured, or
Asian communities are simply not broadcast. Through its extensive
"radio services in the Bantu languages" and the two new black-
oriented television channels, TV2 and TV3, the SABC has effectively
narcotized and propagandized large segments of the black majority.
Urban blacks and the English-speaking opposition especially resent
the SABC projection of a Nationalist party view of the world and of
South Africa in particular that reassures the Afrikaner elite. Actually, in recent years, the SABC's political positions have been to the
right of Prime Minister P. W. Botha and his *verligte* followers.

Broadcasting in South Africa mirrors apartheid—separate broadcast services for different ethnic and linquistic groups—English and
Afrikaans services for the whites, "Radio Bantu" with programming
in the varied African languages and separate television services for
whites and blacks. Critics consider this a reflection of the Nationalist
policy of "divide and rule."

The resentments and animosities that so many South Africans
harbor toward the SABC are exacerbated by its monopoly in television and near monopoly in radio broadcasting. With just a single
"white" television channel broadcasting alternately in Afrikaans and
English, the lack of diversity and choice is resented by many.

Finally, prospects for significant change or reform in the SABC are
faint indeed. National party leaders share the view of authoritarian
rulers elsewhere that broadcasting, and especially television, are too
powerful not to be controlled by government.

History of Broadcasting

Several strands run through the SABC story: the impressive technical
developments and expansion of radio broadcasting; the political
struggle between English and Afrikaans speakers over control of
SABC with a key role played by the Broederbond, the secret society of

right-wing Afrikaners; and the long-delayed introduction of television.

As early as 1927, the potential of radio was apparent, and I. W. Schlesinger, the film pioneer, obtained a ten-year license from the government for his African Broadcasting Corporation. By 1934, the ABC was a commercial success, but its reliance on entertainment and the complete lack of any Afrikaans programming were much resented.[1]

Sir John Reith, director general of the British Broadcasting Corporation, visited South Africa on invitation, and on the basis of his report, the South African Parliament passed the Broadcast Act of 1936. This legislation both dissolved the ABC and established the South African Broadcasting Corporation as the monopoly it has been ever since. Expansion of Afrikaans programming became a high priority, but for one reason or another was slow in coming, in part because most Afrikaners still lived in rural areas beyond the reach of the city-based medium-wave transmitters. Essentially, until the National party's political victory in 1948, the SABC was largely an English-language service.

With the Nationalists running the government, Afrikaners began to gain control of the SABC board of governors and to allot more attention to programming in Afrikaans. The SABC established its own news-gathering service and, in 1950, ended the practice of carrying BBC news over SABC facilities. More important, the first commercial service, Springbok Radio, was started in 1950 and generated additional funds for the three medium-wave services. By the mid 1950s, radio was a popular and commercial success, with each of the three services—the English and Afrikaans services and Springbok Radio—receiving an equal share of the seventy hours a day of broadcasting over fifty-two transmitters.[2]

In 1952, a rediffusion system for Africans—officially termed "Bantu"—was started in Orlando Township, outside of Johannesburg. This single-channel, wired loudspeaker system was operated by a British firm and reached 11,910 subscribers by 1957, when the SABC started providing sixteen hours of programming daily for the system.

Technical and cost reasons prevented the SABC from expanding what it called its Bantu service throughout the country via medium and short wave. The development of the transistor radio, however, made possible ownership of low-cost, battery-operated, portable receivers by blacks in the nonelectrified "reserves," later to be called "homelands."

And by 1959, SABC engineers realized the feasibility of a nationwide FM system designed to serve a variety of audiences without mutual interference. FM made possible "Radio Bantu" or programming aimed specifically at Africans, and by 1964 this consisted of seven separate services: the Xhosa service in Cape Province, the South Sotho service in the Orange Free State, the Tswana service in the northern Cape and western Transvaal, the North Sotho service in the central Transvaal, the Zulu service in Natal and southeastern Transvaal, and the Tsonga and Venda services in the northeast Transvaal.[3]

With a low-cost transistor radio, a rural African could for the first time listen to programs and music broadcast in his own language. The political implications of such government-controlled programming were significant, not the least being that a rural African with his cheap FM radio could not pick up a short-wave radio broadcast from the BBC, Voice of America, or Radio Moscow. The Afrikaner elite now in control of broadcasting did not underestimate its potential for political influence.

The latest significant development in the impressive technological growth of radio came with establishment of commercial, white-oriented regional FM services. Radio Highveld for the north central area started in 1964; Radio Good Hope for the western Cape in 1965; and in 1967, the third of the white regional stations, Radio Port Natal, for the Natal coastal area. Each was on the air for 133 hours a week, and before long the commercial FM stations proved quite popular throughout the Republic.[4] Radio broadcasting has been so successful and pervasive in South Africa in large part because radio, until 1976, did not have to compete with television.

But no history of the SABC, however brief, would be complete without reference to the covert influence of the Broederbond. Na-

tional party influence over the SABC undoubtedly would have increased greatly after 1948, but the infiltration by the Broederbond
into SABC's higher echelons undoubtedly accelerated the process.
Recent revelations about the Broederbond by the English-language
press, especially the *Sunday Times*, and by journalists Hennie Serfontein, Ivor Wilkins, and Hans Strydom have filled out factual details
long suspected and rumored.

The secret, all-male, white Afrikaner Broederbond (organization of
brothers) has been called the real force behind the scenes in South
African public life. Founded in 1918 by a handful of young Afrikaners, it reached a membership in the 1970s of twelve thousand organized into some eight hundred cells, called divisions. Only Afrikaners
who are loyal supporters of the National party government could
belong. Not only prime ministers and cabinet members but top
leaders in the church, education, labor, police, the media, universities, and the farming community are Broeders. No Afrikaner government can rule South Africa without its support. P. W. Botha, current
prime minister, is a member, as were his four predecessors.[5]

According to secret Broederbond documents and speeches of its
leaders, the organization's aims can be summarized as follows: first, to
maintain a separate pure-white Afrikaans *volk* (nation), seemingly at
all costs; second, establishment of Afrikaner domination and rule in
South Africa; third, as part of that process, the subtle but definite
afrikanerization of English-speaking South Africans; and, finally, the
maintenance of a white South African nation built on the rock of the
Afrikaner *volk* with the Broederbond as the hard core of that rock.[6]

The SABC, as one of the strongest opinion-forming and cultural
institutions in South Africa, has been under Broederbond influence
for many years. In their book *The Super Afrikaners*, Wilkins and
Strydom sketch in that influence beginning with Dr. Piet Meyer, who
was chairman of the Broederbond from 1960 to 1972. During most of
that time, Meyer was also chairman of the SABC. At least three SABC
board members, W. A. Maree, S. J. Terreblanche, and H. O. Mon-
nig, were also Broeders. Other top corporation executives at the time
were: Jan Swanepoel, director general; Steve de Villiers, director of
English and Afrikaans radio; T. van Heerden, director of Bantu and
external services, and a dozen or so others—all Broeders. After the

Sunday Times published this information, the paper was deluged with calls from SABC employees who were disappointed that more names had not been revealed. At latest count, Wilkins and Strydom have found at least forty-nine Broeders in influential SABC positions.[7]

The importance of the SABC to the Broederbond–National party alliance and the extent to which it is manipulated for party political ends were apparent in two secret Broederbond documents, according to Wilkins and Strydom. The first, "Masterplan for a White Country: The Strategy," explained the importance of having Broeders in charge of the Bantu service. The master plan called for the use of organizations, including the SABC and its Bantu services and the planned black television service (now in operation), to "compel" compliance with the plan whose main purpose was to see that overwhelming numbers of the blacks live and work in their own homelands as soon as possible.

The second document, dated 1970, dealt with the proposed introduction of television, a controversial issue for some years. Meyer, head of both SABC and the Bond, also headed the commission of inquiry into television. Further, seven of the twelve commission members were Broeders. Consequently, Broeder thinking and aims were to strongly influence early television policy, and, significantly, Meyer informed the Broederbond of his inquiry's findings before passing them on to the government and Parliament.

Although press revelations have removed much of the mystery surrounding the Broederbond, the secret society's influence with SABC remains strong and continues to be controversial. When Steve de Villiers was appointed director general of the SABC, the *Cape Times* editorialized:

That the newly appointed director general of the SABC, Mr. Steve de Villiers, is listed as a member of the Broederbond is hardly surprising. What would be surprising would be the appointment of a non-Broeder to this top and most influential position. As a person he appears to be pleasant and sincere, and as thoroughly bilingual as anyone would wish. The point is that once again a member of the Afrikaner secret elite is to decide what is good and what is not good, for the listening and viewing public. There is no chance of English-speakers gaining admission to this exclusive section of the Afrikaner section of the white section of the total population.[8]

This continued influence of right-wing Afrikaner thinking on broadcasting policies and operations goes far to explain the wide resentment of the SABC by significant portions of South African society. Broederbond fingerprints were all over the crucial policy decisions regarding the introduction of the most complete of all communication media—television.

Introduction of Television

The Republic of South Africa has had a television service only since January of 1976. No other industrialized nation waited longer or debated at greater length over the perils of what one government minister called "that evil black box." The long delay raises two pertinent questions: why the protracted twenty-five-year wait? Why did South Africa proceed with television when it did?

For many years, the ruling National party and the SABC were frankly afraid of television. They were concerned that the little black box would release unsettling forces of change on what is euphemistically called "the South African way of life." The Calvinistic Afrikaners had long perceived numerous dangers in television. They saw a threat to the Afrikaans language and culture because of the expected heavy dependence on American and British programming. They feared the potential psychological and political impact of television on urbanized blacks and were concerned about the potential undermining of traditional moral values of Afrikanerdom and the Dutch Reformed church.

In 1953 the J. Arthur Rank organization was ready to introduce television into South Africa, but the Nationalist government blocked the attempt, saying the time was not ripe. Peter Orlik, a historian of the SABC, writes that a demand for television began to build by 1956. But the Nationalists saw only disadvantages in television for many years, especially the compromising of their cultural independence.

An official of the Broederbond said that, although the struggle against anglicization from without had been won, the battle against the enemy within had just started and must succeed in stopping the non-Afrikaner influences based on English and American ways of life which were infiltrating the Union through the radio, cinema, and popular press.[9] Thus, in the 1950s, Afrikaners were decrying the baleful influences of Anglo-American mass culture in arguments that were strikingly similar to those later voiced by third world advocates of the New World Information Order in the 1980s.

In addition, the Nationalists were concerned about the potential political impact of television on white voters and its potential psychological effects on the urban blacks. Rather than risk such threats, the Nationalists decided that television must be delayed as long as possible.

Dr. Albert Hertzog, long-time minister of posts and telegraphs, was a key figure in this delaying action and, in 1959, argued that television would have a disruptive effect on family life and also that it was practically impossible for the state to effectively police the medium. Television therefore could be a detriment to the moral health of the nation and must be prohibited.

A year later, Prime Minister Hendrik Verwoerd supported Hertzog but stressed the economic arguments: since programming/production costs were prohibitively high, why introduce a nonessential "service" before other countries had carried the full costs of experiment and development? Verwoerd further argued that television should be put off until enough study had been done to show up and cope with the possible evil effects.[10] A correspondent for the *Times* of London commented that "sound programs are to be kept obediently to heel and, for the time being at least, there is to be no television for fear that it might open unwanted windows on the world."[11]

In 1962, Hertzog told parliament again that it was government policy not to introduce television in the near future, and he hinted darkly that it might never be allowed. Among Nationalists, such scare stories as this one reported by Orlik went the rounds: "It is afternoon and the Bantu houseboy is in the living room cleaning the carpet. Someone has left the TV on. The boy looks up at the screen, sees a chorus line of white girls in scanty costumes. Suddenly seized by lust, he runs up stairs and rapes the lady of the house."[12]

Yet public opinion polls showed that most people wanted television, and South African businessmen kept the pressure on. By 1964, a group of firms under the leadership of Harry F. Oppenheimer, head of the giant Anglo-American group, was making plans to establish a television system and to market sets. Dr. Hertzog again blocked the way, saying to an Afrikaans press group: "The overseas money power has used television as such a deadly weapon to undermine the morale of the white man and even to destroy great empires with 15 years that Mr. Oppenheimer and his friends will do anything to use it here. They are certain that with this mighty weapon and with South African television largely dependent on British and American films, they will also succeed in a short time in encompassing the destruction of white South Africa."[13]

One major obstacle to television's introduction was removed when Vorster relieved Hertzog of his portfolio as minister of posts and telegraphs in 1968. Then the first "moon walk" in July 1969 had unexpected political repercussions as white South Africans realized that they were virtually the only people in the developed world unable to observe the historic event. A film showing the landing drew six thousand people to a five-hundred-seat theater in Johannesburg, and the crowd had to be dispersed by police.[14] The United party called for a referendum on television, and in December 1969 the Nationalists named the twelve-man commission of inquiry headed by Meyer to look into the matter and to make recommendations concerning a national television system. By then, it was apparent the government had been considering television for some time. In April 1968, the *Star* reported that the SABC had drawn up architectural plans for television studios as the second stage of its large facility at Auckland Park in Johannesburg.

The commission delivered its fifty-six-page report of recommendations to the cabinet in March 1971, and in late April of the same year the minister of national education informed Parliament that the government had accepted the recommendation that television be introduced within four years.[15] It was clear the Nationalist government and

the SABC had become convinced that they could control the new
medium for their own purposes, both by avoiding its negative features
and by using it as a political tool. The report reflects the carefully
considered policies to be established.

The official *Report of the Commission of Inquiry into Matters Relating
to Television* provided the specific recommendations that charted the
future course for television. Television would be statutorily controlled, and its introduction was to be entrusted to the South African
Broadcasting Corporation which would integrate it with radio broadcasting, thus making it a part of current SABC operations. The
commission recommended:

> This television service should form a supplementary and an in-
> tegral part of the country's pattern of education and should be
> founded on such principles as will ensure the Christian system
> of values of the country, the national identity, and the social
> structure of the various communities will be respected,
> strengthened and enriched—
>   a. by providing wholesome and edifying entertainment;
>   b. by supplying reliable, objective and balanced information;
>   c. by reflecting and projecting the cultural assets of each
> community;
>   d. by stimulating indigenous creative talent; and above all,
>   e. by constantly striving to foster good relations between all
> the people of the country.[16]

The commission recommended against sponsored programs. It
approved of advertisements before and after programs, but deemed
that programs should not be interrupted for commercials and that no
advertisements be broadcast on Sunday.

The first phase of television was to be a combined service for whites
on one channel presented in Afrikaans and English with completely
equal treatment of the two languages, and as soon as possible thereafter a start was to be made on a single-channel Bantu service in Sotho
and Zulu for the Witwatersrand area. In the second phase, it was
recommended that separate white services should be set up in English
and Afrikaans and, as soon as practicable, that the Witwatersrand

Zulu service should be extended to Durban and a Xhosa service introduced in the eastern Cape. (As will be seen, the service has not quite followed these guidelines.)

The commission also was concerned about the technical possibilities and presumably the "dangers" of direct-broadcast satellites to individual receiving sets. It recommended that a suitable ground station be erected in South Africa to pick up television programs via communication satellite from other countries.

The commission also approved specifications for all receivers, including a twenty-six-inch color set priced at R 1,000 retail. By January 1976, this carefully planned and controlled new television service was finally ready to broadcast.

The SABC Today

In its technical facilities for radio and television, hours of broadcast time, size and variety of audiences, amount of staff, and financial support, the SABC is impressive indeed. In the first five years, some R 150,000,000 were spent to launch television, expenditures mainly for the benefit of the five million whites. By 1979, 2,099,596 radio licenses had been sold, although obviously many listened without acquiring a license. (By 1983, licenses were no longer required for radios.) For the services in the African languages, 4,830,000 adults listened from Monday to Friday.

From 1976 to January 1982, SABC offered only one television service—a single bilingual channel broadcasting each evening from six o'clock to about eleven. On a given evening, the first two and a half hours of programming might be in English and the second half in Afrikaans. The following evening, Afrikaans programs would lead off, and so on. With two official languages, it would seem logical to have two channels, one in each language, as most people would have preferred. But it was government (and Broederbond) policy that English speakers should be exposed to Afrikaans-language programming. The SABC claimed that television helped bridge the linguistic gap between the two white language groups and that young English speakers were becoming more proficient in Afrikaans.

Some of the best programming is offered by the Afrikaans service which has better access to imported shows and translates them into Afrikaans. And among SABC-produced programs, those in Afrikaans are considered of better quality than those in English. With the major news programs from 8:00 to 8:30 alternating each evening between the two languages, many English speakers, long reluctant to learn Afrikaans, are listening and learning.

White South Africans took to television with alacrity. The number of sets has steadily increased year by year. At the end of 1979, 1,244,500 television licenses had been issued. By the end of 1982, there were 1,600,000 licensed television sets. SABC estimates that at least three million people watch television at least once a week. Studies showed that 78 per cent of the adult white population in 1983 viewed television from Monday to Friday. And despite the "European" orientation of the programming, 48 per cent of the Coloureds and 71 per cent of adults Asians also viewed during the week. The great African majority was conspicuous by its nonviewing, and only 11 per cent of adult Africans viewed daily.

Now with two more channels (TV2 and TV3) designed for Africans, South Africa has been following the television patterns established in Western Europe and North America: more and more leisure time is devoted to television viewing. The English-language press has been sharply critical of television, in keeping with its long carping at SABC radio (and vice versa); nevertheless, it provides ample news features about television and program logs for its readers.

Yet the public has generally been less than happy with most program offerings, which can best be described as bland, innocuous, and "safe," clearly designed to be unoffensive to the moral and religious values of Calvinistic Afrikaners. In general, SATV shies away from the controversial, expecially any programming including nudity, blasphemy, or interracial contacts. For a considerable time, "Dallas" was extremely popular (some said because of life-style similarities between the Texas city and Johannesburg), but a "Dallas" espisode concerning homosexuality was not shown. Snippets are censored out of some imported American and British shows, but violence as such is not censored.

SATV claims that for 1982 it maintained a ratio of 71.3 per cent local content on the English service and 88.7 per cent local programs on the Afrikaans service. The influence of the Dutch Reformed church is particularly apparent on Sunday evening when most programming is given over to religious services and music. Sports fans have been particularly rankled that telecasting of sporting events is prohibited on Sunday.

Significant insights about SABC policy and attitudes are sometimes revealed in minor controversies. In 1978, for instance, someone suggested that a rabbi, rather than always a Christian minister, be invited occasionally to give the epilogue which ends television programming each evening. Retief Uys, an SABC spokesman, said, "South Africa being a Christian nation, only members of Christian denominations are invited to take part in regular religious programmes." Several religious leaders took exception, including Catholic Archbishop Hurley. He said he shuddered when people said South Africa was a Christian nation: "If one reflected on policies pursued in this country, they were anything but Christian." The final and prevailing word was had by Koot Vorster, brother of the former prime minister and moderator of the Dutch Reformed church, who said it was "completely correct" that South Africa was a Christian nation, and it would not be right to have "Jewish people who had gone against Christ" give the epilogue.[17]

Observers have noted that SABC has long taken positions much closer to those of the most conservative elements of Afrikanerdom than those of the increasingly urbanized and sophisticated *verligte* Afrikaner mainstream. In September 1982, the deputy minister of information, Barend du Plessis, attacked the SABC for broadcasting "propaganda" for the Conservative party. The charge followed a false report that the Conservative party leader, Andries Treurnicht, had been shot.

One observer said, "You must look at the SABC against the backdrop of the *verligte* Afrikaans press. Some Afrikaners look at these papers as the work of the devil with sexy ads, young women in scanty bathing suits, and the *verligte* editorials in *Beeld* and *Transvaler*. So they look to the SABC for safety and assurance." Even then, the SABC is still attacked by the far right for being "too liberal."[18]

Key positions at SABC remain safely in *verkrampte* hands, suggesting that despite personnel changes the Broederbond is still firmly in control of broadcasting. And in the sensitive areas of news and public affairs programs on radio and television, the heavy hand of the National party is most apparent. The SABC cannot be faulted on the quantity of news it provides its radio listeners. Each weekday, more than 269 news bulletins go out over the sixteen radio services in seventeen languages. (Obviously, a good many news items are repeated during a news cycle.) SABC maintains eighteen editorial offices throughout South Africa, and abroad in London and Washington, D.C. SABC boasts that 250 full-time broadcast journalists handle a news intake of five hundred thousand words daily. They also claim to use about a thousand stringers or "correspondents." News services received include SAPA (South African Press Association, which takes the Associated Press), Reuters, UPI, DPA (West German), and AFP (French). In addition, the television news section receives daily five-minute feeds from Visnews in London via satellite and two airmail telefilm packages weekly from UPITN. Seventy television newsmen produce the five-minute news bulletin at 6 P.M. and the main twenty-minute news programs at 8 P.M.[19]

News on radio and television has a professional polish, and the casual or uncritical listener may perceive it to be very good indeed. But critics, such as Professor John van Zyl, think otherwise: "SABC radio's approach to the news is characterized by selection, omission, and placement, and these combine to give a weird picture of the world—a self-centered view of South Africa as a badly misunderstood and wrongly persecuted little nation that is a bastion of Christian democracy. Broadcast news doesn't begin to give a rounded picture of the news either here or abroad." Van Zyl believes that "the SABC has a real fear of the informal, the unpredictable, and the random. The broadcasters always want to be in control of things. The SABC has the technical capability to do a good deal of live, spontaneous broadcasting but only does so with sporting events."[20]

The SABC carries many news items that never appear in the newspapers and vice versa. For example, a leading radio news item on March 9, 1981, concerned a visiting Italian businessman who said the world was unfair to South Africa and that Western nations should give more support to South Africa. Newspapers did not cover the story. SABC news policies are clear to the perceptive listener: report nothing that denigrates or tarnishes the South African image and emphasize any news, however trivial, that enhances Nationalist policies.

The SABC itself does not claim to be neutral in its approach to all news coverage. It is "objective" after being "subjective" in favor of South Africa, according to Dr. Jan Schutte, director general of SABC, in testimony before the Steyn Commission: "The SABC is neutral towards party politics but committed to the general national interest. We are not neutral concerning South Africa and seek to serve the community in its diversification." Schutte admitted it was difficult to decide what was National party policy and what was government policy.[21]

Its reporting of racial unrest tells much about SABC news policies. During one telecast on the school boycotts in Cape Town and elsewhere in 1980, SATV showed no films of student rioting, only "talking heads," and then switched immediately to films of rioting in Miami. On Sunday, July 16, 1978, both radio and television repeated all day long a news item that American Indians were demonstrating in Washington, D.C. Both services quoted actor Marlon Brando's remark that "America is the world's last colonial power. In South Africa, they have even given blacks their land back again in the homelands." The message in both cases was obvious: things are not so bad in South Africa; look at the rest of the world.

SATV's progovernment tilt was apparent in television's coverage of its first major story—the Soweto riots in 1976, less then six months after television began. Radio and television deliberately underplayed the events in which an estimated seven hundred persons were killed. SABC's annual report for 1976 claimed: "Every effort was made to place the disturbances in the black townships in the proper perspective, and to control passions." SABC's 1977 annual report added: "Television news, in reflecting the sporadic unrest in various parts of the country, accepted from the start that its information function demanded precise reporting, but that coverage had to be sober and unemotional, in order to avoid the internationally recognized risk of television only inciting excitement and unrest."[22]

The consequence of this policy was that anxious South Africans, assured by the SABC during the evening that all was quiet, had to read the morning newspapers to find out that more rioting had occurred the night before. On the second anniversary of the Soweto riots, SABC reporters were refused entry to the Soweto church where a memorial service was held.

Clinching proof of the SABC's progovernment bias was provided in early 1978, when Judge Anton Mostert released to the news media the evidence gathered in his investigation of the widespread misuse of secret Department of Information funds. In this key development in the Muldergate scandal (see Chap. 10), which corroborated numerous newspaper stories over the months, South Africa's daily newspapers, Afrikaans as well as English, came out with bold headlines and full coverage. But the SABC chose to downplay the biggest political story in years, because, the SABC said, "it was not sure the law permitted it to report the story." Radio mentioned Mostert's remarks briefly in its 4 P.M. news summary, but on the main news bulletins at 6 and 7 P.M., the SABC simply said that Mostert had given a news conference and then quoted a section from the Commissions Act that it said prohibited publication of Mostert's remarks. By then the afternoon papers were on the streets with the full story.

The next day, the SABC offered the disgraced Connie Mulder the chance to reply on television to the Mostert revelations that SABC had chosen not to report. The *Rand Daily Mail* quoted an opposition leader who said that the "blatant non-reporting by SABC of the information scandal is a scandal in itself." The progovernment *Beeld* commented: "The events underlined the differences between the role of newspapers and the strange role role of radio and television. SABC did not broadcast the substance of evidence under oath of Judge Mostert but was prepared to give Connie Mulder the chance to air his side after the other side had been censored by SABC."[23] Such differences between the press and television as *news* media marked the early years of television.

The SATV, operating as a monopoly and without nearby competing role models, has been hurt by the lack of professional quality of its television news operation. Little vigorous reporting, especially any of an investigative nature, is initiated by the SABC news staffs. Despite considerable resources, SATV news avoids controversy, shows little enterprise, and lags well behind the newspapers in covering most events.

Part of the problem is that television news is a national service, concentrated in the elaborate facilities at Auckland Park. All television news comes into and is telecast from Johannesburg with no local or regional news broadcasts for other distant population centers such as Cape Town, Durban, Port Elizabeth, or Bloemfontein. And because of its close ties to the Nationalists, television and radio news alike exhibit a certain official stodginess, especially when dealing with news about government and public affairs.

However, the SABC has had an access to the prime minister and other cabinet ministers not enjoyed by the opposition English press or even the Afrikaans papers. In fact, a good portion of news shows are devoted to high government figures providing official explanations to sympathetic reporters, who avoid asking embarrassing or probing questions. On one Sunday evening, for example, the first twenty-five minutes of the half-hour news in review show was given over to an obsequious interview with Foreign Minister Pik Botha, who explained the government's views on the continuing unresolved issue of Namibia. No other views were provided. The foreign minister appeared so frequently on the Sunday public affairs program that critics have called it the "Pik Botha Show." National politicians "use" the SABC so adroitly to get across their views that opposition MP Brian Page has called the SABC "nothing more than an agency of the Nationalist Party."[24]

This political use of broadcasting was well established years earlier on SABC radio through the "Current Affairs" commentaries which have long annoyed South Africans critical of the government. One SABC annual report said of them: "The talks are offered as an SABC editorial in which, from a South African point of view, positive comment is made on the affairs of the day. The broad objectives are (1) to project a true picture of South African motives, politics, problems, achievements and goals; (2) to give constructive guidance to listeners on the innumerable situations which are continually developing at home and abroad and which affect the fate of the nation;

and (3) to counteract influences which are hostile to South Africa and which seek to undermine the South African pattern of society."[25]

"Current Affairs," more recently called "Editorial Comment" on radio and usually broadcast immediately after the news bulletin, has been in reality the Nationalists' English-language editorial page—a way to reach English speakers in a land where all English newspapers (until the secretly funded *Citizen*) were in opposition. In any case, over the years the "Current Affairs" talks infuriated a good many South Africans of all races who saw them only as blatant, self-serving propaganda justifying Nationalist policies and excoriating the political opposition. Long before the SABC ties with the Broederbond were confirmed, any claims that SABC was an independent public institution, free of political influences and comparable to the BBC, were considered highly suspect because of the persistent pro-Nationalist tilt of the "Current Affairs" talks. Elaine Potter wrote in 1975, "Increasingly its (SABC) news and current affairs programs have been subject to propaganda. The violence of its attacks on the English-language press and on individual newspapers frequently has not been matched even by the Afrikaans newspapers. The corporation long ago abandoned any pretence at upholding the principles of its charter to act as an impartial public body, and has been used extensively—both inside and outside South Africa—to disseminate the views of the National Party Government."[26]

Some newspaper editors say that television news because of its slow and unprofessional response to breaking news and its official tone has not as yet provided any real direct competition to newspapers in reporting the news. Nevertheless, SABC does enjoy a high credibility with the South African public, a fact dismaying to its critics. A 1974 survey found, for example, that a majority of English-speaking whites thought that SABC radio was the "most reliable and unbiased source" for news on South African politics. Presumably this same credibility carries over to television. Moreover, television is providing direct competition with the press in the use of leisure time. There is certainly less time now to read the afternoon newspapers, and this has been borne out by their falling circulation figures.

The ties between the SABC and the Nationalists are particularly evident during parliamentary elections held at least every five years and sometimes more frequently. SABC's broadcasting monopoly has assured that Nationalist candidates and policy positions receive a preponderance of favorable mention while opposition candidates receive a good deal less attention.

Parliamentary elections were held in 1977 and 1981, and in both campaigns, television entered the fray as a powerful new instrument to help the Nationalists win once again. Newspaper journalists were quick to see the political potential of this new medium. As one observed, from the time television was introduced in 1976, it became obvious that this was to be an even more powerful propaganda medium than radio. In the months leading up to the 1977 general election, virtually every newscast on television featured a Nationalist spokesman. The usual format was a cabinet minister explaining some aspects of state policy to the viewer or answering questions on which he appeared to have been well briefed beforehand or, as some suspected, had even written the questions himself. Opposition views, the journalist reported, received only token airing and black viewpoints none at all.[27]

A survey of the 1977 campaign by the Journalism Department at Rhodes University reinforced these biases noted by the journalist. The study, conducted while candidates were campaigning, found that television devoted more than 80 per cent of its political coverage to government or National party viewpoints. A month-long content analysis found that 32 per cent of news time was given over to political representation—reports pertaining to policies or principles of political parties in South Africa. Of this time, 47 per cent was devoted to showing and hearing government and National party officials. Of the balance, 34 per cent consisted of reports or statements from or news about government or National party figures. Television critic van Zyl commented: "When these figures are combined, it may be seen that 81 per cent of political news was centered on government or National Party officials. It is obvious that the party in power will always have an advantage of newsmaking and newsworthiness, but it is only a television service which is overwhelmingly an *official* service which will provide such an accessible platform for government views which are not tested or probed by informed viewers."[28]

The same SABC support for the Nationalists continued in the parliamentary elections held on April 26, 1981. Prime Minister P. W.

Botha had dissolved Parliament in January, and the political bias of
SABC became an important, if secondary, issue. Opposition leaders
called on the SABC to hold political debates on television in spite of
Botha's rejection of the idea. Vause Raw, leader of the New Republic
party, called on the SABC board to demonstrate that the organization
was not a "bootlicking lackey" of the National party by presenting
debates or panel discussions between political parties which were
prepared to debate, without the National party. The leader of the
opposition Progressive Federal party, Dr. Frederick van Zyl Slabbert, said, "What is becoming a farce is the way in which the government-controlled media are manipulated to promote the image and
interests of the National Party while its opponents are not allowed the
same privilege." No television debates were held.[29]

Opposition party candidates also requested that the SABC provide
equal time for all candidates. In Parliament, MP Colin Eglin asked,
"Is the Opposition going to be treated fairly during the election
campaign? Is the Minister [of Information] going to use taxpayers'
money through the Information Service of South Africa to try to rig
the election in favour of the National Party?"[30] Prime Minister Botha
did not reply, but the SABC refused the request and announced that,
instead, special election reviews would be carried daily on radio and
television. On television these reviews followed the late news and
on radio the morning news on both the English and Afrikaans services.

Next, a plea by the Progressive Federal party to allow political
advertising on television was made to the SABC. But again the SABC
demurred, a spokesman saying, "No advertisement will be accepted
which introduces or incorporates any matter which deals with party,
racial or sexual subjects, or any other matter of a controversial
nature."[31]

Consequently, as in 1977, the Nationalists dominated the election
news on radio and television. A survey taken during the first two
weeks of the campaign showed that National party had received 1,200
per cent more coverage than the opposition Progressive Federal
party. The other parties—New Republic party and Herstigte
Nasionale party—each received less than one minute of television
news time during the two-week period. Despite the outspoken criticisms of SABC's partisan role in the election campaign, widely pub-

licized in the opposition English papers, the SABC did not modify its way of election reporting and continued to reflect Nationalist interests.

In addition to its activities in party politics, the SABC has played an even more pervasive policy role for the Afrikaner minority in its broadcasting to blacks. If the SABC is one of the most controversial institutions in South Africa, then its service to blacks—long known as Radio Bantu—is right at the center of that controversy.

SABC claims that over five million people listen daily to the eight stations broadcasting in the African languages and that over four million letters are received annually from listeners. With a quarter century of broadcasting behind it, Radio Bantu's impact on its African audience has been considerable—and controversial.

Sociologist Heribert Adam calls Radio Bantu "one of the most powerful tools of social control over the urban African."[32] According to Allen Drury, "Radio Bantu is one of the most obvious, and most expensive features of apartheid. It does an undeniable amount of good and, in the minds of its critics, an undeniable amount of bad, in that it of course gives the Government an ideal medium for political propaganda and persuasion." Drury quotes an acquaintance critical of Radio Bantu: "You ought to hear what they tell them all the time about what a wonderful place the Transkei is, and how great the housing developments are, and what a wonderful education they are giving the Bantu, and how perfect the Nats [Nationalists] are and how much they have done for the natives. Then you would know why they are spending so much money on Radio Bantu."[33]

The broadcasting service to blacks undoubtedly reinforces Nationalist policies on apartheid. The extensive broadcasting in the diverse vernacular languages can be seen as an effort to reinforce tribal or traditional differences among Africans—or to "divide and rule"— thus discouraging nationalistic or integrative tendencies among blacks. The SABC takes a paternalistic view of its audience; a few whites have decided for over a quarter century what kinds of radio programs are best for millions of black South Africans.

But quite aside from the paternalistic and propagandistic aspects of Radio Bantu, there is no question that during the many years of the radio service, the SABC has accumulated and preserved a large and valuable archive of cultural materials relating to the major ethnic groups. In the language of an annual report of the SABC: "The various programme Services [of Radio Bantu] once more endeavored to make a contribution to the preservation and expansion of the particular culture of each of the Black peoples by drawing upon their rich traditional heritage and stimulating the modern by giving writers, actors, musicians, and composers ample opportunity. New artists were constantly discovered and encouraged by the award of broadcasting bursaries, and writers were encouraged to produce original works for radio." In that year, the SABC reported that, altogether, 720 original works were broadcast during the year: 58 serials, 48 plays, 150 documentaries, 100 legends, and 314 praise songs.[34] And this pattern has been followed for many years. So at a time when critics of Western broadcasting have decried its destructive influence on the traditional cultures of the third world, the SABC has been preserving and encouraging the traditional music, drama, legends, and folklore of its African tribes.

Among the Africans themselves, the service is perceived in different ways. Among older, more conservative, and perhaps less educated Africans the radio service is widely listened to and accepted. The lives of many Africans are undoubtedly enriched by radio. But among the more sophisticated and politically active younger blacks, the SABC is despised as the voice (and tool) of their oppressors. To them, its propaganda purpose is self-evident.

This split in the black community over the SABC was shown in a major survey done eight months before the black television service was launched. Young blacks believed that the coming black television would be used by the government to intensify propaganda efforts and to "brainwash blacks." The study conducted by a Johannesburg market research firm also found that the "older, calmer and more conforming group" of blacks interviewed believed it was a good idea to have their own television service. But the "younger, aggressive and challenging group" viewed the channel negatively. Among the complaints of young blacks were that certain news items shown to whites would be withheld from blacks and that the black channel would concentrate greatly on the homelands, which were not of interest to urban blacks. Both groups of blacks agreed that the news should not be distorted and they "should stop feeding us with propaganda."[35]

"Black television" came on the air in January 1982 and provided the world with a new wrinkle in state broadcasting monopolies—a television service carefully designed for blacks, quite distinct and separated from another television service intended for a minority white community. Only the architects of apartheid, it was said, could produce such an innovation in broadcasting.

The same policies and mentality that shaped "Radio Bantu" were involved in the planning and implementation of TV2 and TV3, the two channels dedicated to the African majority. TV2 and TV3 (TV2/3) are broadcast entirely in five African languages: Zulu, Xhosa, Tswana, Sotho, and Venda. And to discourage whites from flipping from TV1, the SABC established the strict rule that all programs and commercials must be in these five languages and no others. Although Zulu is the most widely spoken language in South Africa, English is extensively spoken by blacks and serves as a lingua franca of sorts (most black-oriented publications have long been in English). As one black commented, "They [the SABC] are just being consistent. They believe there is no such thing as a black South Africa. We can only be Zulus, Xhosas, or Tswanas."[36]

About a thousand blacks were recruited for staff positions. A spokesman for SABC said black television would faithfully reflect the country's ethnic diversity. With Radio Bantu as a well-established precedent, blacks could be sure that no news or political commentary that in any way challenged the status quo would be aired on TV2/3.

At the time the new service began, a survey found that blacks owned about 235,000 sets. Some observers questioned whether they would accept the new services. Would urban blacks watch the black-oriented shows in vernacular languages instead of the offerings on the English/Afrikaans channel? One advertising man said, "I don't see anyone watching tribal dancing in the Transkei when they can be watching 'Dallas.'"[37]

For a number of reasons, television probably will expand much more slowly among blacks than it has among whites. A R 600 to R 700 television set is expensive for blacks and lags in priority behind a car or a refrigerator. Most black homes do not have electricity, and only recently has the government electrified even the Soweto townships. In the impoverished homelands and rural areas, the lack of electricity is much more pervasive. Further resistence will come from widespread suspicions of the SABC among urban blacks. Many talented black writers and producers will not work for the SABC, and those who do are often suspect among other blacks.

Why then did the SABC proceed with black television? The 1971 Meyer commission of inquiry did call for such a service, and the SABC has generally followed its master plan. Further, the SABC (and the government) were apparently convinced that they could control the black channel and use it for their own purposes.

But television, the most potent of all media, has often produced unexpected effects. Critics of the SABC see TV2/3 not as a humanitarian service for black people but as just another step toward the entrenchment of apartheid. As one letter writer to *The Star* said, "Not only will TV2 and TV3 viewers be subjected to the same bias and government propaganda that characterizes TV1 (especially programs selling the homelands, I am sure) but the very presence of TV2 and TV3 will be a constant reminder of separate development. Instead of providing television channels for all South Africans and bringing communication and understanding between them, the SABC is forcing upon us a television service which can only emphasize racial barriers and disunity, because it is divided into channels on racial lines. SABC tries to excuse its bland adoption of apartheid on television on grounds of language. Why then do Afrikaans and English speaking South Africans not have separate channels."[38]

In fact, pressure is building for a channel entirely in English. The implementation of the two new channels, both in five African languages, has engendered resentment from whites who feel that the TV1 channel, half in English and half in Afrikaans, is too limited and offers far too little choice in programs. English speakers are particularly annoyed that popular shows from Britain and America are translated for the Afrikaans service and never shown in their original English version. Further, the 1971 Meyer Commission recommended that, in the second phase of television development, separate white services should be set up in English and Afrikaans. When and how to do that pose major policy decisions for the SABC. By mid 1983, it was rumored (and not denied outright by SABC) that TV1 would be split into two channels in order to offer more programming to the white audience. Rumor also had it that both TV1 and the new channel would be bilingual to maintain the stimulus for English speakers to use Afrikaans.[39]

International Broadcasting: RSA—The Voice of South Africa

Another policy area of high priority has been the utilization of transnational shortwave broadcasting to improve and enhance the image of South Africa throughout Africa and overseas. Radio South Africa (RSA), the external service of the SABC, has been since 1965 a potent instrument of South African diplomacy and international political communication. As one would expect, the external service is professional, technically proficient, and an effective propaganda tool of the Nationalist government and its policies.

The target areas of RSA have remained constant—Africa first and foremost, followed by Europe, the United States, Canada, Latin America, and the Middle East. Languages used are English, Dutch, Afrikaans, German, Portuguese, French, Spanish, Swahili, Chichewa, Tsonga, and Lozi. Out of a total of 26.5 hours of daily broadcasting, 23 hours are beamed to African nations. From the huge H. F. Verwoerd station at Bloemendal outside of Johannesburg, with its powerful array of two 100-kw and four 250-kw transmitters, strong shortwave signals are directed to the north, northwest, and northeast. There are few periods of the day, from early morning to mid evening, when the RSA signals cannot be picked up throughout Africa. And despite the hostility to South Africa throughout the continent, there is ample evidence that Africans do listen to RSA. The propaganda message is subtle and restrained, and mixed in with a good deal of hard news and interesting programming. Forty-two news bulletins and twenty-one news commentaries are broadcast daily. The news, while selective and self-serving, is accurate and timely; the "comments," as on the domestic SABC, provide the propaganda messages.

Sizes of audiences for international broadcasting are difficult to vali-
date. The SABC claimed that in 1978 it received 53,688 letters, which
if true indicated that a considerable number did listen in. Commenting on these letters in its 1978 annual report, the SABC said, "A
feature of a large number of these letters, particularly from the United
States, West Germany and the United Kingdom, was the support
expressed by listeners for South Africa's efforts to solve her problems
in a peaceful way and the strong criticism expressed against governments which, in the view of the listeners, interfered in the domestic
affairs of South Africa in an improper way."[40]

The external service has been well financed by successive Nationalist governments. In 1981, the *Sunday Express* reported that state
subsidies to Radio South Africa totaled R 81,477,654 between 1969
and 1979. In 1977, the subsidy was R 21,053,300, and there was
evidence that some of this general funding was related to the Muldergate information scandal (see Chap. 10). In commenting on these
figures, the Progressive Federal party spokesman on the media, Dave
Dalling, said it seemed inimical for a statutory body, the supposedly
nonpartisan servant of the different interests in South Africa, to
accept government money to put across a message to the outside
world which merely promoted the policies of the Nationalist government. "Only a distortion of this country can be given to the outside
world if the content of these broadcasts is anything like the biased
service presented internally," Dalling said.[41]

Competition for a Monopoly?

Radio and television broadcasting, which have become such profound
influences in modern societies, are rightly subjected to criticism in
large part because many people are never satisfied with what they see
and hear on the electronic media. However, much of the widespread
unhappiness among South Africans with the SABC stems mainly
from characteristics peculiar to that system:

• The SABC enjoys a monopoly on broadcasting—and a state-run
monopoly at that. That monopoly imposes the narrow Calvinistic
moral and religious values of the minority Afrikaners upon the pro-

gramming for a pluralistic and diverse population. Further, the SABC reflects and strengthens the divisions of apartheid.

• The SABC is clearly used by the Nationalist governments as an instrument of political control. There is selection and omission of news and overt propaganda in both news and commentaries. No one has a right of reply on SABC. Radio and television are not obliged to carry corrections of erroneous statements nor are they required to air the other point of view.

• The SABC's lack of broadcasting competition has resulted in professionally lax and creatively arid broadcasting and a somewhat arrogant and unresponsive bureaucracy that seems convinced it serves the society well.

• SABC staff morale, expecially among creative people, is perennially low and turnover is high. Although technically excellent, the SABC continues to be deficient in programming areas, especially in the English service on television.

South Africans obviously want more choice and diversity in broadcasting. Again and again there have been calls for privately owned television and radio services to compete with the SABC. Yet the responses of the Nationalist government have invariably been negative. Broadcasting has proved too powerful and useful to the Nationalists for them to relinquish control. As one observer said, "There's no way the Afrikaner will allow himself to suffer because of television."[42]

And yet because of new media technology and, ironically, the Nationalists' own policy of establishing "independent" homelands for the Africans, the SABC finally has had to deal with limited competition. The home movie projector and the video cassette player have flourished in South Africa mainly because of the limitations and unpopularity of SABC television offerings as well as the heavy-handed censorship of films. South Africans are considered some of the world's best customers for movies and videotapes, both pirated and legitimate. Lacking other recreational alternatives and bored with television offerings, many South Africans have acquired the illegal "forbidden fruit" of X-rated movies and videotapes of various kinds from Britain and America. As the products of home video or nonbroadcast television become more plentiful and available, South Africans can be expected to spend less time watching SABC television.

Another problem for the government (and the SABC) is that the neighboring independent nations of Swaziland, Lesotho, and Botswana, and also the recently created independent homelands of Transkei, Ciskei, Bophuthatswana, Venda, and so on, have been developing or at least planning radio and television systems whose signals could carry beyond their borders into South Africa itself. For example, guests at the Drum Rock Hotel outside Nelspruit in the eastern Transvaal can watch SATV, Swazi TV, and the hotel's own video film channel. Swazi TV includes top-rated British shows not available to SATV because of British unions' boycott of South Africa. Businessmen in the Lowveld near the Swaziland border have been running advertisements on Swazi television whose surveys have found they have about nine thousand viewers in South Africa.

Bophuthatswana, because of its proximity to the great population center of the Reef area including Johannesburg and Pretoria, offers the greatest potential competition. Radio 702, broadcasting contemporary music out of Bophuthatswana, has proved so popular with South African listeners that SABC's comparable service, Radio 5, has suffered markedly in audience ratings. Another alternative radio service, Capital Radio, was launched in the Transkei with British backing, but because of a variety of technical problems did not really catch on with South African audiences.

South African newspaper publishers, both English and Afrikaans, have been eager to get into television broadcasting but have been shut out by the SABC monopoly. In 1981, a consortium began actively planning a new television service which would emanate from Bophuthatswana. All four press groups, SAAN, Argus, Perskor, and Nasionale Pers, were included in the group negotiating with the Bophuthatswana government. Ironically, the SAAN newspapers, including the *Rand Daily Mail* and the *Sunday Times*, have condemned editorially even the existence of the homelands yet are still eager to go into a television partnership with the Bophuthatswana government. Predictably, the South African government has been reluctant to issue a television frequency to Bophuthatswana, which is not recog-

nized by either the United Nations or the International Telecom-
munications Union, the UN-related body that issues broadcasting
frequencies around the world.

The South African government finds itself faced with an interesting
dilemma. On the one hand, it wants to encourage the homeland
governments to somehow appear independent and has permitted
radio frequencies for both Radio 702 and Capital Radio. On the other
hand, the Nationalists do not welcome incoming radio and television
signals that take away both audience and advertising revenue from the
SABC or in any way weaken the control over South Africa's airwaves
that the SABC has long enjoyed. So far, over-the-air broadcasting
alternatives to SABC have not posed any immediate threat to the
SABC's dominance, but the potential is there.

Considering the political realities, significant change or improvement in the SABC is unlikely. What changes that occur will most
likely be those that are clearly in the political or economic interests of
the ruling Nationalists to implement. Only if there are dramatic
political shifts in South Africa and the Nationalists somehow lose
political power would substantive changes in the SABC take place.
For once power changes hands in nations with politically controlled
media systems, then dramatic changes in the media soon follow.

However, for the present and foreseeable future, the South African
Broadcasting Corporation, and television in particular, should be
viewed as an integral part of "total strategy," or the continuing
attempt by the Afrikaner power structure (including the Broederbond, Afrikaner churches, National party, Afrikaans press, and Afrikaans universities) to exercise semitotalitarian control over all of
South Africa. In the thinking of this power bloc, television must not
ever be allowed to become what Albert Hertzog feared it would
become—the end of the white man in Africa. Total Afrikaner control,
and the very narrow outlook implied by this control on questions of
politics and culture, appear to assure that the SABC will continue to
be a sterile status quo force in South African society.

10 | Muldergate: Covert Efforts to Influence Opinion

Freedom of speech in the West means "the right to lie, deceive, and distort," the South African minister of foreign affairs, R. F. Botha, told a nationwide television audience in March 1983.[1] Botha was reacting to an article in *Newsweek* magazine that argued that blacks still suffered ill treatment in South Africa despite the government's proposed constitutional reforms. The article, said Botha, was "dripping with enmity and hate." Others took up the cry. The Afrikaans Sunday paper *Rapport* complained that the article was a "reprehensible and deliberate denigration of efforts to build a better South Africa . . . part of a campaign that has been waged in so many different ways for so many years." The Johannesburg daily, *The Citizen*, characterized the *Newsweek* article as "mischievous, one-sided and written to detract from the genuine reform plans of the government."[2] What Botha and these newspapers chose to ignore was that the Nationalist government itself had, just several years before, engaged in lies, deception, and distortion to promote its policies at home and abroad. And the sanctimonious *Citizen* was one product of that effort.

Political warfare involves two basic strategies: censorship and propaganda. Confronted with growing hostility abroad and increasing unrest at home, South Africa has, as has been demonstrated in previous chapters, made extensive use of various forms of censorship. It also has used propaganda. South Africa's major propaganda offensive has come to be known as Muldergate, after the senior cabinet minister who promoted it—and for its resemblance to the Watergate debacle in the United States.

In 1978–79 there were revelations in the press, and in subsequent commissions of inquiry, that the South African Department of Information had been conducting a secret propaganda war to sell apartheid to the world. The multi-million-dollar campaign had been attempting for six years to use public funds, without the knowledge of Parliament, to influence media, politicians, and other opinion makers in the United States, Europe, and Africa. When serious abuses in the use of these funds were exposed, first in the English-language press, then in the Afrikaans papers and in the reports of investigating commissions, it rocked the government and the nation. Among those forced from office were Minister of the Interior Connie Mulder, heir apparent to the premiership; Gen. Hendrik van den Bergh, head of the powerful Bureau of State Security; and ultimately State President John Vorster himself. As in the case of Nixon's Watergate, the combined efforts of newspapers and an independent judiciary forced the scandal into the open, despite frantic efforts to cover it up, including threats against the press and against individual journalists involved in the investigation.

This ill-fated enterprise can be understood only within the context of its historical antecedents and the proximate situation that spawned it. From the earliest years of the Nationalist government, spokesmen have fulminated against foreign correspondents who sent "irresponsible" and "slanderous" reports abroad and against the "unpatriotic" or even "treasonous" local newspapers and journalists. Thirty years before the *Newsweek* article mentioned above, the annual report of the State Information Office for 1952 compained that there had been "a resurgence of an organized press campaign against South Africa . . . those who are ever ready to besmirch South Africa seized upon the constitutional crisis and the resistance movement of non-Europeans to put forth a flood of propaganda based on ignorance, prejudice and hostility towards the Union." The Information Office said South Africa was presented as a country where oppression and slavery held sway, and where bloody revolution could break out at any moment: "Overseas newspapers gave their imaginations free play, press representatives closed on the Union, and some South Africans did not hesitate to foul their own nests in communications to the press overseas."

Some of the arguments made at that time are curiously prophetic of criticisms of international news media now being voiced by third world proponents of a "new world information order." The Afrikaners in South Africa had fought their own war of liberation against Britain's colonial yoke. Now they felt that their achievements were being scorned, their shortcomings magnified and held up to ridicule. Foreign Minister Eric Louw told a correspondent of the *Times* of London in 1957 that he was "much concerned about attacks being made on South Africa by some sections of the press and other agencies of public opinion in Britain. They concentrated entirely on criticism and gave no credit for what the South African government had accomplished on the positive side for the African."[3] Two years later the South African Information Department prepared an analysis of British newspapers, which purported to show that three-quarters of their items about South Africa were concerned with "negative subjects," which created "an unfortunate impression in the British reader."[4] Like today's supporters of the New World Information Order, the Nationalists wanted to improve the quality of news about their government presented abroad. During the 1950s several motions in Parliament called for a more energetic campaign to better inform people overseas and to counter malicious criticism. But it took the flood of unfavorable publicity that followed the Sharpeville massacre in 1960, and the subsequent declaration of a state of emergency, to spur the government into specific action.

In November 1961, after South Africa had withdrawn from the British Commonwealth and found itself in a state of increasing international isolation, the government decided to create a full-fledged department of information to replace the underfunded and ineffectual State Information Service, set up in 1937 by a previous Nationalist prime minister, Gen. Barry Herzog. The new minister of information, Frank Waring, told Parliament he would strive for "better understanding" between the government and the press and hoped that the English-language press would "do some soul-searching." These newspapers, he said, should realize that on occasion they had overstepped the mark. "They do not have to support the government if they do not want to, but when it comes to a question of South Africa's interests they should not do what they have done in the past to hamper the government's efforts," Waring said. He suggested that the newspapers declare a moratorium on criticism of the government "until the country's present crisis is over."[5]

Waring elaborated on his views in an interview with a London *Times* correspondent in January 1962. The opposition press in many countries sought to diminish achievements of the government, he said. But in South Africa the position was different from anywhere else, "in that the people who cannot understand Afrikaans cannot balance their views by reading pro-government newspapers, all of which appear in the language." This condition in South Africa, he said, imposed an unusual responsibility on newspapers published in English. "I believe they have a special duty in these circumstances to be balanced and fair-minded in both their news and editorial columns and to give credit where credit is due. In the past they have not lived up to this." The role of the new Information Department, Waring said, would be to contribute toward an informed and balanced public opinion on South African affairs at home and abroad.[6] In a speech later that month, Waring remarked that "Sharpeville was regrettable and was overemphasized in comparison with the millions that have been spent on social services and housing for the non-whites . . . there should be a basis of reasonableness with regard to the dissemination of news from our country."[7] Waring's statements contain the genesis of the idea that media should focus on the positive, on process-oriented and developmental news, rather than on negative, event-oriented reports. They also contain the seeds of Muldergate.

Waring was not alone in expressing these sentiments. The *Times* ran an editorial the same day as the Waring interview, commenting that "it really is time that this little band of white men, marching resolutely out of step with humanity to the certain disruption of their nation, should cease to protest that they are misunderstood." These remarks infuriated *Die Burger*, which protested that "it is this exclusive and negative concentration on differences, this delight in mutual divisions and bitterness, which—even more than the enemy's efforts—will send the West into decline." The next day *Die Burger* pointed out why it objected to negative reports about South Africa:

"Governments abroad are forced to act by their local opinion, not by facts, and this opinion is at least partly formed by sensational and biased news reporting."[8]

Meanwhile the Press Commission appointed in 1950 (see Chap. 3) was still laboring away at its report. The first part, published in 1962, included an extensive study of four international news agencies and of dispatches to and comment carried by newspapers in Europe, North America, Israel, and India. With few exceptions, it contended, the news was "unfair, unobjective, angled and partisan."[9] The second part of the report, released in 1964, complained that many foreign correspondents, apart from making untrue statements, failed to give an account of the problems the government faced in restoring law and order; gave undue prominence to statements by opponents of the government; and played down government statements.[10]

The task of the new Information Department was to rectify this imbalance. At first its efforts were strictly orthodox. It published news digests and feature magazines in several languages for distribution abroad. The department also published magazines for domestic circulation, especially to blacks in the vernacular. It prepared educational films, books, and pamphlets. And it encouraged foreign journalists and other opinion leaders to visit South Africa. One project involved airmailing hundreds of copies of the strongly conservative, progovernment weekly *South African Financial Gazette* to prominent individuals and media abroad. The *Financial Gazette*, published by the Nationalist-controlled Perskor publishing company, depended heavily on this hidden subsidy to survive.

The department's message was straightforward. Given the huge flight of capital from South Africa after Sharpeville, it was essential to portray the country as a stable, profitable environment for investment and a desirable place for Europeans with useful skills to immigrate to. It stressed the importance of South Africa to the West—as a guardian of the strategic sea routes around the Cape; as a reliable source of minerals essential to the industrial nations of Europe and North America; as a bastion of Western civilization at the tip of a darkening continent. The claim of whites to South Africa was explained— archeological evidence to the contrary notwithstanding—in terms of their ancestors' having settled a virtually uninhabited land at the same time, or even before, the black tribes were moving down from the north. This was used also to justify the claim by whites to 87 per cent of the land, leaving the homelands with only the 13 per cent traditionally occupied by blacks.[11]

Once the echoes of the Sharpeville shootings died away, South Africa experienced renewed growth as investors regained confidence in the country's potential. The 1960s was a period of high economic activity: sustained growth in personal income, a high level of employment, and a large influx of white immigrants from Europe and from newly independent African countries. New foreign capital boosted the country's gold and foreign exchange reserves.

Politically, however, the position was less satisfactory. The growing voice of third world countries in international councils meant that South Africa became more isolated. The country was effectively isolated in the United Nations and expelled from some of its specialized agencies; South African goods were boycotted abroad; sports tours were canceled and South Africans prevented from participating in many international organizations. The Department of Information, despite a huge increase in its funding, was unable to change the policies of the West toward South Africa. The need to do so became particularly acute in the early 1970s when the Portuguese dictatorship collapsed, leaving Angola and Mozambique independent and substituting a *cordon sanitaire* on South Africa's northern border for the previous comfortable buffer of friendly states. This, together with the fall of Richard Nixon with his policy of communication and "selective involvement" with the Republic, aroused concern that was exacerbated by penetration of Russians and their proxies, the Cubans, into southern Africa. The country was in effect at war, the Nationalists felt. And in time of war the rules of war must apply. Not only should the military and armaments industry be built up, but also the propaganda machinery. Since South Africa's enemies were waging an all-out propaganda war against the country, the Nationalists felt justified in using any means to counter them.

South Africa's secret propaganda operation began in earnest in 1972 when the minister of the interior and of information, Cornelius "Connie" Mulder, appointed Eschel Rhoodie as secretary for information—the department's top administrative post. Rhoodie's appointment was made over the heads of several more senior officials and caused some bitterness in the department. But he had the support of powerful patrons, including Mulder, Prime Minister Vorster, and Gen. van den Bergh, head of the Security Police and Vorster's close confidant. Rhoodie, after some experience on a Defense Force magazine and the Nationalist newspaper *Die Vaderland*, and armed with a doctoral degree in sociology, had joined the Information Service in 1956. He served as an information attaché in Australia, the United States, and The Netherlands before returning to South Africa in 1971 as deputy editor of a new weekly news magazine, *To the Point*. This magazine, it turned out later, was one of the department's first secret projects.

While serving in Holland, Rhoodie had cultivated the friendship of Herbert Jussen, a director of the Dutch publication *Elseviers*. Jussen, a political conservative, had long wanted to launch an international newsmagazine, in the style of *Time* or *Newsweek*, to counter what he perceived as the left-wing orientation of much of the world's mass media. Rhoodie arranged for Jussen to visit South Africa where he met Vorster and Mulder, among others. Vorster agreed to the idea of starting *To the Point*.[12] The South African government gave secret funds to Jussen to get the magazine off the ground, then undertook to buy copies for distribution abroad. Its initial subsidy was about R 1 million a year, rising later to about R 2.8 million. Altogether more than R 17 million in secret government money was funneled to *To the Point*, although this was strenuously denied at the time.

According to evidence before the Erasmus commission of inquiry into the Information Department's affairs, after the scandal broke, the intention of the magazine was to give "an objective picture of South Africa; it would not engage in party politics, and it had to be critical of the government."[13] It clearly was not to be too critical, however, since Rhoodie was moved into the editorial offices to direct policy.

First launched in South Africa, *To the Point* added an international edition, based in Antwerp, in 1974. The magazine never did become economically self-sufficient. Its international edition was abandoned in 1977, after British journalists working on it walked out in protest against taking instructions from Johannesburg. The South African

edition limped on for two years after its links to the Information
Department were revealed, and finally closed in 1980. It was, said the
Rand Daily Mail, which helped bring about its demise, a fitting end
for a publication "born in sin and with a lie nailed to its masthead."[14]

Another early venture of the department was to try covertly to buy
an existing English-language newspaper in South Africa. The *Natal
Mercury*, Durban's morning daily, was one of the few English papers
not owned by either Argus or SAAN. In May of 1973 the chairman of
the board of the family-controlled *Mercury* announced that he had
been offered R 7 million for the paper. The bid came from Lawrence
Morgan, ostensibly acting on behalf of a group of English-speaking
businessmen. Morgan had worked for the *Mercury*, but later had
joined the progovernment *Financial Gazette* and broadcast regularly
for the SABC. His bid stirred a storm of protest—from the staff of the
Mercury, from some major shareholders, and from other newspapers
that suspected there were sinister political motives behind the offer.
They were right. After the Information Department's house of cards
collapsed in 1978, Rhoodie admitted that he had been behind the bid,
along with Pieter Koornhof, a Nationalist cabinet minister, and Gen.
van den Bergh.[15] The offer was refused, and instead SAAN bought a
majority share in the *Mercury* to add it to its stable of morning papers.

Another of the department's early secret projects was the use of a
front organization, dubbed the Club of Ten, that bought pro–South
African political advertisements in elite newspapers in Britain, North
America, Europe, Australia, and New Zealand. The expensive advertisements, usually occupying a full page of the newspaper, were
highly provocative. A frequent theme was to attack double standards
and hypocrisy in the West. The United Nations, the World Council of
Churches, and other important institutions and individuals who had
publicly opposed South African policies were excoriated in advertisements placed in papers like the *Daily Telegraph*, the *Guardian*, and the
Observer in London, the *New York Times* and the *Washington Post*,
and the *Montreal Star*. The Club of Ten had only one visible member:
a former British lawyer and writer named Gerald Sparrow. The other
members were supposed to be anonymous South African businessmen concerned with improving their country's image abroad. In fact
there was only Sparrow, placing the advertisements written by the

Information Department and paid for out of carefully laundered secret funds.[16] The campaign spurred much speculation about the membership and backing of the Club of Ten. Both Sparrow and Rhoodie publicly denied that it had any links with the South African government. Only after the bubble burst in 1978 did Sparrow admit his role as a front man in a covert campaign to sell apartheid through some of the world's most respected newspapers.

Encouraged by the success of these early operations, Rhoodie began to plan more ambitious projects. In February 1974, Rhoodie met with Vorster, Mulder, and Finance Minister Nico Diederichs to sell his idea of an extensive covert compaign. Vorster needed little persuasion. He had previously written an approving foreword to Rhoodie's book *The Paper Curtain*, which called for just such a campaign as he was proposing now. Mulder was firmly behind Rhoodie. Diederichs's assistance was essential to provide the necessary funds and to launder them through his contacts with Swiss banks. Rhoodie's pitch, he told reporters years later, was that if South Africa was to break out of its isolation it would have to act on two fronts. Internally, it would have to revise those laws and practices that affronted the dignity of the blacks. And externally it would have to establish a secret propaganda network, based on the premise that having others speak for South Africa was more effective than having the government speak for itself. Rhoodie told Vorster he wanted his approval for a propaganda war where no rules or regulations would count. Vorster agreed to Rhoodie's request for R 64 million to be spent over the next five years. Diederichs decided the money would best be channeled through the budget of the Department of Defense, which controlled enormous funds for the acquisition of arms abroad, and which was tightly shielded from public scrutiny in the interests of national security. The object of the exercise was to project a "true image" of South Africa; to counter hostile attacks from abroad; and even, if possible, to swing world opinion around in the Republic's favor. This was the start of what Les de Villiers, Rhoodie's top assistant in charge of secret projects, was to call a "masterplan for bribery, deceit and infiltration in the media, political circles, churches, labor unions, publishing houses, and every other possible avenue of influence peddling."[17]

The first major application of the department's license to undertake secret projects with government funds was aimed at a longtime enemy, the English-language press. Les de Villiers paints a vivid picture of the department's attitude toward the English newspapers in a self-serving book, *Secret Information*, written after the debacle. Invite a few Afrikaners to a social gathering and politics will soon crop up in the discussion, de Villiers writes. "Next the English-language press will be dragged in by its tail and kicked around the room in anger. After all, this is the animal that has torn the Afrikaner and his reputation to shreds ever since the days of President Paul Kruger and has never let go despite futile attempts to declaw and tame it." The Afrikaner, says de Villiers, sees the English press as "internally destructive, attempting at all times to prevent moderate blacks, Coloureds and Indians from coming to a reasonable agreement with the white, predominantly Afrikaner, government." What is more, he writes, if the world views South Africa unsympathetically through dark, distorted glasses, it must be the fault of the English-language press. The English newspapers have not only "ground, polished and tinted the lenses, but provided the basic material for the picture show, with its regular expose of 'hardships,' 'oppression,' and 'tyranny' in South Africa. Those who speak and write in English have the eager ears of the world and its media."[18]

The most outspoken of the English papers were those belonging to S.A. Associated Newspapers, particularly the *Rand Daily Mail* and the *Cape Times*, and the nationally distributed *Sunday Times*. The controlling interest in SAAN—about 40 per cent—was held by trustees of the estate of one of the founders of the group, mining magnate Abe Bailey. SAAN was not doing well financially, and the trustees wanted to get out of the newspaper business and invest their funds more profitably elsewhere. In 1968 they had offered to sell their shares to the powerful Argus company, but the move was blocked by Vorster on the grounds that it would create an undesirable monopoly. Argus did, however, later negotiate a share exchange that gave it a 33 per cent holding in SAAN. In 1975 SAAN was losing money, seemed likely to lose more, and, with its share prices dropping, seemed ripe for a takeover bid.

The offer came from an unlikely source. In October 1975, an Afrikaner millionaire, Louis Luyt, announced that he would make a bid for the entire issued share capital of SAAN for R 4.50 a share, or a total of about R 9 million. This was more than double the current trading price. Luyt had enjoyed a meteoric rise to success in South Africa. From a start as a fertilizer salesman, he had built up his own marketing company, then a fertilizer factory, and by 1975 he virtually controlled the country's fertilizer market. He was also, he said, "a Nationalist, and proud of it." Luyt was on record as saying that SAAN publications had damaged South Africa's reputation abroad through their reporting of events that got publicity overseas. So he wanted moderation: a bad international image made things difficult for a major exporter of fertilizer. Asked if SAAN papers would be more conservative under his control, he replied that he "would expect them to be a bit more to the right." There was, he said, no involvement by any political party—a claim echoed by Vorster, who said he had nothing to do with the takeover bid.[19]

The offer infuriated the South African English establishment. English papers denounced the bid as an attempt by the National party to take over the English press. The *Rand Daily Mail*, the real target of Luyt's offer, said in a front-page editorial that if he were to succeed, "a devastating blow will have been dealt to the cause of press and public freedom in South Africa and a wide range of public opinion stifled." Journalists on the SAAN papers said the takeover could spell the end of a sector of the South African press—"five newspapers, all vigorous and provocative and a leader in press opposition to the threat of a totalitarian state."[20]

Afrikaans newspapers took a very different line. *Die Burger* editorialized that from the point of view of broad South African interests, the political role of the SAAN papers over the years had been more destructive than constructive. "As a whole they are a negative factor in our affairs. Any change of control that would bring an improvement here would be in the national interest."[21]

Faced with strong opposition, Luyt increased his offer to R 6.00 a share, or three times their former market value. And he announced that he was being joined in his bid by two foreign newspaper moguls.

One was John McGoff, American publisher of a string of midwestern newspapers, who had been bitterly criticized in the United States for forcing his editors to publish articles expressing his ultraconservative views. The other was the controversial West German publisher Axel Springer. McGoff confirmed that he was negotiating with Luyt. "My interests in SAAN are basically financial," he said. "I also have a political interest. I believe you hold a key role in the future of the West. I believe your country has been badly maltreated, mainly by your own press." Although the Nationalist government previously had complained about foreign influences on the English-language press, it made no move to block Springer and McGoff from taking a 25 per cent share in SAAN if Luyt's offer succeeded. There was a further complication when Sir De Villiers Graaff, leader of the opposition United party, accounced that one of the companies he directed would join Luyt in taking over SAAN if shareholders agreed to Luyt's offer. Graaff was no friend of the SAAN papers, which for years had criticized his leadership and had pressed for a more liberal stance by the United party—a campaign that led the reform wing of the party to break away to form the Progressive party. According to Graaff, he had intervened at Luyt's invitation, so as "to guarantee press freedom in the best sense of the term and ensure that the group would not be taken over by any one political party."[22]

The offer was rejected. G. K. Lindsay, chairman of the administrators of the Bailey estate, declared that in considering any offers more than financial factors would have to be considered: "In other words, money alone is not enough." And if Luyt were allied to political Afrikaner nationalism, "then there are those who would fight to the end to make sure his hands are never placed on the levers of power in SAAN."[23] To secure the newspapers against further takeover bids, a group of businessmen set up a trust to buy a 20 per cent stake in SAAN from the Bailey interests. This, together with the Argus company's 33 per cent holding, effectively buttoned up control of the group.

Thus spurned, Luyt announced that he would start a new English paper in Johannesburg—a morning daily in direct competition with the *Rand Daily Mail* to be edited by Martin Spring, former editor of the *Financial Gazette*, and printed by Perskor.[24] The first issue of the new tabloid, *The Citizen*, appeared in September 1976. Spring's tenure as editor lasted less than two weeks. He was replaced by M. A. Johnson, who as former editor of the *Sunday Express* had backed the far-right wing of the United party, essentially the party of English-speaking Nationalists. Johnson's editorials in *The Citizen*, couched in breathless, brief sentences, occasionally criticized the Nationalists and especially the Security Police for their harassment of black militants. But for the most part *The Citizen* read like an English translation of the progovernment Afrikaans newspapers. Its front page often featured official "leaks" that portrayed the government in a favorable light. It splashed no-holds-barred investigations of allegedly anti-South African organizations like the Rockefeller Foundation. When Steve Biko, the black nationalist leader, died in police custody, *The Citizen* sought to support the government's claim that he had died as a result of a hunger strike. When an autopsy showed Biko had died of massive injuries, *The Citizen* suggested he had killed himself by banging his head against a wall.

The paper attracted little advertising. But it did appeal to some readers who objected to the liberal line of the *Rand Daily Mail* and *The Star*. Conservative white English speakers, and Afrikaners accustomed to reading an English newspaper, switched their allegiance to *The Citizen*, which was claiming a circulation of 70,000 copies daily just eighteen months after its debut.[25] Readership surveys showed that *The Citizen* was attracting almost as many white readers as the *Mail*, which had a large circulation in the black townships. *The Citizen*'s support for the National party in the elections of November 1977 helped Voster gain enough support from English speakers to win by the biggest margin in the country's history.

But the *Mail* was not taking the competition lying down. From the first announcement, despite repeated denials by Luyt, there were suggestions that *The Citizen* was getting secret support from the government. Raymond Louw, editor of the *Mail*, also distrusted *The Citizen*'s claimed circulation figures. A team of *Mail* reporters he assigned to follow the paper's distribution trucks found that up to thirty thousand copies were being dumped at a wastepaper depot and on a farm outside Johannesburg.[26] Reporters were also chasing leads on other activities thought to be linked to the Department of Information. The *Sunday Times* and the *Sunday Express*, both SAAN stable-mates of the *Mail*, each had investigative reporters digging for dirt. But fear of prosecution under the Official Secrets Act, and other pressures, prevented them from publishing anything specific at first. There were good reasons to be cautious. In 1974 *Rapport* had run a story suggesting that there were hidden links between the Department of Information and *To the Point* magazine. The report was picked up by *Beeld* and by the *Sunday Express*. Rhoodie reacted violently. He hauled the newspapers before the Press Council and swore under oath that he and the Information Department had no connection with the magazine. The newspapers were found guilty of contravening the code, assessed with heavy fines, and ordered to print a retraction and an apology. Vorster and Mulder, who knew the reports were true, made no effort to intervene.

The first break in the case, however, was not related to the Information Department's media activities. Rumors of careless spending by department officials led to an audit of its books by the state auditor general, Gerald Barrie. Rhoodie tried to block the audit, on the grounds that the department's activities were covered by the Official Secrets Act. When that failed, he ordered his deputies to destroy sensitive documents relating to its secret funds. The auditor's report, presented to Parliament in February 1978, criticized unnamed officials of the department for taking unnecessary and extravagant trips abroad. In April the *Sunday Express* ran a front-page report on a trip taken by Rhoodie, his family, and an entourage of ten people to the Seychelles at government expense. Shortly thereafter, the *Express* obtained a secret report to the prime minister from the auditor general, severely critical of "irregularities" in the department's spending. The *Express* agreed to a request by Mulder to delay publication for a week while he investigated aspects "touching on the interests of the state." Rhoodie, tipped off by Mulder, went on the offensive. He issued a statement accusing the auditor general of destroying secret operations financed by the department. The propaganda war, he said, was overseen by a three-man cabinet committee who approved secret projects. In the report the *Express* was about to publish, said Rhoodie, the auditor general referred to irregularities he described as unique in civil service history. "This is correct," said

Rhoodie, "only in the sense that the country has never yet been fighting an equally no-holds-barred propaganda war against its enemies in which normal rules cannot be applied." Two days later Vorster revealed to Parliament that funds allocated for "combating the psychological and propaganda onslaughts against the Republic" had been channeled to the Information Department through other departments. "The purpose was to withstand the subversion of our country's good image and stability." It was clear, said Vorster, that the effectiveness of the department had been destroyed by the allegations of misuse of funds. He announced that the department would be restructured and that Rhoodie would retire on pension. Later in the debate Mulder, responding to strong criticisms, told Parliament that "the Department of Information owns no newspaper in South Africa and runs no newspaper in South Africa. The Department of Information and the Government do not give funds to *The Citizen*."[27]

The *Rand Daily Mail*, meanwhile, had sent a reporter to Europe to track down rumors of Information Department activities there. Gerald Sparrow, figurehead of the Club of Ten in London, had by then become disenchanted with the South African government. He sold his story to the *Mail* for nine hundred pounds, detailing how he had been recruited by Rhoodie to place pro–South African advertisements in the world's leading newspapers.[28] But he failed to back up his story with documentary evidence, and the iceberg of which his operation was but one tip remained concealed.

The *Sunday Express* and the *Mail* meanwhile continued to investigate *The Citizen*. Both carried reports alleging that it had been financed by public money channeled through secret government funds. But they lacked proof, until it was provided by a totally unexpected source. A Supreme Court judge, Anton Mostert, had been appointed a one-man commission to investigate possible violations of the country's foreign exchange control regulations. In the process he stumbled upon funds laundered through European banks to pay for the Information Department's schemes. Mostert took statements from several people connected with the department and discovered that large sums of money from secret funds had been used to finance *The Citizen*. Luyt himself appeared before Mostert and revealed how he, Mulder, Rhoodie, and others had plotted to buy out

SAAN and, when that failed, had launched *The Citizen*.[29] Mostert, despite heavy pressure from the government, revealed at a press conference that he had uncovered evidence of "the improper application of taxpayers' money running into millions of rands; moreover, there are indications from the same sources of corruption in the widest sense of the world, relating to public funds."[30] He then released the documentary evidence.

Mostert's revelations hit the country like a bombshell. "IT'S ALL TRUE," the *Mail* trumpeted in huge type across the top of page one on November 3, 1978. Luyt's evidence implicated Mulder, Vorster, and van den Bergh as key figures in the secret project to finance *The Citizen*. According to the evidence given by Luyt before Mostert, and by Luyt and others before the subsequent Erasmus commission of inquiry into irregularities in the Information Department, Mulder and Rhoodie had become convinced that tremendous harm was being done to South Africa by reporting and comment in the English-language papers. Mulder and Rhoodie pointed out that in addition to reports sent abroad, thousands of immigrants and tourists in South Africa were totally dependent on the English papers for their evaluation of the situation there. The two men believed, said the commission, that there were only two alternatives to counter these problems: either press censorship or the establishment of an English-language daily paper that would "print the objective facts to English-speakers objectively." Mulder's view, said the commission, was that "the eventual cost to the state of *The Citizen* was in a sense the price South Africa had to pay to avoid press censorship."[31]

At the beginning that price was estimated at about R 8 million. Rhoodie granted Luyt a loan of R 12 million that he invested in his Triomf Fertilizer company, which paid the interest to a subsidiary company, S.A. Today. This interest was intended to finance *The Citizen*. The amount proved totally inadequate to meet the costs; by the time the Erasmus Commission looked into its finances, the paper had cost the taxpayers about R 32 million.

The function of the new paper was made quite explicit in one of the documents released by Mostert, an "editorial charter," signed by Luyt and by Rhoodie in April 1976, providing for total editorial control of *The Citizen* by the Department of Information. It stipulated that the paper would not publish anything that would endanger the political, social, or economic position of the white population, or publish anything that would endanger the constitutionally chosen government, and would strive for the preservation of the identity and political authority of the whites. The paper, said the charter, "supports the broad objectives of the present elected government in respect of separate political development of the black and white populations of the Republic, as well as the Republic's anti-communist and security legislation." The Erasmus Commission, commenting on the charter and on issues of *The Citizen* that appeared during the 1977 election campaign, said it "could come to no other conclusion than that it was the intention that the newspaper should support the party policy in regard to separate development of the ruling political party."[32]

All this was gleefully carried by the newspapers, despite attempts by the government to prevent publication. Just hours after Mostert's press conference, the prime minister issued a note to editors over the wires of the South African Press Association warning them that by the terms of the Commissions Act the evidence could not be published. Mostert disagreed, and every major newspaper in the country, English and Afrikaans, ignored the injunction and splashed the story. Port Elizabeth's *Evening Post*, for example, ran its report under a huge headline, "LIES, LIES, LIES." The outstanding exception was the SABC. It mentioned in an afternoon news bulletin that Mostert had held a press conference and had alleged corruption in high places. But those who tuned in to the main evening news bulletins heard no word of one of the most sensational news stories of the decade. The Afrikaans press was, if anything, even more indignant than the English. *Beeld* called for the dismissal of those responsible for the scandal: "Their immediate departure from public life would certainly not be enough, but an essential first step." *Die Transvaler* said it was essential to deal with an "iron hand" with those who had so grievously abused the nation's confidence.[33]

But even before Mostert's revelations, the political repercussions had begun. In September 1978, two months before Mostert's press conference, Vorster had announced that he was stepping down as prime minister after twelve years in office and would be available for election to the largely ceremonial post of state president. Cynics suspected he was trying to duck responsibility for the Muldergate affair before determined digging by the press revealed his complicity since, by law, state presidents are shielded from public criticism. Mulder, as the powerful leader of the National party in the Transvaal, the traditional launching ground for Nationalist prime ministers, was the front-runner to take over as premier, even though he had been under attack for his supervision of the department since the critical report of the auditor general. But although he had been "cleared" of any wrongdoing by a Vorster-ordered audit by the Security Police, the Nationalist caucus, alerted by insiders that more irregularities would be revealed, rejected Mulder by a narrow margin. It chose instead P. W. Botha, minister of defense and leader of the National party in the Cape Province.

Mostert's revelations put severe pressure on Botha, who in his inaugural speech as premier had promised a "clean and honest administration." Now Mulder, his rival and still a member of his cabinet, stood accused by Luyt and others of lying to Parliament about his involvement in *The Citizen.* Faced with demands from all sections to expose the full extent of the malpractices uncovered by Mostert and the press, Botha appointed a three-man commission under the chairmanship of Justice Rudolf Erasmus to investigate and report to Parliament. Meanwhile, Mostert announced his intention of taking more testimony—and in public hearings—on the activities of the Information Department. Botha promptly dismissed Mostert, saying he was exceeding his authority and would be duplicating the work of the Erasmus Commission. That same day, November 7, 1978, Mulder was forced by the disclosures to resign from the cabinet and later from the leadership of the party in the Transvaal. Rhoodie, earlier forced to retire by Vorster in his attempts to put a lid on the scandal, fled overseas.

The Erasmus Commission presented its first report to Parliament in December 1978. It confirmed press charges that the department had grossly misused public funds. It said there were "irrebuttable indications of large-scale irregularities and exploitation of the secret fund" and gave details of some of the wasteful expenditures. Rhoodie, for example, regularly drew large sums of cash from the secret fund to pay "anonymous collaborators." But no vouchers were filed to show that the money was in fact paid out. The commission was strongly critical of the use of government funds to launch and sustain *The Citizen*. It singled out Mulder, Rhoodie, and van den Bergh for special blame. Mulder was accused of acting irregularly by lending Luyt R 12 million to start the paper; of being lax and negligent in giving Rhoodie unlimited discretion in dealing with public funds; and of exercising "improper pressure on others in order to secure favorable results for himself." The commission found Rhoodie guilty of neglect of his duty and of gross negligence. Rhoodie's orders to destroy documents, the commission said, were "an attempt to conceal irregularities pointing to fraud and theft." It criticized Van den Bergh for being an "enthusiastic participant" in Mulder's and Rhoodie's schemes. The commission recommended that Rhoodie and his brother, Denys, who had served as his deputy in the department, be investigated on charges of fraud and theft. But it absolved both Vorster and Botha of blame, suggesting that the secret projects, including *The Citizen*, had been undertaken by Rhoodie and Mulder without their knowledge or consent. The only criticism that could be leveled against Vorster, the commission said, was failing to take steps to get rid of *The Citizen* once he became aware of its secret funding. In the commission's opinion, however, "his integrity is unblemished."[34]

The commission also corroborated the evidence given before Mostert about subsequent developments concerning *The Citizen*. Within six months of its appearance, Luyt and Rhoodie had fallen out over Luyt's use of the funds loaned to him to start the paper, and over Rhoodie's attempts to influence its content. It was turned over to the two other front men for the department, Jan van Zyl Alberts and Jussen, in February 1978. The agreement was that the department would continue to fund it for two years, after which they could try to run it for their own profit. After the disclosures, the paper was sold to Perskor for the discounted price of the press it owned. By this time it was on the verge of breaking even, and Perskor obtained virtually as a giveaway a paper whose start-up costs had been covered by taxpayers to the tune of R 32 million.

In August 1979, Rhoodie was extradited to South Africa from France and tried and convicted on charges of fraud. He was sentenced to six years in prison for using part of the secret funds for his own purposes. The conviction was overturned by the appeals court a year later, and Rhoodie emigrated to the United States.

If the government expected that the Erasmus Commission report would end the rumors and investigations, it was mistaken. The newspapers dug up new leads, in South Africa and abroad, suggesting that the Information Department's activities extended far beyond funding of *To the Point* and *The Citizen*. More important, those who had taken the major share of the blame for the debacle—Mulder and Rhoodie—were determined that the Erasmus Commission's exoneration of Vorster should not go unchallenged. The public too was determined that the top man should not escape censure. Van den Bergh was openly contemptuous of the commission's report. He called it a farce and said it contained blatant lies. Rhoodie, in exile and on the run, was threatening to reveal all he knew if he were taken back to South Africa and prosecuted.[35] He got in touch with van den Bergh, saying that he had recorded all he knew about the secret projects on forty-one tapes that were hidden in Europe and would be released if anything happened to him. Van den Bergh flew to Europe to see Rhoodie and struck a deal. Rhoodie, in exchange for keeping his mouth shut, would be given employment by a rich South African businessman, and van den Bergh would intercede with the government on his behalf. But Botha rejected the idea.

Meanwhile Rhoodie was tracked down in South America by *Rand Daily Mail* reporters Mervyn Rees and Chris Day. He confirmed all they knew and revealed details of other secret projects besides. In interviews with the *Mail* team, and with reporters from British media, Rhoodie asserted that Vorster had known all along about *The Citizen* and other secret schemes, and had formed an unofficial three-man committee with Mulder and Finance Minister Owen Horwood to supervise the operations.[36] One of the articles the *Mail* reporters filed quoted Rhoodie as saying that the minister of justice, James Kruger, had been aware of *The Citizen* project. The *Mail* called Kruger for comment on the allegation. He responded by obtaining an injunction at midnight from the Supreme Court. A court official telephoned the *Mail* and demanded that it delete several paragraphs referring to Kruger from its front-page story.[37] The paper's final edition appeared with six inches of white space on page one. The restraining order was later set aside by the court, which found that the reference to Kruger was not defamatory and ordered that he personally pay the court costs since he had filed the suit in his personal capacity. The judge took a strongly liberal line. "Matters of government policy," he said, "may be freely criticized and condemned even if such criticism and condemnation is unfounded and unfair."[38] Nevertheless, police later called at the offices of the *Cape Times*, which picked up the *Mail*'s report, and told the editor they were investigating criminal charges against the newspaper.

Mulder, forced by the scandal to resign also from his parliamentary seat, fought back too. He gave the press precise dates and times when he had discussed with Vorster the Information Department's projects. Vorster, in an unprecedented move for a state president, issued a statement without consulting the government. He called Rhoodie a liar and denied that he had discussed the projects in advance with Mulder. Mulder, in turn, issued a press statement calling the state president a liar. Meanwhile, the Erasmus Commission, working on a supplementary report, specifically was instructed by Botha to investigate whether any cabinet members had known of irregularities in the Information Department before the facts were made public. The commission, too, tried to stop the *Mail* and the *Cape Times* from printing further disclosures by Rhoodie until it had completed its investigations. The commission's application for a restraining order was rejected by the Supreme Court in Johannesburg.

The supplemental report was published in June 1979, and Botha told a stunned Parliament that Vorster had resigned as state president. The commission, reversing its earlier finding, accused Vorster of giving false evidence before it and of complicity in covering up misspending of the secret funds. "For more than a year," the report said, "Vorster, together with Dr. Mulder, kept his knowledge of irregularities in the administration of the country from his cabinet colleagues, at a time when the Press and the Opposition were already making serious insinuations and accusations of maladministration against the government." Discussing why Vorster had kept the facts from the cabinet, the report said Rhoodie had blackmailed him, threatening to bring down the government if action were taken against him. The commission cleared Botha and Finance Minister Horwood of blame. It said Botha had objected from the start to the secret funds.[39]

The supplementary report also detailed a large number of projects undertaken by the Information Department, most of which had already been reported piecemeal in the press. The major scheme disclosed in the report was an audacious attempt to buy control of the *Washington Star*, using McGoff, the conservative American publisher, as front man. Early in 1979 the *Mail* and the *Sunday Express* had revealed that McGoff, together with Rhoodie, Mulder, and other Information Department figures, owned shares in a large farm in the Transvaal—a farm they equipped with a helicopter pad so that Mulder could use it as his "Camp David" when he became prime minister.

McGoff owned six daily papers in Michigan and Illinois and more than forty weekly papers and radio stations. He had visited South Africa in 1968 at the invitation of Les de Villiers of the Information Department. During his visit, said the commission, he "discovered an affinity with South Africa and her people, which he cultivated further." De Villiers testified to the commission that when the Information Department wanted to get a message across to Americans, McGoff would send the article to his editors and say, "Look, this article has to be published." And it would be. McGoff was helpful in other ways. Mulder visited the United States in May 1971, and through McGoff's good offices was able to meet Vice-President Gerald Ford and other influential Americans. In addition to backing the Information Department's bid to take over SAAN, as previously mentioned, he helped the department arrange seminars for American businessmen that stressed the folly of disinvesting in South Africa. Meanwhile he was enjoying a life-style more affluent than the precarious financial condition of his newspaper chain would seem to justify. He had the use of a luxurious beach house in Miami, and a hundred-foot yacht.

In 1974 McGoff told South African officials that the *Washington Star* was in financial trouble and could be bought. The opportunity held considerable attraction for South Africa. As de Villiers told the Erasmus Commission, the *Washington Star*'s influence extended throughout the United States. If it were to adopt a supportive line toward South Africa, this would help to offset the hostility of the *Washington Post* and the *New York Times*. McGoff thought he could buy the *Washington Star* for about $25 million. He wanted South Africa to contribute $10 million, saying he could raise the rest. The money was transferred from the South African Defense Department's special account to Thesaurus Continental Securities Corporation, a shell company used for laundering secret funds. Thesaurus in turn transferred the money to McGoff, making it look like a legal loan from the bank. Representatives of the *Washington Star*, however, were not impressed by McGoff's financial credentials, and sold the paper to a Texas millionaire. Later, McGoff spent $6 million of the South African loan to buy the *Sacramento Union*, and used the balance to run the paper.[40] But Mulder and Rhoodie, who had expected McGoff to invest only the interest on the loan to buy the California paper, needed the money to cover the losses they were incurring on *The Citizen*. At a meeting in Montreal in September 1976, they told McGoff to sell the *Union*. But McGoff had become involved in a lawsuit with the owners of the rival *Sacramento Bee*, which he accused of antitrust violations. He was subpoenaed to appear in court in August 1979 to testify whether he had used South African funds to buy the *Union*. Minutes before he was due to take the stand, McGoff dropped his suit, thus avoiding having to answer questions about the purchase.[41] He eventually sold the paper and returned about $5 million of the $10 million loan to Thesaurus. The rest of the debt, including interest, was written off by South Africa.

The California newspaper was not McGoff's only investment on behalf of the Information Department. According to the Erasmus Commission, South Africa gave him $1.7 million in secret funds in 1975 to buy 50 per cent of UPITN, the world's second-largest producer and distributor of television newsfilm, serving more than a hundred clients in eighty countries. The company was owned by Paramount Films, which held a 50 per cent share, and by United Press International and Britain's Independent Television Network, which had 25 per cent each. McGoff used the South African funds to buy Paramount's share in his own name, but he assured de Villiers that "I realize that I represent you in the company." McGoff became chairman of the board and appointed half the directors. The intention was to distribute pro–South African newsfilm from the SABC television service through UPITN. After the Erasmus Commission disclosures, however, McGoff's share in UPITN was bought by Independent Television News, which was disturbed by McGoff's financing.

Yet another joint venture between McGoff and the Information Department involved a printing company, Xanap, that he set up in South Africa in 1974. McGoff's associate in this was Jan van Zyl Alberts, who was as previously mentioned a leading figurehead for the Information Department and, like van den Bergh, a close friend of Vorster. All three had spent time in a concentration camp during the Second World War for their pro-Nazi sympathies. One of Alberts's companies, Afri-Comics, was given secret funds by the government to publish comics featuring a black Superman who supported separate development in South Africa. The comics were printed by Xanap.

The Erasmus Commission's disclosures brought McGoff some unwelcome attention. Both the United States Justice Department and the Securities and Exchange Commission began to look into his dealings with South Africa. The SEC was concerned with allegations that McGoff had failed to disclose that the South African government was helping to finance his media acquisitions. In September 1983 the SEC obtained a permanent federal court injunction prohibiting McGoff and his Global Communications corporation from falsifying any filings with the regulatory agency. In effect McGoff avoided a court battle by agreeing not to violate SEC rules in the future, but did not admit or deny that he had done so in the past. In late 1983 he was, however, still being investigated by a federal grand jury that was looking into allegations that he had acted illegally as an unregistered agent of the South African government.[42]

In 1980 McGoff sold most of his newspaper holdings and sought a new career in the travel and recreation business. But although McGoff had failed in his attempt to buy the *Washington Star* with South African money, he still appeared to have some influence on Washington media. After the *Star* folded in 1981 a new newspaper, the *Washington Times*, was launched by the Rev. Sun Myung Moon's Unification Church in 1982. The paper is a forum for some of the most conservative writers in the United States. The editor of the *Washing-*

ton Times, James R. Whelan, had previously worked for McGoff as editorial director of Panax Newspapers, and as editor of the *Sacramento Union* that McGoff bought with secret South African funds. And in 1983 McGoff was a member of the editorial advisory board of the *Washington Times.*

The disclosures in the South African press and the Erasmus Commission reports spurred extensive digging into the Information Department's activities in Africa, Europe, and the United States. Top investigative reporters on newspapers and magazines like *Newsweek,* the *New York Times,* the *Nation,* the *Columbia Journalism Review,* the *Guardian,* the *Observer,* and *Le Canard Enchaîné* discovered that the department's tentacles had penetrated dozens of countries. The United States seems to have been a priority target. Some department activities were aboveboard. In 1974 South Africa hired a Washington lobbyist, Donald de Kieffer, and in 1976 added the New York public relations firm of Sydney S. Baron for an annual fee of $365,000.[43] The firm's budget for its pro–South Africa work was doubled in 1977 to $650,000. Les de Villiers, Rhoodie's top aide in charge of secret projects, left the department to join Sydney Baron in New York soon after the contract was increased. Between them, Sydney Baron and de Kieffer were paid at least $3 million. Both made regular reports to the Justice Department about their activities on behalf of a foreign client. Among the projects Baron funded was a series of conferences on investment in South Africa for American businessmen. Gerald Ford was paid $10,000 to address one of them.

However, other attempts by South Africa to buy influence in the United States were more covert. Rhoodie, in a summary distributed to potential buyers of the tapes he had made concerning the department's secret operations, alleged that South Africa had secretly funneled $250,000 to a successful campaign to unseat Senator Dick Clark of Iowa in the 1978 elections. As chairman of the Senate Foreign Relations Subcommittee on Africa, Clark had been an influential critic of U.S. policy toward the Republic. Another $150,000 had been used to help defeat California Senator John Tunney, who had opposed United States aid to South Africa and UNITA during the 1975 Angolan war. South African newspapers reported that almost $4 million had been channeled into Ford's 1976 presidential campaign.

Rhoodie said also that he had given more than $100,000 to American trade union leaders to dissuade them from joining an international week of action against South Africa. The people who were alleged to have benefited from this largesse denied receiving South African funds. But the funds could have been channeled through third parties, making them difficult to trace.

Yet another approach adopted by the department was to encourage American congressmen, businessmen, journalists, and other opinion leaders to visit South Africa, all expenses paid. Since federal law prohibits members of Congress from accepting gifts from foreign governments, Rhoodie set up front organizations to fund the junkets. One was the Foreign Affairs Association, established in 1975. According to the Erasmus Commission report, the FAA was "to represent itself as an academic body doing research, which was to be financially independent of the State and the Department." Apart from publishing books, said the report, the FAA's function was "to invite Americans, especially American politicians, to the Republic to get a better picture of the country." The FAA was headed by Casper F. de Villiers, who the Erasmus Commission said was more interested in living sumptuously and in chasing women around Europe than in tending its affairs.[44] The organization was disbanded in 1978 after its cover was blown. Another front organization active in bringing Americans and others to South Africa was the Institute for the Study of Plural Societies. It was set up as part of the Department of Sociology at the University of Pretoria—a department that happened to be headed by Rhoodie's brother, Professor Nic Rhoodie. Like the FAA, the institute was secretly funded by the Information Department to do research for publications and to arrange conferences—all aimed at boosting the image of the Republic abroad. The Erasmus Commission found that there had been "nothing irregular" in the institute's activities, but recommended that they be continued overtly, instead of secretly. Two other organizations active in this field were the South African Foundation and the South Africa Freedom Foundation, both of which sponsored visits to the Republic by influential Americans.

Although the United States appears to have been the primary target of the Information Department's covert campaign, it was active also in Britain, Europe, and Japan. The most prominent front organization in London was the Club of Ten. But there were other devious projects as well. In 1975 the Information Department tried, through covert means, to buy the influential magazine *West Africa* from the Daily Mirror group. When news of the South African involvement broke in the British press, the magazine's entire staff walked out, and the bid failed.

A more successful operation involved the purchase, through a front organization, of a major shareholding in the British publishing company Morgan Grampian.[45] The publishing house owned a stable of magazines in Europe, as well as Britain's most prestigious medical and engineering journals, and the successful women's magazine *Over 21*. The front man in the Morgan Grampian deal was from a very different background from that of most of those involved in the Information Department's schemes. David Abrahamson was a well-known Johannesburg businessman and a leading member of the opposition Progressive Federal party. He had made a fortune running a mutual fund during the stock market boom of the late 1960s. Through his business dealings he had become acquainted with Finance Minister Diederichs—a useful contact when he needed permission from the Reserve Bank to transfer funds out of South Africa. Abrahamson wanted to buy into Morgan Grampian. He approached van den Bergh, who introduced him to Rhoodie and Mulder. Rhoodie jumped at the chance of getting an interest in the company, whose publications could serve as a conduit for pro-South African information to the British elite. Rhoodie's plan, he explained later, was to use the company to buy up a string of newspapers and magazines, including possibly the *Daily Telegraph* and the *Observer*.[46] The Information Department gave Abrahamson an interest-free loan of $4.6 million, laundered through a company registered in Bermuda. Abrahamson used the money to buy a 20 per cent interest in Morgan Grampian. Rhoodie advanced a further $1.5 million to buy more shares, and by November 1976 Abrahmason and his associate Stuart Pegg had a 27 per cent interest in the company. There is no indication that the South African connection influenced material in the Morgan Grampian publication, and before Abrahamson and Pegg could consolidate their control another British company, Trafalgar House, offered to buy their shares in Morgan Grampian at a substantial profit. They sold their shares for $10 million, with half of the $4 million profit going to the Information Department, which used it to keep *The Citizen* afloat. Abrahamson and Pegg pocketed $1 million each.

The following year, Abrahamson tried to buy the influential British financial publication, the *Investors Chronicle*. But its owners, the *Financial Times* and the Mirror Group, were warned of the South African connection and pulled out of the deal. He then bought a 50 per cent share in a smaller version of the *Investors Chronicle* called the *Investors Review*, apparently with the intention of turning it into a pro-gold, pro–South African publication.

Similar efforts were being made in Europe, with France and Germany as particularly important targets. In France, the Information Department gained control of a weekly journal, *France Eurafrique*, and of a Paris firm that published travel magazines, including the holiday magazine *Vacances*. Attempts to buy the well-known journals *Paris Match* and *L'Express* failed. Large sums were funneled into a pro–South African organization, the French Institute of Studies of the Contemporary World, and into the French–South Africa Association.

The department is reported to have spent $60,000 to help finance a newspaper that supported a right-wing Norwegian politician, Anders Lange, who visited South Africa at the department's expense in 1972.[47] His party won four seats in the Norwegian parliament, giving the Republic its only sympathetic political voice in Scandinavia. The party collapsed after Lange's death. In Germany, the department spent more than $1 million on junkets for journalists, and on support for the German-Afrikaans Association. In Japan, departmental funds were channeled to two members of the Japanese Diet who were influential with trade union leaders. Other organizations it funded in Europe and black Africa were not directly concerned with media, and are beyond the scope of this study.

While most of this activity was aimed at influencing public opinion abroad, the Information Department also was active inside South Africa, as *The Citizen* and the *To the Point* projects demonstrate. Abrahamson and Pegg used government funds, laundered through a complicated maze of foreign bank accounts, to buy control of South Africa's biggest firm of commercial printers, Hortors. The department also launched a magazine, *Pace*, aimed at black readers.

Another secret domestic project involved an elaborate scheme to control the manufacture and distribution of films intended for black audiences.[48]

A memorandum sent by Mulder to Finance Minister Horwood in 1974, and revealed in *The Star* in 1981, provided a blueprint for the creation of a Bantu film industry. Marked "top secret," the memorandum stated that the cabinet had already consented to the use of funds to make films that would "promote the government's policy of self-development." The Department of Information would control the funds, and "also exercise an ideological control over the project." The memorandum is revealing also in that it explicitly sets out the role of the SABC in internal propaganda. Execution of the film project, said the memorandum, would be done in consultation with the SABC, because the new film industry could "play a valuable role in the eventual Bantu television service." To carry out the policy of separate development, it said, "the idea of multi-nationalism must be conveyed to the different Bantu population groups. Therefore not only must new communications channels be created to these groups, but the channels must be placed under proper control." The memorandum pointed out that three of the most important channels are radio, television, and film: "The first two are, or will be, effectively controlled by the SABC and the giant success of Radio Bantu is generally known." Now the same control was to be exercised over films. Mulder suggested that no film project—production, distribution, building of theaters, or screening rights—be granted without prior consultation with Rhoodie. "In a nutshell," he wrote, "we must in the first place organize an effective control over film show facilities . . . by means of front organizations."[49]

The idea, as Rhoodie later explained to *Rand Daily Mail* reporters, was to combine censorship and indoctrination. Concerned that South African blacks were becoming Americanized by watching "B-grade" movies, the department planned to counteract that influence by creating local black heroes. Showing them in action against an ethnic background would help put across the idea of separate development. Rhoodie's front man in this exercise was South African film producer André Pieterse. He was given R 825,000 in secret funds to establish a black film industry, including a chain of theaters, in South Africa. The project was delayed by bureaucratic indecision, however, and

Pieterse began work on a private commercial film, *Golden Rendez-vous*. When that ran into financial difficulties, Pieterse used the Information Department funds as security for loans to pay his debts. It was, said the Erasmus Commission report, "an example of the ill-considered manner in which money in the secret fund was expended."

The Information Department's links with the SABC went beyond using it to complement its propaganda activities. In 1981 Kitt Katzin, the *Sunday Express* reporter who broke many of the Muldergate stories, revealed that the SABC has received secret state funds over a period of several years. Rhoodie told the *Express* that he had paid the SABC "hundreds of thousands" for several undercover propaganda projects. Rhoodie described the broadcasting corporation as being "quite simply, an Information front." He said he made the disclosures because the SABC had refused to accept TV advertisements for a book he was writing about the Information Department.[50] SABC officials at first strenuously denied receiving the funds. But Minister of Information R. F. Botha, in reply to formal questions in Parliament, admitted that the SABC had been given a total of R 840,000 in secret funds—of which R 365,000 came from the Information Department. This was in addition to the R 81 million in subsidies paid to the SABC by the state for its external services between 1969 and 1979. The money, the SABC said, was used to provide audio news and magazine programs to foreign radio organizations. It appears, however, that some of the money was used to fund a joint secret project involving the Information Department, the Department of Defense, and the SABC. It involved setting up a counterinformation radio station that operated from a South African navy ship off the coast of South West Africa/Namibia. Purporting to be a voice of the South West Africa Peoples Organization (SWAPO), it sought to demoralize Cuban forces working with SWAPO and to build up the morale of local blacks.

As in the case of Watergate, the Muldergate scandal was forced into the open largely as a result of aggressive digging by the press. Much of the credit lies with the English newspapers. Allister Sparks, editor of the *Rand Daily Mail*, and Rex Gibson, editor of the *Sunday Express*, both received awards as "International Editor of the Year" from the

Overseas Press Club in the United States. Kitt Katzin of the *Sunday Express* won South Africa's top journalism award. But the Afrikaans press also played a significant role in investigating and exposing the story. This was not the case when the English papers first began their exposé. The Afrikaans editors tended to stand back, suspicious that it was simply another attempt by the opposition newspapers to embarrass and discredit the government. They reported with approval the steps Vorster took to clean up the mess, including disbanding the Information Department and shunting Rhoodie into retirement. But once the scandal was documented by Judge Mostert, and by the Erasmus Commission, they became as fierce in their criticism as the English papers.

Part of the reason for this was a sense of betrayal. Afrikaners have a strong respect for authority, especially when it is associated with political power. And however misguided and narrow Afrikaner leaders may appear to outsiders, they have always been respected for their sincerity and honesty. Corruption and graft in high places were considered typical of the rulers of developing countries to the north, not of a government of God-fearing Calvinists. Now it was evident that these leaders, like politicians elsewhere, could lie, deceive, and perhaps line their own pockets. So the Afrikaners were incensed. Thus *Die Transvaler*, mouthpiece of the National party in the Transvaal, complained in a front-page editorial about the "amazing abuse of power." And the party organ in the Free State, *Die Volksblad*, demanded that "this festering sore . . . be rooted out without sparing any person's name, position, status or personal relationship." Eventually the Afrikaans papers were to turn against even the revered and respected John Vorster, who for twelve years had led the country as prime minister before becoming state president. When Mulder, infuriated at being made the scapegoat for the Information debacle, revealed that Vorster and other members of the cabinet had known all along about the secret projects, *Rapport* carried his statement under a huge front-page headline, "MULDER: VORSTER LIES." As Les de Villiers put it, the Afrikaans press, once alerted, "found themselves not following but leading the English-language press and their supporters in carrying Mulder, Rhoodie and the others to the stake."[51]

A second reason for the aggressive probing by the Afrikaans papers had to do with political and commercial factors. The Information Department scandal became a major issue in the struggle for power between the Transvaal and the Cape wings of the National party, supported respectively by the Perskor newspapers and the Nasionale Pers papers. Mulder at the time was the leader of the party in the Transvaal, and a director of Perskor. P. W. Botha, minister of defense and Mulder's chief rival for the premiership vacated by Vorster, was leader of the party in the Cape, and had the support of Nasionale Pers. This rivalry, and the political infighting that ensued, meant that the Afrikaans papers, instead of closing ranks and ignoring the story, which would have made it easier for the government to stifle the English papers, were in the forefront in reporting it. In addition, there was cutthroat competition between Perskor's Johannesburg daily, *Die Transvaler*, and *Beeld*, started by Nasionale Pers in Johannesburg in 1974 to capture a share of the lucrative and politically important Transvaal market. Neither could afford to sit back while the other captured readers with stories that were political dynamite.

In at least one instance, the Afrikaans papers were even more daring in probing a highly sensitive matter than their English counterparts. One of the still unresolved mysteries that may be linked to the Information Department is the murder of Robert Smit, a brilliant economist, and his wife. Smit was a National party candidate in the 1977 elections. But he was rumored to have discovered, perhaps through his service as South Africa's representative on the International Monetary Fund, that gold bullion was being smuggled out of the country to finance the secret projects. It was rumored also that he planned to go public with his findings. But Smit and his wife were brutally murdered before the election, and before the story broke. Several Afrikaans papers openly linked the Smit murders to Muldergate. *Rapport* was hauled before the Press Council for suggesting, in a carefully worded story, that there was some connection. The crime reporter who wrote the story later had his police press credentials withdrawn. A reporter for *Beeld* wrote a secret memorandum to her editor about the Smit murders, and was charged in court to give the source of her information, even though the story had not been published. She refused, and the editor of *Beeld* accused the police of tapping the newspaper's telephones and planting a spy in his office.

The Afrikaans papers were not alone in being subjected to pressure of this kind. Kitt Katzin of the *Sunday Express* was ordered by a court to reveal his sources for a report that Smit had been killed by two hired German hitmen. Editors all over the country, and even parliamentary correspondents in Cape Town, were interrogated by police.

Shaken to its foundations by the revelations, the government moved to prevent any further publication of allegations of state corruption and maladministration. In May 1979 the government introduced into Parliament its Advocate General Bill. It proposed to create the post of advocate general to investigate any allegations of bribery or corruption. It proposed that no newspaper be allowed to report about such matters without the prior permission of the advocate general. It said that if anyone suspected that state moneys were being misapplied, he should bring it to the attention of the advocate general who would, if necessary, refer the matter to the police. Anyone who went ahead and published such allegations without permission would be liable to a fine of R 5,000, or a year in jail, or both. If the bill had been in force a year earlier, the Information Department scandal might never have come to light, and Mulder, van den Bergh, and Rhoodie would have been running the country.

The "Press Gag Bill," as it came to be known, set off a storm of protest in the press, both Afrikaans and English. Faced with this united opposition, the government backed down. It dropped the most contentious sections of the bill, including the restrictions on reporting. But the idea was retained in an attempt to control any similar investigations in future. And Prime Minister Botha warned journalists to make sure that their reports were accurate, or he would take steps to discipline them.

Despite the threats and intimidation, however, it is significant that the press was in fact permitted to pursue the story even though the result was serious embarrassment to the government. And in virtually every instance where government attempts to restrain publication resulted in court action, the courts sided with the newspapers. As Stephen Mulholland of the *Sunday Times* noted, it is fair to say that "if South Africa can let it all hang out this way, it can rightly claim that it is not, racial matters aside, a totalitarian state even if it is an authoritarian one."[52]

11 | Changing Media in a Changing South Africa

The Republic of South Africa, with its deep divisions and racial tensions, is in the early 1980s a dynamic and changing society. Among the black majority, the powerful influences of demographic change, increasing urbanization, continued industrialization, rising personal income, and spreading education and literacy are affecting all facets of the society, including mass communication. The press and other media, quite independently of the pressures from the Nationalist government, have been undergoing far-reaching modifications in their content, the nature and size of their audiences, and their relationships with each other.

What future changes the media may go through will be shaped in part by political events and shifts as they have in the past. The South African political system is itself unstable, with almost every major political faction—the ruling Nationalists, the moderate Progressive Federal party, and the outlawed African National Congress—advocating sweeping, albeit different, changes in the political structure. And the Afrikaner ultra-right-wingers—the new National Conservative party and the Herstigte Nasionale party—by stubbornly urging maintenance of the status quo in such a volatile political environment, might be offering the most radical political program of all.

Mass media in South Africa traditionally have been produced primarily by and for the white elite. The earliest newspapers, the first radio services, and television when it was introduced in 1976 were directed at whites. Other population groups, in the early stages of

262

each medium, were essentially eavesdroppers. That has changed.
Today the bulk of newspaper readers and radio listeners are African,
Coloured, or Indian. There still are more whites who watch television, but that too is changing. Special newspapers are directed at the
different population groups. There are separate radio and television
channels for blacks. A large proportion of the readers of even those
publications directed primarily at white audiences are drawn from
other population groups. This growing diversity of media audiences is
a major reason for the government's determination to control their
content. Black publications that venture into active politics are likely
to be suppressed. And English-language newspapers, with their large
black readerships, likewise must be curbed. In a land of segregated
schools, suburbs, churches, and colleges, the English newspapers are
one of the few experiences the diverse groups have in common. And
therein lies their vulnerability.

Media usage in South Africa is strongly influenced by demogra-
phy—a population characterized by a wide diversity in race, culture,
language, and religion. The four main African racial groups between
them speak some sixteen different languages. Zulu is the most widely
spoken among adults, with about 3.5 million native speakers. Next is
Xhosa with some 2.8 million and then Afrikaans with about 2.5
million. Tswana has some 1.5 million speakers, just ahead of English,
which has about 1.5 million. The numerical advantage of the black
languages over English and Afrikaans is increasing. In 1980, about 70
per cent of the population was black, 17 per cent white, 9 per cent
Coloured, and 3 per cent Asian. By the year 2000, the population is
projected to reach almost 50 million. By then the fast-growing black
population will account for some 75 per cent of the total.[1] Yet English
is, and is likely to remain, the dominant language for newspapers,
since it serves not only the whites but as a lingua franca for diverse
black groups.

Media usage is affected also by an increasing tendency toward
urbanization in all groups. In 1980, about 90 per cent of whites and
Asians lived in towns and cities, as did about 77 per cent of Coloureds.
For blacks the figure was about 38 per cent, and it would no doubt
have been much higher were it not for the government's policy of
controlling black influx into the cities.[2]

Even though only little more than a third of blacks live in the urban areas, they represent almost half of all urban dwellers. They are being drawn to the cities by the demands of industry for labor and the inability of the black homelands to provide jobs for their burgeoning populations. Black birthrates remain high in the cities, while death rates are decreasing as a result of improved living standards and medical care. It is estimated that by the year 2000 almost 80 per cent of blacks outside the homelands will be living in cities and will account for two-thirds of South Africa's urban inhabitants. The government's efforts to decentralize industries and to provide more employment opportunities in the homelands may slow the process, but cannot reverse it.

Almost 80 per cent of the total population is concentrated in only four large metropolitan areas centered on Johannesburg, Cape Town, Durban, and Port Elizabeth. The remaining urbanites live mainly in Bloemfontein, the Free State goldfields, East London, or Kimberley. Of these urban areas, the Witwatersrand, with Johannesburg as its focal point, is by far the largest. Almost half the total population lives and works there.[3]

The physical distribution of the population favors the development of mass media. The fact that most people are concentrated in a few densely populated urban areas means that newspapers can reach them easily. The SABC can cover most of the population with transmitters in key centers. In some areas, however, the population is very thinly spread. Parts of the Karroo and the northwest Cape have a density of less than one person per square kilometer—and nonelectronic media are correspondingly thin.

Media consumption patterns are affected also by the educational attainment of different groups. The whites have, by any standards, an unusually high level of education. More than half of white adults have completed high school, and a third have some form of advanced education. Primary and secondary schooling are free and compulsory. Ten residential universities for whites have a combined enrollment of some eighty thousand students. The average education of the whites outstrips that of other race groups—and much more is spent on their education on a per capita basis. The Indian community ranks second in educational attainment. Indians in South Africa traditionally have a high regard for education, and by 1970 some 96 per cent of Indian children were attending school. Schooling became compulsory for all Indians up to the age of fifteen in 1973. About 15 per cent of Indian adults have completed high school, and 8 per cent have some college education. A university specifically for Indian students was established in Durban in 1961. By 1980, it had an enrollment of almost five thousand students. Some six thousand more were attending white universities or studying by mail through the University of South Africa, said to be the world's largest correspondence university.

The Coloured community is relatively less well educated, as a group, than the Indians, but is making quick progress. In 1971, about 90 per cent of Coloured children were receiving five years or more of schooling. In 1974, school attendance became free and compulsory for all Coloured up to the age of sixteen. By 1980, there were 745,000 pupils in primary and secondary schools. About 10 per cent of adults had completed high school, and some 4 per cent had college educations. A separate university for Coloureds in the western Cape had a 1980 enrollment of about 3,600 students. Another 3,000 were enrolled at white universities or at the University of South Africa.

The biggest population group, the blacks, have the lowest average level of education. In 1955, only 45 per cent of school-age blacks were enrolled for classes. By 1975, this figure had increased to 75 per cent, but few were progressing beyond the primary grades. In the next five years, however, the government, unable to meet its skilled manpower needs by white immigration alone, made education for blacks a major priority. Whereas the latest phase of the country's industrial revolution was powered by the importation of some half million skilled workers, mostly from Europe, the new expansion will have to be manned largely by blacks. Compulsory education for urban blacks was introduced in 1980. There was a fourfold increase in the number of black pupils enrolled in secondary schools, despite serious unrest and boycotts at times. Also by 1980, the proportion of black children attending school had increased to 75 per cent, and a third of those who started primary school were progressing to secondary school. In that year, three black universities had an enrollment of about six thousand, while another ten thousand were studying at white universities or through the University of South Africa. In November 1983, the government pledged to provide equal educational opportunities for each child, regardless of race, and to improve training for black teachers.[4]

Nevertheless, because of the numbers involved, the pace of change is slow. A recent government commission found that 40 per cent of male black workers in urban areas were functionally illiterate, and in rural areas the figure rose to 65 per cent. But clearly a whole new generation of literate, urbanized blacks is developing. It likely will have the same impact on media growth in South Africa as did the 1870 Education Act in Britain that brought free and compulsory education to the masses for the first time—also, as it happened, to meet the country's need for skilled industrial labor. Analysis of 1980 census figures indicated that the literacy rate for the country as a whole was 60.5 per cent. The literacy rate for whites was 87 per cent; for Asians 78 per cent; for Coloureds 70 per cent; and for blacks 51 per cent.[5]

The disparity of education between the different groups is reflected also in income distribution, a major determinant of media usage. Again the whites form a privileged minority. In 1980, the average white household had a monthly income of about $900. For Indians the figure was about $450, for Coloureds about $310, and for blacks $130. The average figure for blacks was depressed, however, by the large rural population, most existing in a subsistence economy. In the cities the picture was rather different. During the 1970s, a deliberate policy of narrowing the gap between the wages of whites and those of other population groups brought Coloured and Indian salaries for equivalent jobs to much the same level as those of whites. A severe shortage of skilled black workers led to big increases in their wages also. Between 1970 and 1976, the real earnings of whites rose less than 4 per cent; for blacks the figure was over 50 per cent. In the first half of 1978, as the country recovered from an economic downturn, white wages rose 8 per cent while those of blacks shot up by 28 per cent. During the 1970s, real income of black mine workers increased by more than 400 per cent—admittedly from an appallingly low base. For whites the corresponding figure was 80 per cent. As a result, blacks' share of total personal income rose from 22 percent in 1970 to almost 30 per cent in 1980. By the end of this decade it is estimated that blacks will account for half of all consumer spending. Expenditures on black advertising trebled during the 1970s.[6]

As mentioned in the Introduction, this diverse population is served by twenty-one daily newspapers, eight Sunday or weekly papers, about a hundred weekly or biweekly county papers, and about five hundred different periodicals ranging from family entertainment magazines to highly specialized journals. The wide range of publications, in relation to the size of the population, is due to a variety of social, political, and geographic factors. Johannesburg, for example, needs not just one morning and one afternoon paper, but separate papers in English and Afrikaans—plus a daily and a weekly aimed specifically at the large black readership. Two more dailies are published in Pretoria, the administrative capital just thirty miles away, making a total of eight dailies in the Reef complex alone.

Johannesburg clearly is the hub of the country's mass media system. When the Pretoria circulation figures are included almost 60 per cent of the country's daily papers are sold there. Johannesburg is the headquarters for three of the four major newspaper chains, of the SABC radio and television services, and of the South African Press Association. The city dominates South African media in much the same was as Paris does in France or London in Britain. Cape Town and Port Elizabeth each have three dailies, Durban and Bloemfontein have two each, while East London, Pietermaritzburg, and Kimberley have one each. In centers with two morning or two afternoon papers, one is in English, the other in Afrikaans. The combined circulation of these dailies amounted to about 1.4 million copies in 1982—or 50 papers sold per 1,000 population. This puts South Africa well below the advanced industrial nations, but above most developing countries.

Three of the four main Sunday papers are published in Johannesburg, two in English, one in Afrikaans. A third English Sunday paper is published in Durban. Several daily papers publish special weekend editions that appear on Saturdays because of the blue laws, carry typical Sunday features and supplements, and usually have bigger circulations than their daily counterparts. One of the fastest-growing fields in South African journalism is that of weekly papers aimed at

specific race groups. The banned *Weekend World*, published in Johannesburg for an almost exclusively African readership, was the country's third-largest weekly, with a circulation of more than 200,000 and
growing fast. The *Cape Herald*, a Cape Town weekly aimed at a
Coloured readership, with three-quarters of its circulation in the
western Cape, has already been mentioned (see Introduction), as has
the *Post/Natal*, catering to Indians, *Ilanga*, a Zulu publication, and
Imvo Zabantsundu, a Xhosa weekly published in the eastern Cape.

All the daily papers are essentially regional in distribution. Not one
qualifies as a national paper. Each circulates in appreciable numbers
in the urban center in which it is published and in a comparatively
small surrounding region. English dailies tend to have a greater
concentration of circulation in the center of publication than Afrikaans dailies, while the Afrikaans papers have a proportionately
higher circulation in smaller communities and rural areas. One reason
for the relatively limited circulation zones of South African papers is
the concentration of the population into a few large urban areas
separated by considerable distances. Another is the ownership structure. Since the large newspaper groups each have papers in most of
the major centers, publishing a national paper would mean competing
with their own publications in other cities. The only exceptions are
the two biggest Sunday papers, the *Sunday Times* and *Rapport*. Both
are published in Johannesburg, but use facsimile transmission to
printing plants in coastal cities for local production and distribution
and thus achieve a truly national circulation.[7]

Associated with the limited circulation area of the dailies is their
relatively small circulation in terms of numbers. The biggest daily
paper in 1982 was *The Star* in Johannesburg with a circulation of
about 172,000—down from a peak of just under 200,000. The small-
est dailies, like the *Friend* in Bloemfontein or the *Diamond Fields
Advertiser* in Kimberley, had circulations of less than 10,000. The
average daily circulation was about 60,000. Circulations were limited
by the local character of the papers, each serving essentially its own
community, by the fact that a large proportion of the population was
illiterate or unable to afford a newspaper, and by the duplication that
arises when a country has two official languages, with newspapers
dividing the English and Afrikaans readership between them.

One striking characteristic of newspaper circulation is the predominance of English-language papers. Although Afrikaans-speaking whites outnumber English speakers in the ratio of about six to four, the English papers account for no less than three-quarters of total daily circulation and two-thirds of Sunday circulation. This discrepancy results from several factors. For one thing, there are fifteen dailies in English and only six in Afrikaans. Some cities—Durban, East London, Kimberley, and Pietermaritzburg—have one or more English dailies but no Afrikaans paper. Afrikaners living in those cities must perforce buy an English paper for local news and advertising. No city has Afrikaans papers alone. The traditional dominance of English speakers in terms of education, income, and occupational status also has been a factor, although in the 1970s Afrikaners achieved income parity for the first time. Nevertheless, surveys show that English speakers still outnumber Afrikaners in most professions and in white-collar jobs—groups in which readership traditionally is highest. Discrepancies still exist in the relative educational achievement of the two groups and in the proportions of each who are urbanized. The English have always been a largely urban population, with more than 95 per cent living in urban complexes at present. But the past fifty years have seen a significant move by Afrikaners from rural areas to towns and cities. In 1936, less than half the Afrikaner population lived in urban areas. Today the figure is close to 90 per cent. Because of their larger numbers, there actually are more Afrikaners in the country's towns and cities than English speakers. But in the big cities, where daily newspapers find their largest markets, English speakers still are in the majority.

The influence of these factors shows up clearly in data collected for national readership surveys. Among other things, the data show that:

• About two-thirds of the white population read a daily paper regularly.

• A far higher proportion of Afrikaans speakers do not read a daily than English speakers. In 1980, about 73 per cent of English speakers read a daily; the figure for Afrikaners was 57 per cent.

• English-language newspapers have a high proportion of Afrikaans readers. About 22 per cent of the readership of English papers is

Afrikaner. Conversely, few English speakers read Afrikaans papers. In 1980, the figure was less than 8 per cent.

• Newspaper readership is declining among members of both white groups, a trend that was accelerated by the introduction of television in 1976, as Table 1 demonstrates.[8]

Table 1. *Daily newspaper readership among white adults (%)*

	1962	1968	1972	1975	1980
English	87	85	84	82	73
Afrikaners	66	64	66	70	56

Differing patterns of media use among whites are, however, not nearly marked enough to explain the large differences in circulation between English and Afrikaans papers. Again the readership survey data provide an answer. A large and growing proportion of the total readership of daily papers is not white but black, Coloured, and Indian. The composition of the readership has changed rapidly over the past few years, as Table 2 shows.

Table 2. *Readership of all dailies by race (%)*

	White	Black	Coloured	Indian
1975	63	16	14	7
1980	45	38	11	6

There is, however, an enormous difference in the use of English and Afrikaans dailies by nonwhites. Eight out of ten readers of Afrikaans papers are white, as opposed to only four out of ten for English papers (see Table 3).

Table 3. *Readership of English and Afrikaans dailies by race in 1980 (%)*

	White	Black	Coloured	Indian
English dailies (excluding *Sowetan*)	40	39	12	8
Afrikaans dailies	77	11	12	0

Figures for individual newspapers demonstrate this even more clearly. In Cape Town, the *Argus* and the *Cape Times* have far more Coloured readers than white. Durban's *Daily News* has a predominantly Indian readership. In Johannesburg, *The Star* has twice as many black readers as white; the *Rand Daily Mail* has three times as many. Afrikaans papers, by contrast, draw relatively few nonwhite readers, the exceptions being *Die Burger* in Cape Town, which has a substantial Coloured readership, and *Beeld* and *Die Vaderland* in Johannesburg that each have several thousand black readers.

The preference shown by nonwhites for English papers is overwhelming. In 1980, of all Indians who read a paper, 99 per cent read it in English. The figure for blacks was about 95 per cent, for Coloureds about 75 per cent. The preference of Indians for English papers is easy to explain: most live in Natal where there are no Afrikaans dailies. They have English as a home language or as a second language after an Indian language. This does not hold true for blacks, particularly in the densely populated Reef area where there are as many Afrikaans as English papers and where blacks learn both English and Afrikaans at school in addition to their home language. The preference shown by Coloureds for English papers is even more unexpected, since 90 per cent have Afrikaans as their home language. Obviously, other factors are involved.

One explanation is that for many blacks and Coloureds, English is a prestige language—a window on the outside world. Many regard Afrikaans as the language of the oppressor—the language of apartheid, of the police, the pass office, the courts. Hence the decision by the new homeland governments that the medium of instruction in schools should be English, not Afrikaans. The riots in Soweto in 1976 were triggered, in part, by resentment at pupils' having to learn some subjects through the medium of Afrikaans.

This attitude is found even among some Coloureds, despite their Afrikaans linguistic roots. Adam Small, the renowned Coloured poet, refused to write in Afrikaans at all. Furthermore, the more liberal position on race relations espoused by the English papers is more in accord with the aspirations of blacks and Coloureds than the progovernment line adopted by Afrikaans papers. While the English papers, with the exception of *The Citizen*, are unanimous in calling for change, for an end to apartheid, most Afrikaans papers support the status quo, although some editors are trying to prepare their readers for the inevitable changes the country faces. But Afrikaans papers, no matter how liberal, are not likely to find widespread acceptance among politicized blacks and Coloureds who consider even the English papers not fully responsive to their needs.

Impact of Television

The rapid industrialization and urbanization of all population groups in South Africa since World War II has led to a much-enlarged potential audience for printed news. Over the past twenty-five years, there has been a very high correlation between newspaper circulation and the growth in population, in per capita income, and in enrollment in primary and secondary schools. Yet circulation has not increased in proportion to the growth of these variables. In the twenty years between 1958 and 1978, circulation grew by about 55 per cent, while the population increased by 60 per cent, real disposable income per capita by 123 per cent, and school enrollment by 150 per cent.

One reason for the lag in newspaper sales is the impact of competing media. During the same period, the number of radio licenses issued increased by about 180 per cent, despite a substantial rise in the number of "pirate" listeners who did not buy licenses. New regional radio services were introduced, along with several channels in the vernacular for blacks. Even more significant has been the impact of television. Data gathered for the national All Media Product Survey show clearly how swiftly television penetrated the market after its introduction in 1976. Whites, with their relatively high incomes, were the first to adopt the new medium in large numbers, but other groups were not far behind (see Table 4).

Table 4. Television viewing "yesterday" by race group (%)

	1976	1977	1978	1979	1980	1983
Whites	46	59	66	71	73	78
Coloureds	13	24	30	35	37	48
Indians	24	34	43	58	61	71
Blacks	1	1	2	3	4	11

As television viewing among whites increased, so their use of newspapers declined. But newspaper circulations remained stable, largely because of the growing numbers of nonwhite readers. Most blacks could not afford television sets or the relatively high annual license fee; those that could often had no electricity available to their homes. Their extra spending power was channeled instead into heavier use of radio and print media.

As mentioned in Chapter 6, editors of English-language newspapers adopted two basic strategies to deal with the changing demographics of their readership: they chose either to generalize or to specialize their appeal. The Argus Printing and Publishing Company, with mainly afternoon papers and the largest aggregate circulation in the country, chose to specialize and established separate papers for each nonwhite ethnic group. The Argus mainstream dailies, although they may have a larger nonwhite than white readership, are directed primarily at the affluent white market prized by advertisers. Argus executives see the division as being based not necessarily on race, but on class. Other newspapers, notably the *Rand Daily Mail* and the *Daily Dispatch*, consciously aim at an integrated readership. Allister Sparks, while editor of the *Mail*, said, "We see ourselves as a most important bridge, the last means of interracial communication."[9]

The attempt to be inclusive rather than exclusive has its perils. In cities where a newspaper has no direct competition, it can get away with running a large portion of news relevant to black readers in its editions intended primarily for whites. But in Johannesburg, where the *Rand Daily Mail* competes head-on with the progovernment *Citizen*, the situation is very different. The *Mail*, like other mainstream South African papers, originally paid little attention to news of groups other than whites. Few black names appeared in the news columns. Apart from references to "the Native problem," blacks generally were not treated as a political force with spokesmen of their own. One of the first editors to challenge this was John Sutherland, then editor of the *Evening Post* in Port Elizabeth. Under his guidance, the *Post* began, in the mid 50s, to reflect more closely the totality of South African society. But the *Evening Post* was a small paper with little circulation outside the Eastern Cape. The new inclusiveness Sutherland pioneered became far more visible when starting in 1957 Laurence Gandar took a similar approach in the much larger *Mail*.

This trend was continued and developed by Gandar's successors,

Raymond Louw and Allister Sparks. According to Sparks, the first and most dramatic thing Gandar did was to drop the word "Native" in favor of "African." It caused an outcry, he says, and the biggest wave of cancellations in the newspaper's history. Gandar appointed the first African affairs reporter in South Africa, Benjamin Pogrund, who began focusing on black politics and such social injustices as malnutrition and forced removals of blacks from white areas.

The attempt by the English papers to report as much as they legally could about the development of black politics both reflected the growing numbers of black readers and encouraged more. It also discomforted conservative white readers who resented having their shortcomings pointed out in the *Mail*. Some apparently stopped reading papers altogether, turning instead to the more comfortable news offered by the new television service. Others switched to *The Citizen*, which noted proudly that, despite its much lower circulation, it had by 1982 outstripped the *Mail* in numbers of white readers. White readership of the *Mail* peaked in the mid-70s, then began to decline. Black readership continued to increase, particularly after the banning of the *World* and *Post* and the Soweto unrest of 1976 and its aftermath. In 1972, the *Mail* had some 400,000 white readers and 150,000 black. (Totals for readers are several times that of circulation or copies sold.) By 1983, white readership had dwindled to some 219,000, while that of blacks had quintupled to 715,000.[10]

To some advertisers, however, the new black readers are not an asset but, because of their lower spending power, a liability. The chairman of a large advertising agency told the *Financial Mail* in 1981 that during the previous five years coverage in the *Rand Daily Mail* had been "angled at scoring political points, as opposed to reporting the news in as objective a way as possible." And the bottom line was that if readers did not find news content "satisfying, stimulating and presented in a way that holds them they are not going to see our ads."[11] Faced with increasing losses as a result of declining circulation and advertising revenue, the directors of the *Mail* abruptly fired Sparks in 1981, despite his protests that "I told them the *Mail*'s loss of white readers was due to there being five papers competing for the white market, and the newspapers catering for the black market had been halved by the banning of *World* and *Post*. It was natural that we should pick up more black readers. But according to the marketing people, these are economically inactive readers and advertisers don't want to aim at them." The editorial team chosen to replace him, says Sparks, had a different political coloring, reflecting management's hope for a softer protesting voice: "If the voice is lowered it is less discomforting. They think if there is less emphasis on black views there will be an increase in white readership. I don't believe it."[12]

In a sense, then, the government's decision to spend some $30 million in secret funds to establish *The Citizen* as an English-language mouthpiece to muffle the outspoken *Mail* has paid off. Just as the banning of its black newspapers forced the Argus company to tone down criticism of the government in its surviving *Sowetan* lest that too be banned, so legal, political, and economic pressures have subdued the voice of the Nationalists' arch enemy, the *Rand Daily Mail*. In 1983 the *Mail* was still losing money and its future was in doubt.[13]

Government attempts to control the parameters of political debate are succeeding in other ways as well. If the growth of black newspaper readership over the years has been remarkable, the increase in usage of broadcast media by all race groups has been spectacular. And both radio and television are firmly in the hands of the government. As has happened in other countries where first radio and then television have been introduced, the new media have largely replaced newspapers as the primary source of news for many people. Surveys show also that they are regarded as being more credible than print media. The implications for South Africa are more consequential than for other countries, however, because the government has a virtual monopoly of radio and television. As the electronic media have expanded, therefore, a growing proportion of the population has been getting its news and opinions from media with an avowedly progovernment bias. At the same time, the English newspapers, while acquiring more black readers, are being intimidated into toning down their criticisms of the government and have a diminished influence on public opinion.

Foreign Journalists in South Africa

One segment of journalism that the Nationalists have not been able to control are the foreign journalists in their midst who report on South

Africa to the outside world. Many in South Africa have long believed that the overseas media, especially those in Britain and the United States, have given a distorted and biased picture of the Republic.

The Muldergate affair, of course, concerned covert and illegal efforts to improve that tarnished overseas image. The Nationalists, from their prime ministers on down, have not liked foreign journalists, but do not quite know what to do about them. Sometimes foreign correspondents are harassed or interfered with, but most of the time authorities leave them alone and wish they would go away. The relationship between the government and the foreign journalists is abrasive and uneasy. On the other hand, Western reporters are criticized as well by the opponents of the South African regime.

But however objective reporting from South Africa may or may not be, its impact on the outside world cannot be denied. Western journalists, especially the British and more recently the Americans, have been reporting on South Africa for a long time, and global attitudes toward the apartheid regime have been largely shaped by the words, and more recently the television images, coming out of Johannesburg.

For Johannesburg, the industrial dynamo of South Africa, has had, since the late 1970s, the largest concentration of foreign journalists anywhere in Africa. With excellent air connections and communications facilities (the SABC has the only capability in black Africa to transmit television newsfilm by communication satellite), "Joburg" has been the most convenient base from which to cover not only the tumultuous events in South Africa itself but such major nearby events as the Rhodesian civil war and emergence of the new nation of Zimbabwe, guerrilla wars and new independent governments in Angola and Mozambique, and the protracted negotiations and low-level guerrilla war over Namibia.

The Foreign Correspondents Association, which had only six members in 1974 amd thirty in 1977, has burgeoned to eighty-five journalists (eighteen or twenty of them Americans) representing fifty-three organizations from ten Western countries, Japan, and Taiwan. All major U.S. media are present, including *U.S. News and World Report, Time, Newsweek,* the *New York Times, Washington Post, Los Angeles Times, Christian Science Monitor, Business Week,* Associated Press, United Press International, National Public Radio, and the major broadcasting organizations, ABC, CBS, and NBC. Other publications such as the *Wall Street Journal* have reporters visiting regularly.[14]

Such a concentration of journalists has assured that South Africa (and southern Africa generally) was the most thoroughly reported area of Africa. (During the same period, Western news coverage of sub-Saharan Africa generally declined.) However, this pattern may not continue. If southern Africa quiets down and produces less news, then certainly many in the foreign press will depart. Furthermore, the neighboring black governments have made reporting more difficult for South African-based reporters. In August 1983, information ministers of Angola, Botswana, Mozambique, Tanzania, Zambia, and Zimbabwe agreed to put their countries off limits to all correspondents based in South Africa. Officials at the meeting in Zimbabwe said the reporters, because they live in South Africa, tend to give "a distorted view and misrepresentation of our region" and to support "Pretoria's view of reality in southern Africa."[15] The following day, the Zimbabwean government ordered a BBC television team to leave the country. This action showed that the "frontline governments" also distrusted the Western reporters, but for reasons quite different from those of the Nationalists.

While they enjoy more freedom than in most African countries, foreign journalists do work under a variety of pressures in South Africa. First, they must contend with a government generally hostile to their work, that sees them "as a bunch of Marxist agitators, who stir up trouble. The government is only dimly aware of what the press does but still blames the press for the world's attitudes toward South Africa. They don't understand the press. They're dumb and they don't help the press and themselves in getting out the news."[16]

For example, when Vere Stock returned to South Africa in 1980 after five years as consul general in New York, he expressed a common Afrikaner viewpoint when he said he believed that "American prejudice is artifically contrived, mainly by the press, and particularly by the *New York Times*. That newspaper positively refuses to give credit where credit is due. It always presents a prejudiced and slanted view of the country."[17] A veteran American correspondent says, "I consider the government totally incompetent on its information policy. They are suspicious with much animosity to the foreign press but they still want a positive image in the media. But their view of what is positive news is way to the right of what Western newsmen consider to be news."

Government officials complain that foreign journalists are hostile to the Nationalists and work too closely with the opposition English press in South Africa. There is some truth to this, for often an opposition paper will give a story it can't print to a foreign journalist, and then after the story is published abroad it will be picked up by South African papers.

Foreign journalists agree that access to government leaders and official news sources is their major problem. One complaint is that it is particularly difficult to interview cabinet ministers and others high in government. One American journalist who has reported from Moscow says that South Africa is on a par with the Soviet Union in the difficulty of getting interviews with high officials. (It should be noted that local journalists, including even some Afrikaans reporters, also have problems gaining access to Nationalist leaders.)

On the other hand, correspondents agree that they are free to move around the country to gather news though they run into the same difficult access problems as do local reporters. Foreign correspondents are not exempt from the same myriad of laws that restrict access by South African journalists. However, some foreign newsmen make a calculated decision to violate some of these laws. For example, foreign journalists will sometimes quote banned persons or discuss the aims of the outlawed ANC and PAC—both actions specifically against South African law. Gaining access to imprisoned black leaders and to the military activities on the Namibia/Angola border were two particular problems for newsmen. Foreign newsmen, especially those with television cameras, are often barred from trouble areas during protests or riots.

Prime Minister P. W. Botha is considered by journalists to be hostile to the foreign press in part because he can't control or intimidate them, because "all he can do is expel them, and this can lead to bad international publicity with Western embassies lodging protests, etc. So the price to retaliate is too high." Yet foreign journalists must work and live with the constant threat of expulsion. To work in South

Africa, foreign journalists need a visa, a work permit (renewable every six months), and an accreditation card signed by both the foreign minister's office and the police. Police store up resentments against foreign journalists and, in recent cases of five reporters, refused to sign their accreditation cards. However, nonrenewal of the six-month work permits is the most direct control the government holds over the foreign journalists.

Authorities keep track of what foreign journalists report for their media abroad, usually through clipping services and through press attachés in South African overseas embassies who will on occasion complain to the reporters' editors. Some journalists say their telephones have been tapped and that incoming mail is often read as are stories sent out by telex. A few journalists, considered particularly hostile to South Africa, have been subjected to much more intense surveillance and even harassment.

These actions against foreign newsmen reflect the recent relations between the government and the foreign press:

Daniel B. Drooz, a part-time reporter for the *Chicago Sun-Times* and *Maariv*, an Israeli newspaper, was denied renewal of his work permit when it expired on August 31, 1978. Drooz was told that some of his reports amounted to a "distortion of reality."

Eight West German journalists were denied visas to visit South Africa in June 1980.

Nat Gibson, a UPI correspondent, was charged under the Defense Act for reporting that soldiers had been deployed against racial rioting in Port Elizabeth. In October 1981, without a word of explanation, the government dropped the charges.

A few days earlier, Cynthia Stevens, an AP correspondent, was forced to leave the country after the Department of Internal Affairs refused to renew her work permit. While no official explanation was given, it was generally felt that her contacts with black leaders were the underlying cause of the order.

In a similar incident in October 1982, Gerard Jacobs, a Dutch radio and television correspondent, was expelled when the government refused to renew his work permit. Jacobs said he had been given no reason for the decision nor had any complaints about his work been made to him.

Sometimes harassment can take more subtle forms. In November 1982, the producer of an ABC News television documentary on black labor unions said that the film his crew had shot was ruined in a way that led the network's technical experts to conclude that the destruction was sabotage. Circumstantial evidence indicated that twelve thousand feet of film shot in Port Elizabeth had been deliberately exposed to light after it was checked through on a South African airways flight. The clear implication was that the sabotage was carried out by the Security Police who had monitored the film crew's activities at Port Elizabeth.[18]

On occasion, harassment becomes prosecution. In March 1983, Bernard Simon, a correspondent for AP–Dow Jones News Service, was detained by security police and accused of "defeating the ends of justice." Police charged that Simon took documents from the office of Allister Sparks, former *Rand Daily Mail* editor and part-time correspondent for the *Washington Post*, just before police arrived to conduct a six-hour search of Sparks's home and office. Police were looking for evidence that Sparks had quoted Winnie Mandela, wife of the imprisoned leader of the ANC, Nelson Mandela. Mrs. Mandela was a banned person and under South African law may not be quoted. Simon and Sparks's wife, Suzanne, were accused of obstructing justice.[19] In March 1984, charges were dropped.

These incidents indicate that the government recently has become less tolerant of the foreign correspondents, and clearly any newsman who tries to investigate and report on the political activities among blacks is particularly vulnerable to expulsion.

The abrasive relationships between the Nationalists and the foreign journalists may result in some self-censorship by the journalists. They know they face expulsion if they dig too deeply into certain kinds of stories, and there is the constant problem of dealing with the unpredictable and arbitrary Security Police. Yet the flow of news is indisputably negative because that is the kind of news South Africans are making. Western media can be faulted, perhaps, for being too optimistic at times: Botha's promises of the easing of apartheid were given too much uncritical coverage as have the unfounded hopes that South Africa is indeed ready to give up its hold on South West Africa/Namibia. Nuances and subtle analysis may be sometimes lacking, but the foreign newsmen in South Africa are reporting to the outside world all the major, significant developments in its long, tragic drama.

Political Prospects

The form and substance—and comparative freedom—of public communication in the years ahead will be influenced as in the past in large part by the political news coming out of the Republic. South Africans often seem preoccupied with the future—the prospective modifications in the power structure that they either hope for or dread. For a common agreement exists across the political spectrum that "things cannot go on the way they have," even though they seem to be doing just that. Despite the hazards, conjuring up scenarios for a South Africa of the future has been a favorite pastime for many years. Within cellular South Africa, each group—radical blacks, right-wing Afrikaners, ruling Nationalists, liberal English speakers, and others—has its own blueprint for the years ahead.

Several recent trends in South African politics will have a bearing on both political prospects and mass communication changes—and perhaps ultimately on which scenario will play. After becoming prime minister in 1978 amidst the wreckage of Muldergate, P. W. Botha raised expectations by warning his white electorate, "We must make adaptations, otherwise we will die." "Adapt or die" became a popular slogan. White survival, Botha stressed, depended on making changes that would satisfy the political aspirations of the majority Africans, as well as the Indians and Coloureds. One cabinet minister, Piet Koornhof, even told a U.S. audience in 1979 that his country had reached a "turning point in our history. Apartheid, as you came to know it in the United States, is dying and dead."[20] The opposition press and media abroad reported all this with uncritical enthusiasm, and there was a widespread feeling that changes were indeed in the offing.

However, aside from a few cosmetic alterations, Botha and his *verligte* followers have not delivered—basic changes have not been made in the apartheid apparatus. Many Nationalists realize that their apartheid policies will not work much longer, but they are fearful of dismantling the pervasive controls. Further, most whites are unyielding about one man, one vote. The blacks insist on some significant share of political power; they will settle for nothing less. Hence, the impasse.

A political journalist, Hennie Serfontein, said in 1982 that no fundamental changes were taking place in the policy of apartheid and, further, that the Afrikaners had no intention of making such changes. "We are dealing," he said, "with methods to remove the ugly face of apartheid. Perhaps, to use a phrase, moving from a crude van der Merwe style of apartheid to a more English-style [Ian] Smith-type apartheid."[21] In fact, the Botha government has moved to strengthen some key apartheid laws. In August 1982, new legislation was proposed to tighten laws aimed at keeping the number of blacks in urban areas to the minimum needed to meet labor requirements.

On the other hand, the promised reforms have resulted in some diminution of overt racial discrimination, and certain features of "petty apartheid" have been somewhat eased. Further, increasing numbers of Afrikaners have become uneasy with long-standing Nationalist policies. For example, the Dutch Reformed church has for many years provided moral and theological support for apartheid, but recently 123 white ministers of the church declared in a letter to a religious journal that the nation's official racial policies "cannot be defended scripturally" and called for racial equality.[22] The letter, which caused a furor within the church, urged repeal of several basic laws of apartheid, including the ban on mixed marriages, race classification, and group area laws.

Nevertheless, it is apparent that Botha's Nationalists have become preoccupied with appeasing the right-wing Afrikaners, inside and outside the party, and are abandoning most of their promised reforms. Afrikaners have long feared a split in their party ranks, raising as it does the specter of political control by the English speakers once again. Hence Botha has felt he must mollify his right-wing supporters.

But a showdown may come in the opposition of Dr. Andries Treurnicht, a cabinet minister who has fought against the "heresy" that white power, which he calls "white self-determination," can survive racial mixing in the political and social spheres. In 1982

Treurnicht led a rebellion of sixteen Nationalist Parliament members. But Botha won a test of strength against Treurnicht's supporters in the Transvaal, and "Dr. No," as the English press called him, was ousted from his cabinet seat. Treurnicht formed the new Conservative Party of South Africa, committed to continued total separation along racial lines. He even started a newspaper, *Die Patriot*, to espouse his views. By its own count, the new right-wing party already has 1,100 branches, and political commentators predict that it could take enough seats from the Nationalists in future elections to become an important opposition party. However, the resounding support that Botha received from the national referendum for his constitutional reforms in November 1983 indicated that right-wing opposition to the Botha government was less widespread that expected.

These developments underline a basic dilemma of the reform minded: even though *verligte* Nationalists control the government, *verkrampte* Afrikaners retain a veto power over any significant reform of the apartheid structure. Yet continued National party control of the government seems quite likely.

Another trend has been the militarization of South African politics. Since retaining control of Parliament in the 1981 elections, Botha has been seeking military, rather than political, solutions to the "total onslaught." Instead of implementing political reforms within South Africa, he has embarked on military adventures into neighboring countries. There is clear evidence that the Botha government is trying to destabilize the black governments in Zimbabwe, Zambia, Angola, and Mozambique.

During 1981 and 1982, the efficient South African Defense Force, by far the most effective military force in the sub-Sahara, made a series of raids into neighboring Mozambique, Angola, and Lesotho. Their targets have been the SWAPO guerrillas in Angola and various elements of the ANC in Maseru, Maputo, and other cities. These military incursions were a response to another trend—the rising level of terrorism and violence directed at persons and installations within South Africa. South Africans will have to accept certain levels of discomfort, disruption, and even violence in their daily lives, the chief of the South African Defense Force, Gen. Constand Viljoen, told a conference in Pretoria in June 1983. It was essential, he said, that South Africans prepare themselves psychologically without becoming alarmist or dispirited.[23]

Just a few days earlier, the minister of defense, Gen. Magnus Malan, had urged all industrialists, businessmen, and employers to protect their premises against sabotage by terrorists. He told a gathering in Johannesburg that South Africa—being a highly industrialized country but also limited in manpower and finance—had a range of industrial targets for which the armed forces could not possibly provide guards or impregnable defense measures.[24] These warnings reflect official concern that South Africa has, over the past few years, been slipping into an Ulster-like pattern of low intensity civil war. Incidents of political violence and sabotage have increased not only in frequency but in severity. Although these acts provide no immediate threat to the stability of white rule, they are a reminder that a black resistance movement exists, that some kind of political accommodation may be reached with it, and that a modern industrial state is vulnerable to attacks on its infrastructure.

As the bearer of the news of military incursions and terrorist (or guerrilla) attacks, the press has come in for considerable and contradictory criticisms according to the perspective of the critic. The government's attitude on reporting of terrorism has been ambiguous. One response has been to use the media to mobilize the population for what amounts to a state of siege. White South Africans are urged to forget their political differences and unite to oppose the "total onslaught by Communist-inspired black terrorists." Where it suits the government's purpose, the media are permitted, even encouraged, to report on some aspects of terrorism. For the most part, however, reporters are kept in the dark until well after the event, and then only the government version of the news is available.

Many blacks, on the other hand, perceive military incursions and acts of terrorism very differently from whites. While most whites approve of attacks on "terriorist bases" across international borders, many black South Africans consider such raids as naked war against fellow South Africans. After the December 1982 raid into Lesotho in which twenty-nine South African blacks were killed, the *Sowetan* expressed its "total abhorrence," and used such words as "odious," "indefensible," and "obnoxious" in its condemnation.[25] Among blacks generally there is increasing acceptance of revolutionary violence and a resurgence of support for the African National Congress as well as a growing interest in radical ideology.

The rising level of violence raises questions as to where South Africa is headed in the years ahead. For many years, opponents of the apartheid regime have warned that a violent, widespread and bloody upheaval was imminent unless headed off by strong measures from outside South Africa. After Sharpeville in 1961 and again after Soweto in 1976, many felt strongly that South Africa was about to explode—yet it has not.

Peter Duignan and L. H. Gann in a recent book were critical of what they call "the Jericho complex" of those who have been so long predicting the imminent collapse of the South African regime: "South African cities are not powder-kegs about to explode, cauldrons about to boil over, or boilers about to burst." The white minority, they argue, is too well equipped, trained and armed, resolute and ruthless. And the black majority is too unorganized, divided, and weak to mount a revolution—at least, for the present.[26] Other observers, including the Study Commission on Policy toward Southern Africa, tend to agree with Duignan and Gann that, under present conditions, the prospects for a violent overthrow of South Africa's white regime— either by a foreign invasion or by internal or external guerrilla assaults—are not in the realm of military probability.[27] Nevertheless, conditions can change, and it should be remembered that among blacks there is a growing conviction that only violence will bring about meaningful change in South Africa. However, at this time, this is not a likely scenario.

Slow, gradual, but peaceful change is another prediction that is no longer considered realistic because of the growing impatience and militancy of blacks and the intransigence of most whites who stubbornly refuse to share political power with blacks. The rising level of sabotage, plus continued repression of even the most moderate black political expression as well as police repression of black activism, seems to have made this scenario obsolete. This option is especially unrealistic if one accepts, as many South Africans do, that a low-level civil war has been going on inside South Africa for many years now.

The two most realistic scenarios appear to be either (1) slow, evolutionary change marked by a growing level of sporadic violence, or (2) a slow descent into civil war. These two alternatives seem to be the most realistic eventualities largely because they represent continuation of current trends. The Study Commission on U.S. Policy toward Southern Africa concluded that it does not believe in imminent revolution but does believe in the possibility (no more than that) of peaceful change. As Franklin A. Thomas, head of the commission, put it, "The alternatives, as our group came to see them, are not either slow, gradual peaceful change or violent revolution; they are slow, sporadically violent evolutionary change or slow descent into civil war. Of these last two, the former was infinitely preferable."[28]

Whether by civil war or evolutionary change, most observers believe that time is on the side of the majority blacks and that events will lead to a changeover from white to black rule as has happened in Zimbabwe, Angola, and Mozambique. But it is impossible to predict when and how this political transformation will occur. Either scenario would in time lead to some kind of significant power sharing, but both represent turbulent and stressful times ahead for all South Africans.

Continued repression of civil rights, including freedom of expression, would probably accompany any rising level of sabotage and terrorism. In view of these political realities, then, the future for mass communication and freedom of the press in South Africa promises more of the same. The "total onslaught" against the press will undoubtedly continue. Government pressures on the opposition press will probably include greater restraints on journalists along with more restrictive legislation. Newspapers will be under strong pressure to conform and support a government which is itself under increasing stress. English-language newspapers, for their part, will probably exercise even more self-restraint through self-censorship, as the black majority turns to greater violence and the government to ever more repression. As Tertius Mybergh, editor of the *Sunday Times*, puts it, "Anyone thinking this is the thirteenth round in a bout with history is wrong. The government hasn't begun to tap its resources of unused naked power."[29] In the years ahead, it is unlikely that the opposition papers will be able to stand up to such pressures; what freedom of the press remains will decline even further for economic as well as political reasons.

The real demise of press freedom in South Africa, some have said, will occur when the government bans or shuts down a major English newspaper opponent, such as the *Rand Daily Mail*. But because of the growing propensity of the English press to censor itself, such a drastic action may never be needed. The Nationalists may win their long struggle against the press by default.

Black journalism—or any publications that seem to carry a political message to blacks—will continue to be repressed and suppressed. Black journalism may find its only political outlet in ephemeral, underground pamphlets and newssheets considered subversive by government. Yet black-oriented publications, devoid of political content, will probably increase in numbers and readers. Ironically, the newspapers of dissident Afrikaners—the Conservative party's *Die Patriot* and the Herstigte Nasionale party's *Die Afrikaner*—probably will be subjected to the same harsh restraints as the English and black papers have suffered.

For economic as well as political reasons, the newspaper press will likely decline in size and influence, while the electronic media, led by an expanded SABC television service, will play a greater role in news dissemination and public affairs. And with radio and television thoroughly controlled by the government, the ruling Nationalists need fear neither dissent nor criticism from that quarter.

The tragedy of South Africa offers certain painful lessons. The unwillingness of the dominant white minority to create a just society with equal political rights for all has created an authoritarian regime in which all freedoms become jeopardized. South Africans are learning the truism that "freedom is indivisible." When civil and political rights are denied to any significant group, then in time the rights of all are curtailed, as the English-speaking liberals and dissident Afrikaners have been finding. Freedom of the press or simply independence from government intrusion can be abridged, not only by arbitrary government actions, but also by a slow whittling away through legislation duly enacted by an elected parliament.

Acknowledgments and
Reference Matter

Acknowledgments

Many persons in South Africa have assisted the authors in the preparation of this book. Because of their different backgrounds, Giffard and Hachten have each drawn on different kinds of sources.

Anthony Giffard was born in South Africa and worked on the SABC and the Friend Newspapers in South Africa, as well as the *Times* of London and the Seattle *Post-Intelligencer* before he joined the faculty of Rhodes University in Grahamstown. There he organized and headed for ten years the first program in journalism education at an English-speaking university. Since 1979, he has been at the University of Washington.

William Hachten, a specialist on mass communication in Africa, has visited South Africa five times—in 1965, 1968, 1974, 1978, and 1980–81—and obtained information about mass communication there from a wide range of South Africans. Interviews and documents for this study were collected during his most recent visit. Over seventy-five persons provided useful information and some have not been cited because they prefer not to be quoted directly.

The following persons were particularly generous with their help: Raymond Louw, Benjamin Pogrund, Joel Mervis, Les Switzer, Arnold DeBeer, H. P. Fourie, Guy Butler, Graeme Addison, Wally Langschmidt, Harvey Tyson, D. A. S. Herbst, Gerald Shaw, Robert Chancellor, Robin Knight, Gary Thatcher, William Nicholson, Ton Vosloo, Peta Thornycroft, James McMillan, Mervyn Rees, Zubeida Jaffer, Louise Silver, Frans van der Vyver, Anthony Mathews, G. G.

A. Uys, John van Zyl, Louis Louw, David Thomas, Graham Hayman, Ian MacDonald, and Randy Speer. These persons, of course, are in no way responsible for the findings and conclusions of this study.

The authors are indebted as well to Anthony L. Johnson, who provided helpful comments on the manuscript. Major assistance was provided by Harva Hachten, who perceptively edited several versions of the entire manuscript. As a journalist and "fellow traveler" on the journeys to South Africa, her insights are found particularly in her husband's chapters. Christina Giffard provided invaluable assistance in translating documents and preparing the manuscript. Finally, Hachten thanks the Research Committee of the Graduate School of the University of Wisconsin-Madison for support of his 1980–81 field research.

The authors, whose professional and personal association dates from 1974, worked closely together in the planning and execution of this study. Hachten wrote the Introduction and Chapters 1, 4, 5, 6, 7, and 9. Giffard wrote Chapters 2, 3, 8, and 10. Giffard also did the first half of Chapter 11 and Hachten the second half. Each edited and commented at length on the other's chapters. They both stand fully behind the book as a whole.

Notes

Chapter 1

1 Interview with Benjamin Pogrund, Johannesburg, July 18, 1978.

2 *Survey of Race Relations in South Africa 1980* (Johannesburg: South African Institute of Race Relations, 1979), p. 234.

3 C. A. Giffard, "Media Trends in South Africa," Paper presented to "The Road Ahead" Conference, Grahamstown, South Africa, July 1978, pp. 11–12.

4 Anthony Mathews, *The Darker Reaches of Government* (Johannesburg: Juta, 1978), p. 169.

5 See Robin Hallett, "The South African Intervention in Angola, 1975–76," *African Affairs*, July 1978, pp. 347–86.

6 Interview with Joel Mervis, Johannesburg, January 16, 1981.

7 Barry Rubin, "Media under Pressure," *IPI Report*, January 1981, p. 8.

8 *Rand Daily Mail*, November 20, 1980, p. 4.

9 "World Press Freedom," *IPI Report*, December 1980, p. 13.

10 Ibid.

11 Interviewed in Johannesburg, January 15, 1981.

12 *The Star*, January 6, 1981, p. 2.

13 Coetsee and Tyson were quoted in *The Star*, January 24, 1981, p. 4. Vosloo was quoted in *Beeld*, January 21, 1981, p. 7.

14 *Report of the Commission of Inquiry into the Mass Media*, PR 89, 3 vols. (Pretoria: Government Printer, 1981, 1982).

Chapter 2

1 W. W. Bird, *State of the Cape of Good Hope in 1822* (London: John Murray, 1823), pp. 58–61.

2 Thomas Pringle, *Narrative of a Residence in South Africa* (Cape Town: C. Struik, 1966), p. 174.

3 *Papers Relating to the "South African Commercial Advertiser" and its Editor Mr. Greig*, London: January 1827 (Command Paper 470). For the early history of the press, see also G. M. Theale, *History of South Africa from 1795 to 1872*, Vol. 1 (London: George Allen and Unwin, 1927), pp. 416 ff., and G. E. Cory, *The Rise of South Africa*, Vol. 2 (London: Longmans, 1913).

4 Pringle, *Narrative*, p. 180.

5 L. H. Meurant, *Sixty Years Ago* (Cape Town: Africana Connoisseurs Press, 1963), p. 52.

6 Pringle, *Narrative*, p. 189.

7 Anthony Delius, "Journalism and the Press," address delivered at 60th anniversary celebrations, Rhodes University (Grahamstown, 1964).

8 W. M. MacMillan, *Bantu, Boer and Briton* (London: Faber and Gwyer, 1929), p. 115.

9 Robert Godlonton, *A Narrative of the Irruption of the Kafir Hordes* (Grahamstown: Meurant and Godlonton, 1936), pp. 85–87.

10 J. H. Hofmeyr, *Het Leven van Jan Hendrik Hofmeyr* (Cape Town: Van de Sandt de Villiers, 1913), p. 45.

11 J. du P. Scholtz, *Die Afrikaner en sy Taal* (Cape Town: Nasou, n.d.), pp. 41–42.

12 *De Mediator*, July 18, 1837.

13 L. E. Neame, *Today's News Today: The Story of the Argus Company* (Johannesburg: Argus Printing and Publishing Co., 1956).

14 T. Shepstone, *Shepstone's Letters*, Vol. 3, 1878 (University of Pretoria Library), p. 798.

15 Neame, *Today's News Today*, p. 41.

16 Quoted in Johan de Villiers, "South African Community and Its Newspapers: A Socio-Historical Study," Ph.D. diss., University of the Orange Free State, 1976. This dissertation reproduces many valuable source documents in Afrikaans, Dutch, and English.

17 See W. F. Butler, *Sir William Butler: An Autobiography* (London: Con-

stable, 1911), p. 392. Also the *Transvaal Leader*, January 29, 1887, and the *Standard and Diggers News*, May 31, 1900.

18 *Rand Daily Mail*, September 22, 1902.

19 *Sunday Times*, February 4, 1906.

20 H. E. O'Connor, "The Changing Role of the Press," *Communications in Africa*, Vol. 1, No. 2 (Grahamstown: Rhodes University, 1974).

21 H. L. Smith, *Behind the Press in South Africa* (Cape Town: Stewart, 1945), pp. 72–73.

22 T. R. H. Davenport, *South Africa: A Modern History* (London: Macmillan, 1977), pp. 148ff.

23 De Villiers, "South African Community."

24 Davenport, *South Africa*, p. 185.

25 F. P. Scannell, ed. *Keeromstraat 30* (Cape Town: Nasionale Boekhandel, 1965).

26 Neame, *Today's News Today*, p. 266.

27 Smith, *Behind the Press*, p. 163.

28 Neame, *Today's News Today*, pp. 279ff.

29 *Ibid*, pp. 280–281.

30 Davenport, *South Africa*, p. 252.

Chapter 3

1 Commission on the Freedom of the Press, *A Free and Responsible Press* (Chicago: University of Chicago Press, 1947).

2 Royal Commission on the Press, 1947–49, *Report*, Cmnd, 7700 (London, 1949).

3 *Hansard*, February 24, 1948.

4 *Times* (London), November 29, 1949.

5 The motion was debated on January 31, February 3, 10, and March 4, 1950.

6 Britain's Lord Iliffe bought a large block of shares in Eastern Province Newspapers in September 1949. The company said there would be no change in the policy of local control (see the London *Times*, September 12, 1949).

7 *The Star*, February 11, 1950.

8 *The Star*, October 24, 1950.

9 S.A. Press Board of Reference, *First Periodical Report* (Johannesburg, 1964), p. 6.

10 *Times* (London), August 18, 1954.

11 *Hansard*, February 6, 1957.

12 *Times*, September 17, 1959.

13 *Times*, April 8, 1960.

14 *The Star*, April 6, 1960.

15 *Die Burger*, April 7, 1960; *Times*, April 8, 1960.

16 *The Star*, April 20, 1960.

17 *Hansard*, April 14, 1961.

18 *Rand Daily Mail*, April 15, 1961.

19 S.A. Press Board of Reference, *First Periodical Report*, p. 7.

20 *The Star* and the *Rand Daily Mail*, March 14, 1962.

21 Quoted in the *Sunday Times*, April 6, 1962.

22 S.A. Press Board of Reference, *First Periodical Report*.

23 *Ibid.*

24 S.A. Press Commission 1950–64, *First Portion of the Report of the Commission of Inquiry into the Press* (Cape Town: S.A. Department of the Interior, 1962).

25 S.A. Press Commission 1950–64, *Second Portion of the Report of the Commission of Inquiry into the Press* (Cape Town: S.A. Department of the Interior, 1964). See the London *Times*, May 12, 1964.

26 S.A. Press Board of Reference, *Second Periodical Report* (Johannesburg, 1968).

27 S.A. Press Board of Reference, *Third Periodical Report* (Johannesburg, 1972).

28 S.A. Society of Journalists, *The Journalist*, December 1971.

29 *The Journalist*, December 1971, and *Eastern Province Herald*, September 15, 1972.

30 *Daily Dispatch*, September 6, 15, 1973.

31 Quoted in the *Daily Dispatch*, September 15, 1973.

32 *Eastern Province Herald*, September 20, 1973.

33 *Daily Dispatch*, October 31, 1973.

34 The *Argus*, July 20, 1974, and author's notes of the meeting.

35 South African Press Council, *Constitution*, (Johannesburg, July 1974).

36 *Daily Dispatch*, September 25, 1974.

37 *Die Transvaler*, August 7, 1974, and *Die Vaderland*, August 7, 1974.

38 *Cape Times*, December 16, 1975.

39 Republic of South Africa: Newspaper Bill (B.82–1977).

40 *The Star*, March 14, 1977.

41 *Die Transvaler*, March 15, 1977.

42 South African Press Council, *Annual Report*, 1979.

43 *The Star*, June 6, 1981.

Chapter 4

1 *Report of Commission of Inquiry into the Mass Media.*

2 *Pretoria News*, June 26, 1980, p. 1.

3 Quoted in *The Star*, December 3, 1980.

4 *Rand Daily Mail*, December 3, 1980, p. 16.

5 *Rand Daily Mail*, November 26, 1980, p. 1.

6 *The Star*, December 6, 1980, p. 2.

7 *Rand Daily Mail*, March 7, 1981, p. 2.

8 *Rand Daily Mail*, December 9, 1980, p. 3.

9 *Rand Daily Mail*, November 28, 1980, p. 1.

10 *Rand Daily Mail*, December 3, 1980, p. 16.

11 *Rand Daily Mail*, December 6, 1980, p. 3.

12 *East Province Herald*, March 20, 1981, p. 11.

13 *Rand Daily Mail*, October 25, 1980, p. 3.

14 *NPU Memorandum to Commission of Inquiry into Mass Media*, January 5, 1981, reported in *Rand Daily Mail*, January 22, 1981, p. 2.

15 SASJ Memo to Commission of Inquiry into Mass Media, January 1981.

16 *The Star*, December 13, 1980, p. 1.

17 *The Star*, February 28, 1981, p. 13.

18 *Rand Daily Mail*, January 16, 1981, p. 3.

19 *New York Times*, February 2, 1982, pp. 3 and E2.

20 Ibid.

21 *Rand Daily Mail*, February 2, 1982, p. 1; *The Star*, February 6, 1982, p. 10.

22 *New York Times*, February 3, 1982, p. 5.

23 Ibid.

24 Allister Sparks, "South Africa Relents on Press Curbs," *Washington Post*, July 1, 1982, p. A20.

25 *Report of Commission of Inquiry into the Mass Media*, p. 67.

26 Ibid., pp. 72–73.
27 Ibid., pp. 74–75, 76.
28 Quoted in *New York Times*, January 7, 1982, p. E3.
29 Ibid.
30 *Rand Daily Mail*, February 5, 1982.
31 *Report of Commission of Inquiry into the Reporting of Security News from South African Defense Force and Police*, RP 52 (Pretoria: Government Printer, 1980), para. 469.
32 Les Switzer, "Steyn Commission 1: The Press and Total Strategy," Paper, Rhodes University, 1980, p. 6.
33 William Hachten, *World News Prism* (Ames: Iowa State University Press, 1981), p. 14.
34 *The Journalist*, June, July, September 1983.
35 *The Star*, September 5, 1983.
36 *The Journalist*, September 1983.

Chapter 5

1 These five points were made by Anthony Mathews, "Banned," *Sunday Tribune* (Durban), January 4, 1981, p. 1.
2 Interview with a South African journalist, Johannesburg, January 1981.
3 Much of the material for this section is drawn from John Dugard, *Human Rights and the South African Legal Order* (Princeton: Princeton University Press, 1978).
4 Ibid., p. 7.
5 Ibid., p. 36.
6 J. D. van der Vyver, "The Function of the Press in the Face of Excessive Governmental Power," Paper presented at conference on censorship, University of Cape Town, April 1980.
7 Ibid, p. 4.
8 Dugard, *Human Rights*, p. 181.
9 Mathews, "Banned," p. 1.
10 Elaine Potter, *The Press as Opposition*, (Totowa, N.J.: Rowman and Littlefield, 1975), p. 102.
11 Interview with Mathews, Durban, March 10, 1981.
12 Benjamin Pogrund, "The South African Press," *Index on Censorship*, August 1976, p. 11.

13 Ibid.

14 Kelsey Stuart, *The Newspaperman's Guide to the Law*, 3d ed., (Durban: Butterworth, 1982), p. 140.

15 Pogrund, "South African Press," p. 12.

16 Ibid., p. 13.

17 Dugard, *Human Rights*, p. 223.

18 Frene Ginwala, "The Press in South Africa," *Index on Censorship*, no. 3, 1973, p. 27.

19 Interview with Keith Lister, Johannesburg, February 2, 1981.

20 G. E. Devenish, "A Critical Review of Inroads into Press Freedom in South Africa," *Business SA* 15 (May 1980): 31.

21 "Is This Act Really Necessary?" *Black Sash* 23, no. 4 (February 1981): 15.

22 Devenish, "Critical Review," pp. 34–35.

23 *Rand Daily Mail*, June 13, 1980, p. 1.

24 Interview with McMillan, Durban, March 9, 1981.

25 Pogrund, "South African Press," p. 13.

26 Interview with McMillan, Durban, March 9, 1981.

27 Interview with Shaw, Cape Town, April 1, 1981.

28 *The Star*, April 4, 1981, p. 5.

29 *Journalist*, December 1980, p. 4.

30 Interview with Mathews, Durban, March 18, 1981.

31 Interview with Shaw, Cape Town, April 1, 1981.

32 Interview with Switzer, Grahamstown, March 15, 1981.

33 Interview with Grogan, Grahamstown, March 16, 1981.

34 Anthony Mathews, "Censorship, Access to Information and Public Debate," *Theoria* 55 (October 1980): 23.

Chapter 6

1 That view was clearly expressed in a group interview with twelve black journalists of the MWASA chapel at the SAAN building, Johannesburg, February 24, 1981. No journalist present disagreed.

2 Giffard, "Media Trends in South Africa," p. 14.

3 C. A. Giffard, "The Impact of Television on South African Daily Newspapers," *Journalism Quarterly*, Summer 1980, p. 223.

4 *Washington Post*, July 28, 1978.

5 This view was expressed frequently in our talks with nonwhite journalists.

6 Quoted in *New York Times*, May 1, 1978.

7 Interview with Switzer, Grahamstown, July 20, 1978.

8 *Rand Daily Mail*, September 19, 1980, p. 5; Interview with Jaffer, Cape Town, March 25, 1981.

9 Graeme Addison, "The Union of Black Journalists: A Brief Survey," Paper, Journalism Department, Rhodes University, September 1977.

10 Hennie Serfontein, "Press War in South Africa," *Africa*, February 1981, p. 64.

11 *Rand Daily Mail*, July 3, 4, 1978.

12 Quoted by Caryle Murphy in *Washington Post*, July 28, 1978.

13 Serfontein, "Press War," p. 64.

14 Ibid.

15 Denis Becket, "The MWASA Strike," *Frontline* 1, no. 7, p. 5.

16 Interview with Louw, Johannesburg, December 19, 1980.

17 Interview with Pogrund, January 12, 1981.

18 Interview with Thornycroft, Johannesburg, February 5, 1981.

19 MWASA chapel interview.

20 Ibid.

21 Les Switzer and Donna Switzer, *The Black Press in South Africa and Lesotho*, (Boston: G. K. Hall, 1979), p. vii. Throughout this section, we have relied heavily on this authoritative study.

22 Quoted in SASJ Memorandum to Commission of Inquiry into Mass Media, January 3, 1981.

23 Gwendolen Carter, *The Politics of Inequality* (New York: Praeger, 1958), p. 43.

24 T. J. Couzens, "A Short History of the *World* and Other Black South African Newspapers," Paper, University of the Witwatersrand (Johannesburg), 1977, p. 2.

25 David Bristow, "The Black Voice That Knows Only Harassment," *The Star* (Johannesburg), May 16, 1981, p. 12.

26 Switzer and Switzer, *Black Press*, p. 1.

27 Ibid., p. 4.

28 Ibid., p. 8.

29 Ibid.

30 Graeme Addison, "The Drum That Roused the Black Consciousness," *The Star* (Johannesburg), May 16, 1981, p. 14.

31 Switzer and Switzer, *Black Press*, p. 16.
32 SASJ Memorandum to Commission of Inquiry into Mass Media, January 1981, p. 143.
33 Quoted in *Sowetan*, February 2, 1981, p. 5.

Chapter 7

1 Nadine Gordimer, "New Forms of Strategy—No Change of Heart," *Critical Arts*, June 1980, p. 27.
2 Dorothy Driver, "Control of the Black Mind Is the Main Aim of Censorship," *South African Outlook*, June 1980, p. 10.
3 André Brink, "Censorship and the Author," *Critical Arts*, June 1980, p. 16.
4 C. A. Giffard, "Censorship by Intimidation," unpublished paper, Madison, Wisconsin, November 1975, p. 3.
5 Dugard, *Human Rights*, pp. 191–92.
6 John Dugard, "A National Strategy for 1980," Presidential Address to S.A. Institute of Race Relations, Johannesburg, 1980, pp. 8–9.
7 Mathews, "Censorship, Access to Information and Public Debate," pp. 22–23.
8 Dugard, *Human Rights*, p. 193.
9 Ibid., p. 194.
10 Ursula Barnett, "Censorship in South Africa Today—From Bad to Worse," *Publishers Weekly*, September 22, 1975, p. 78.
11 Dugard, *Human Rights*, p. 194.
12 Reuters story in *New York Times*, February 10, 1974.
13 Interview with Louise Silver, Center for Applied Legal Studies, University of the Witwatersrand, January 25, 1981.
14 Nadine Gordimer et al., *What Happened to Burger's Daughter, or How South African Censorship Works* (Johannesburg: Taurus, 1980), p. 69.
15 Wessel Ebersohn, "Edging toward the Light," *Frontline*, March 1982, p. 28.
16 See Gordimer, *What Happened to Burger's Daughter*.
17 *Survey of Race Relations in South Africa, 1982* (Johannesburg: South African Institute of Race Relations), p. 265.
18 Paul Fussell, "The Smut Hounds of Pretoria," *New Republic*, February 23, 1980, p. 21.

19 Barnett, "Censorship in South Africa Today," p. 80.

20 Dugard, chapter in *What Happened to Burger's Daughter*, p. 71.

21 Louise Silver, "Criticism of the Police," *South African Law Journal* 95 (1978): 580.

22 Quoted by Dugard in *What Happened to Burger's Daughter*, p. 72.

23 Louise Silver, "The Statistics of Censorship," *South African Law Journal* 96 (1979): 120.

24 Helen Zille, "South Africa Gags 2 Student Journalists, Bans Their Anti-Apartheid Paper," p. 12.

25 Helen Zille, "Student Press is the Chief Victim of South Africa's Censorship Law," *Chronicle of Higher Education*, April 28, 1982, p. 19.

26 Memo of SASJ to Commission of Inquiry into Mass Media, January 1981, p. 148.

27 Brink, "Censorship and the Author," p. 23.

28 Quoted in *Rand Daily Mail*, March 3, 1981, p. 5.

29 Interview with Coetzee, Johannesburg, January 21, 1981.

30 *Sunday Tribune*, February 22, 1981, p. 12.

31 Deon du Plessis, "White Liberals Getting It from All Sides," *Sunday Tribune* (Durban), January 25, 1981, p. 8.

32 Ibid.

33 Dugard, *Human Rights*, p. 202.

Chapter 8

1 Willem Wepener, "The Role of the Afrikaans Press," in *Survival of the Press* (Grahamstown: Rhodes University, 1979).

2 Johan de Villiers, "South African Community and Its Newspapers: A Socio-Historical Study," Ph.D. diss., University of the Orange Free State, 1976.

3 Scannell, *Keeromstraat 30*, p. 44.

4 Potter, *Press as Opposition*, p. 181

5 Schalk Pienaar, "Afrikaners en hul Koerante: Vriendskap in Spanning," *Die Burger*, September 15, 1973.

6 Ebbe Dommisse, "The Changing Role of the Afrikaans Press," in Edwin S. Munger, ed. *The Afrikaners* (Cape Town: Tafelberg, 1979), p. 101.

7 Wepener, "Role of the Afrikaans Press."

8 *Dagbreek en Landstem*, November 22, 1970; *Beeld*, November 1, 1970; *Sunday Times*, November 1, 1970; Wepener, "Role of the Afrikaans Press."

9 *Beeld*, September 16, 1974.
10 *The Star*, September 26, 1983.
11 *Sunday Times*, January 4, 1981.
12 *The Journalist*, September 1982.
13 *The Star*, October 23, 1982.
14 *Beeld* and *Die Transvaler*, February 9, 1983.
15 *Oggendblad*, September 20, 1973.
16 Quoted in *Sunday Times*, September 19, 1973.
17 *Die Vaderland*, August 7, 1974.
18 *Die Transvaler*, August 8, 1974.
19 *Die Burger*, August 22, 1974.
20 *Die Transvaler*, August 20, 1974.
21 *Die Vaderland*, March 11, 15, 1977.
22 *Die Vaderland*, March 15, 1977.
23 *Die Transvaler*, March 15, 1977.
24 *Beeld*, March 20, 1979.
25 *Hoofstad*, May 21, 1979.
26 *Die Volksblad*, May 24, 1979.
27 *Rapport*, May 13, 1979.
28 *Beeld*, May 20, 1980.
29 *Die Transvaler*, October 10, 1979.
30 *Die Burger*, June 30, 1980.
31 *Beeld*, June 30, 1980.
32 *Beeld*, January 9, 1981.
33 *Beeld*, March 5, 1980.
34 *Beeld*, January 21, 1981.
35 *The Star*, May 1, 1982.
36 Heribert Adam and Hermann Giliomee, *Ethnic Power Mobilized: Can South Africa Change* (New Haven: Yale University Press, 1979).
37 Quoted in the *Rand Daily Mail*, April 11, 1981.
38 *Die Vaderland*, June 16, 1975.

Chapter 9

1 Peter Orlik, "Southern Africa," in Sydney W. Head, ed., *Broadcasting in Africa* (Philadelphia: Temple University Press, 1974), p. 141.
2 Ibid., pp. 142–43.
3 Ibid., p. 144.
4 Ibid., pp. 144–45.

5 Ivor Wilkins and Hans Strydom, *The Super Afrikaners* (Johannesburg: Ball, 1978), p. 1.

6 J. H. P. Serfontein, "The Afrikaner Mafia," *Africa*, December 1978, p. 68.

7 Wilkins and Strydom, *Super Afrikaners*, pp. 11–12.

8 "Broeder Domination," *Cape Times*, March 23, 1981, p. 6.

9 Peter Orlik, "South Africa: How Long without TV?" *Journal of Broadcasting*, Spring 1970, p. 246.

10 Ibid., p. 247.

11 Ibid.

12 Ibid., p. 248.

13 Ibid., p. 249.

14 Orlik, "Southern Africa," p. 149.

15 See *Report of the Commission of Inquiry into Matters Relating to Television* (Pretoria: Government Printer, 1971).

16 Ibid., pp. 46 ff.

17 William A. Hachten, "Policies and Performance of South African Television," *Journal of Communication*, Summer 1979, p. 68.

18 Interview with U.S. Embassy official, Johannesburg, March 10, 1981.

19 Interviews with Jan Pretorius and Ken Hamman of SABC news department, Johannesburg, January 25, 1981.

20 Interview with Van Zyl, Johannesburg, January 13, 1981.

21 Quoted in *The Star*, February 25, 1981, p. 3.

22 See *Annual Report of SABC*, 1977, p. 61.

23 *Rand Daily Mail*, November 7, 1978, p. 3.

24 Interview with U.S. embassy official, Johannesburg, March 10, 1981.

25 See *Annual Report of SABC*, 1967, p. 50.

26 Potter, *Press as Opposition*, p. 49.

27 Hachten, "Policies and Performance of South African Television," pp. 67–68.

28 Ibid.

29 Quoted in *Rand Daily Mail*, February 4, 1981, p. 3.

30 *Rand Daily Mail*, January 30, 1981.

31 *Sunday Times*, Feburary 15, 1981.

32 Heribert Adam, "The Political Sociology of South Africa: A Pragmatic Race Oligarchy," in Ian Robertson and Phillip Whitten, eds., *Race and*

Politics in South Africa, (New Brunswick, N.J.: Transaction Books, 1978), p. 47.

33 Allen Drury, *A Very Strange Society* (New York: Trident Press, 1967), p. 117.

34 *Annual Report of SABC*, 1976, pp. 13, 69.

35 "Johannesburg Survey of Blacks on TV," *The Star*, May 30, 1981, p. 2.

36 Joseph Lelyveld, "And Now, Separate TV for South African Blacks," *New York Times*, December 9, 1981, p. 8.

37 Ibid.

38 Letter to *The Star* by Ian Barnard, January 23, 1982, p. 7.

39 *The Star*, April 16, 1983, p. 8.

40 *Annual Report of the SABC*, 1978, p. 97.

41 *Sunday Express*, February 1, 1981, p. 3.

42 Interview with U.S. embassy official, March 10, 1981.

Chapter 10

1 *S.A. Digest*, March 25, 1983.

2 *Rapport*, March 20, 1983; *The Citizen*, March 21, 1983.

3 *Times* (London), July 5, 1957.

4 *Times* (London), September 17, 1959.

5 *Times* (London), November 13, 1961.

6 *Times* (London), January 2, 1962.

7 *Times* (London), January 26, 1962.

8 *Die Burger*, January 6, 7, 1962.

9 S.A. Press Commission, 1950–64, *First Portion of the Report of the Commission of Inquiry into the Press.*

10 S.A. Press Commission, *Second Portion of the Report of the Commission of Inquiry into the Press.*

11 For details of propaganda themes, see John C. Lawrence, *Race Propaganda and South Africa* (London: Victor Gollancz, 1979).

12 Mervyn Rees and Chris Day, *Muldergate* (Johannesburg: Macmillan, 1980), pp. 41 ff.

13 *Supplementary Report of the Commission of Inquiry into Alleged Irregularities in the Former Department of Information* (Republic of South Africa, 1979), p. 49. (Subsequently referred to as Erasmus II.)

14 *Rand Daily Mail*, December 11, 1980.

15 *Report of the Commission of Inquiry into Alleged Irregularities in the Former Department of Information* (Republic of South Africa, 1978), p. 52. (Subsequently referred to as Erasmus I.)

16 Les de Villiers, *Secret Information* (Cape Town: Tafelberg, 1980), pp. 54 ff.

17 *Ibid.*, p. 58.

18 *Ibid.*, p. 117.

19 *The Star*, November 1, 1975, and the *Argus*, October 28, 30, 1975.

20 *Rand Daily Mail*, October 29, 1975.

21 *Die Burger*, November 4, 1975.

22 *Weekend Argus*, November 1, 1975, and *Cape Times*, November 10, 1975.

23 *The Star*, October 24, 1975.

24 Erasmus I, pp. 52 ff., and Erasmus II, p. 26.

25 C. A. Giffard, "Newspaper Circulation Trends in South Africa," *Journalism Quarterly* (Spring 1980), pp. 86–91.

26 Rees and Day, *Muldergate*, p. 10.

27 Rhoodie's order to destroy documents is noted in Erasmus I, p. 30. The role of the *Sunday Express* is described in Rees and Day, *Muldergate*, pp. 18 ff. Vorster made his statement in Parliament on May 8, 1978, and Mulder on May 10. The charges against Mulder are listed in Erasmus I, pp. 76 ff.

28 De Villiers, *Secret Information*, p. 149.

29 Erasmus I, pp. 24 ff.

30 *Rand Daily Mail*, November 3, 1978.

31 Erasmus I, p. 152.

32 *Ibid.*, pp. 52-66.

33 *Beeld*, November 3, 1978, and *Die Transvaler*, November 3, 1978.

34 The commission's findings concerning dishonest use of funds are in Erasmus I, pp. 34–51; concerning *The Citizen*, on pp. 52–66; concerning Mulder, Rhoodie, and Van den Bergh, on pp. 76–93; and concerning Vorster, on pp. 68–74.

35 *Africa*, May 1979.

36 Rees and Day, *Muldergate*, pp. 185 ff.

37 *New York Times*, March 13, 1979.

38 The ruling by the Judge President of the Cape, J. W. van Zyl, was reported in *The Star*, April 11, 1979.

39 Vorster's role is discussed in Erasmus II, pp. 6–11; Horwood's on p. 53.

40 Karen Rothmyer, "The McGoff Grab," *The Columbia Journalism Review*, November/December 1979, pp. 33–39.

41 *Editor & Publisher*, August 18, 1979, p. 12.

42 *Rand Daily Mail*, August 30, 1980; *Milwaukee Journal*, September 18, 1983; *Editor & Publisher*, September 24, 1983.

43 Karen Rothmyer, "The South African Lobby," *The Nation*, April 19, 1980, pp. 455–58.

44 Erasmus II, pp. 16–20.

45 *Wall Street Journal*, January 16, 1979.

46 *Newsweek*, April 2, 1979.

47 Ibid.

48 Erasmus II, pp. 39 ff.

49 *The Star*, October 4, 1981.

50 *Sunday Express*, January 25 and February 1, 1981.

51 For Afrikaans press reaction, see Erasmus I, p. 26; *Rapport*, March 3, 1979; Les de Villiers, *Secret Information*, p. 166.

52 Mulholland's comments appeared in *Wall Street Journal*, January 16, 1979.

Chapter 11

1 E. J. Marais, *Demographic Trends in South Africa: Report of the President's Council* (Cape Town, 1983).

2 W. J. de Klerk, "Some Realities of the South African Situation" (Johannesburg: S.A. Forum, 1982).

3 Human Sciences Research Council, *Research Report S82* (Pretoria: HSRC, 1982).

4 United Press International, November 25, 1983. See also the S.A. Forum position paper "Education for Blacks Now a Major Priority" (Johannesburg, 1982).

5 *The Star*, November 10, 1982.

6 *Sunday Tribune*, February 1, 1981; *Sunday Times*, June 5, 1983; *Business Day*, October 11, 1983.

7 C. A. Giffard, "Circulation Trends in South Africa," *Journalism Quarterly*, Spring 1980, pp. 86–91.

8 S. A. Advertising Research Foundation, *All Media Product Survey*, 1972–1982.

9 Interview with Sparks, September 1979.

10 SAARF, *All Media Product Survey*, 1976–1980.

11 *The Journalist*, July 1981.

12 Ibid.

13 *Advertising Age*, August 8, 1983.

14 Interview with William Nicholson, AP bureau chief and president of the Foreign Correspondents Association, Johannesburg, February 17, 1981.

15 AP story from Harare, Zimbabwe, *New York Times*, August 1, 1983, p. 5.

16 This quotation and others that follow were obtained from interviews with four U.S. correspondents in Johannesburg, February 1981. Two of them did not wish to be quoted directly.

17 *S.A. Digest*, May 30, 1980, p. 6.

18 *New York Times*, November 24, 1982, p. 3.

19 *Wall Street Journal*, March 17, 1983, sec. 2, p. 29.

20 Conor Cruise O'Brien, "How Long Can They Last," *New York Review of Books*, November 5, 1981, p. 26.

21 "Nat Reform Is still Apartheid," *Race Relations News*, August 1982, p. 2.

22 *New York Times*, June 10, 1982, p. 4.

23 South African Press Association, June 28, 1983.

24 *The Citizen*, June 17, 1983.

25 *New York Times*, December 11, 1982, p. 3.

26 L. H. Gann and Peter Duigan, *Why South Africa Will Survive* (London: St. Martin's Press, 1980).

27 See *South Africa: Time Running Out*, Report of the Study Commission on U.S. Policy toward Southern Africa (Berkeley: University of California Press, 1981).

28 Quoted in "Time Running Out," *New Yorker*, August 31, 1981, p. 27.

29 *Wall Street Journal*, December 13, 1982, p. 20.

Glossary

Afrikaans A language, derived from Dutch, spoken as a home language by about 60 per cent of the white population and most Coloureds in South Africa.

Afrikaner South African citizen, usually of Dutch descent, whose home language is Afrikaans.

ANC African National Congress. Although outlawed, a major voice of Africans' opposition to white rule.

Apartheid A policy of strict racial segregation in all spheres; implemented especially by the National Party after 1948.

Argus The Argus Printing and Publishing Company. The largest chain in South Africa, it is primarily engaged in the English-language afternoon newspaper field.

Banning An action by the Minister of Justice to restrict a person's freedom of movement, association, and expression. In some cases, it includes house arrest. Organizations and publications can also be banned.

Broederbond A secret organization dedicated to promoting Afrikaans interests; has considerable influence on cultural, educational, and political policies.

HNP The Herstigte Nasionale Party. A right-wing offshoot of the ruling National Party, it is dedicated to maintaining traditional apartheid and opposes any liberalizing reforms.

Homelands Areas designated by the government as homes for the various African ethnic groups. There are ten, including Transkei, Ciskei, and Venda.

Laager A camp marked out by a circle of wagons used for defensive purposes by Dutch settlers in the nineteenth century. Now used metaphorically.

Nasionale Pers   Cape Town–based Afrikaans press and publishing company; has daily papers in several major cities.

National Party   The ruling party in South Africa since 1948. Traditionally representative of exclusively Afrikaner interests, it now occupies a centrist position with opposition from both the left and the right.

NPU   The Newspaper Press Union, a voluntary association of newspaper publishers. Magazine and periodical publishers can be associate members. The NPU regulates advertising, and operates the Audit Bureau of Circulations and the South African Media Council.

PAC   Pan-Africanist Congress. An outlawed political party that represents African interests.

Perskor   Afrikaans newspaper, printing, and publishing company based in the Transvaal.

PFP   The Progressive Federal party. The official Opposition in the South African Parliament, the party draws most of its support from English-speaking business and professional classes. It calls for a national convention of all race groups to negotiate a new multiracial constitution.

SAAN   South African Associated Newspapers. The country's second-largest newspaper chain, it owns or controls most of the English-language morning and Sunday papers.

SAPA   South African Press Association. A nonprofit cooperative news agency jointly owned by daily and Sunday newspaper companies, SAPA receives the bulk of its news from members. Most external news comes from Reuters and the Associated Press, with which it has exchange agreements.

Townships   Designated residential areas for Africans in South Africa, generally located near white cities. The largest is the southwest township, or Soweto, near Johannesburg.

Uitlander   A foreigner or alien; originally applied to British fortune-seekers of the nineteenth century who went to the Transvaal Republic after the discovery of gold there.

Verkramp   Narrow, rigid, or bigoted; a term applied to right-wing, ultra-conservative Afrikaaners.

Verlig   Literally, "enlightened"; a term applied to more liberal Afrikaners.

Volk   Afrikaans word for "the people" or "the nation"; refers to the Afrikaner nation.

Bibliography

Adam, Heribert, and Giliomee, Hermann. *Ethnic Power Mobilized: Can South Africa Change?* New Haven: Yale University Press, 1979.

Addison, Graeme. "Black Press: A Selected Bibliography." Journalism Department, Rhodes University.

Addison, Graeme. "The Drum That Roused the Black Consciousness." *The Star* (Johannesburg), May 16, 1981, p. 14.

Addison, Graeme. "'Total Strategy' and the News of the Angolan War." Journalism Department, Rhodes University, May 1979.

Addison, Graeme. "The Union of Black Journalists: A Brief Survey." Journalism Department, Rhodes University, September 1977.

Ainslie, Rosalynde. *The Press in Africa: Communications Past and Present.* New York: Walker, 1966.

Annual Report of the South African Broadcasting Corporation. 1976, 1977, 1978.

Ascherson, Neal. "Selling Apartheid: The Facelift in South Africa." *Ramparts*, July 1975, pp. 11–13.

"Banned in South Africa." *More*, December 1977, pp. 12 ff.

Barnett, Ursula. "Censorship in South Africa Today—From Bad to Worse." *Publishers Weekly*, September 22, 1975, pp. 78–80.

Barton, Frank. *The Press of Africa: Persecution and Perseverance.* New York: Africana, 1979.

Beaubien, Michael. "Inadequate, Infrequent and Insufficient." *Southern Africa*, January 1980, pp. 7–9, 26.

Beckett, Denis. "The MWASA Strike: Beneath the Surface Lie Bottomless Depths." *Frontline* 1, no. 7, pp. 4–7.

Bellwood, W. A. *South African Backdrop.* Cape Town: Nasionale Boekhandel, 1969.

Benson, Ivor. *The Opinion Makers.* Pretoria: Dolphin Press, 1967.

van den Berghe, P. L. *South Africa: A Study in Conflict.* Middletown, Conn.: Wesleyen University Press, 1965.

Bernstein, Peter. "Reporting in Pretoria." *Index on Censorship*, Autumn 1975, pp. 44–48.

"Biko's Friend." *New Yorker*, May 29, 1978, p. 22.

Bird, J. *The Annals of Natal 1495 to 1845.* Cape Town: C. Struik, 1965.

Bird, W. W. *State of the Cape of Good Hope in 1822.* London: John Murray, 1823.

Blackwell, Leslie, and Bamford, Brian. *Newspaper Law of South Africa.* Cape Town: Juta, 1963.

Bosman, F. C. L. *Hollandse Joernalistiek in Suid-Afrika Gedurende die 19de Eeu.* Reprint of articles which appeared in *Ons Land* on April 1, 1930.

Botha, P. R. *Die Staatkundige Ontwikkeling van die Suid-Afrikaanse Republiek onder Kruger en Leyds, 1844–1899.* Amsterdam: Swets en Zeitlinger, 1926.

Boyce, W. B. *Notes on South African Affairs.* London: J. Mason, 1839.

Brink, André. "Censorship and the Author." *Critical Arts*, June 1980, pp. 16–26.

Bristow, David. "The Black Voice That Knows Only Harassment." *The Star* (Johannesburg), May 16, 1981, p. 12.

Brookes, Edgar H. *A History of Natal.* University of Natal Press, 1965.

Brookes, Edgar H., and Macaulay, J. B. *Civil Liberty in South Africa.* Cape Town: Oxford University Press, 1958.

Broughton, Morris. *Press and Politics of South Africa.* Cape Town: Purnell and Sons, 1961.

Brown, Douglas. *Against the World: Attitudes of White South Africa.* Garden City, N.J.: Doubleday, 1968.

Brown, Trevor. "Did Anybody Know His Name? U.S. Press Coverage of Biko." *Journalism Quarterly*, Spring 1980, pp. 31–38.

Brown, Trevor. "Free Press Fair Game of South Africa's Government." *Journalism Quarterly*, Spring 1971, pp. 120–127.

Brown, Trevor. "The South African Press: No News for 170 Years?" Paper presented to Association for Education in Journalism, University of California at Berkeley, August 1969.

Calpin, G. H. *There Are No South Africans.* London: Thomas Nelson and Sons, 1942.

Cape Times. The Cape Times Centenary Supplement. March 27, 1976.

Cape Times. Fifty Years of the Cape Times. November 1, 1926.

Carter, Gwendolen. *The Politics of Inequality: South Africa since 1948.* New York: Praeger, 1958.

Carter, Gwendolen, ed. *Five African States: Responses to Diversity.* Ithaca, N.Y.: Cornell University Press, 1963.

Carter, Gwendolen, and O'Meara, Patrick, eds. *Southern Africa: The Continuing Crisis.* Bloomington: Indiana University Press, 1977.

Carter, Gwendolen, and O'Meara, Patrick, eds. *Southern Africa in Crisis.* Bloomington: Indiana University Press, 1977.

"Censorship Noose Tightens around South African Librarians." *American Libraries,* September 1975, p. 497.

Charles, Jeff; Shore, Larry, and Todd, Rusty. "The New York Times Coverage of Equatorial and Lower Africa." *Journal of Communication,* Spring 1979, pp. 148–55.

Chimutengwende, Chenhamo. "The Media and the State in South African Politics." *Black Scholar,* September 1978, pp. 44–57.

Chimutengwende, Chenhamo. *South Africa: The Press and the Politics of Liberation.* London: Barbican Books, 1979.

Cloete, Bettie. *Die lewe van Senator F. S. Malan.* Johannesburg: Afrikaanse Pers-Boekhandel, 1946.

Coetzee, J. A. *Nasieskap en Politieke Groepering in Suid-Afrika, 1652–1968.* Pretoria: Transvaalse Uitgewersmaatskappy, 1969.

Collins, W. W. *Free Statia: Reminiscences of a Lifetime in the Orange Free State.* Cape Town: C. Struik, 1965.

Corrigan, Edward C. "South Africa Enters into Electronic Age." *Africa Today,* Spring 1974, pp. 15–28.

Cory, G. E. *The Rise of South Africa.* London: Longmans, Green, 1913.

Couzens, Tim J. "A Short History of the *World* and Other Black South African Newspapers." University of the Witwatersrand (Johannesburg), 1977.

Crisp, R. *The Outlanders: The Men Who Made Johannesburg.* London: Peter Davies, 1964.

Cutten, Theo E. G. *A History of the Press in South Africa*. Cape Town: National Union of South African Students, 1935.

Davenport, T. R. H. *The Afrikaner Bond: The History of a South African Political Party, 1880–1911*. Cape Town: Oxford University Press, 1966.

Davenport, T. R. H. *South Africa: A Modern History*. London: Macmillan, 1977.

Davis, Foster. "Percy Qoboza's Nightmare." *Progressive*, January 1978, p. 28.

Devenish, G. E. "A Critical Review of Inroads into Press Freedom in South Africa." *Business SA 15*, (May 1980): 30–35.

Dormer, F. J. *Vengeance as a Policy in Afrikanerland: A Plea for a New Departure*. London: James Nisbet, 1901.

Driver, Dorothy. "Control of the Black Mind Is the Main Aim of Censorship." *South African Outlook*, June 1980, pp. 10-13.

Drury, Allen. *A Very Strange Society*. New York: Trident Press, 1967.

Dugard, John. *Human Rights and the South African Legal Order*. Princeton, N.J.: Princeton University Press, 1978.

Dugard, John. "A National Strategy for 1980." Presidential Address to the S.A. Institute for Race Relations, Johannesburg, 1980. 12 pp.

Dugmore, R. H. *The Reminiscences of an Albany Settler*. Grahamstown: Grocott and Sherry, 1958.

Ebersohn, Wessel. "Edging toward the Light." *Frontline*, March 1982, pp. 28–30.

Edwards, I. E. *The 1820 Settlers in South Africa: A Study in British Colonial Policy*. London: Longmans, Green, 1934.

Erasmus, L. J. *'n Volk Staan op uit sy As: Verhaal van die Afrikaanse Pers (1962) Beperk*. Johannesburg: T. W. Hayne, 1969.

Foisie, Jack; Ryan, John; Akhalwaya, Ameen; and Vosloo, Ton. "Update: The Press in South Africa." *Nieman Reports*, Summer 1982, No. 2, pp. 23–28.

The Friend. A Century of Achievement, 1850–1950: An Official Record of the First 100 Years of The Friend Newspapers Ltd. Special Centenary Supplement to the *Friend*, June 10, 1950.

Fussell, Paul. "The Smut Hounds of Pretoria." *New Republic*, February 23, 1980, pp. 20–23.

Galbraith, J. S. *Reluctant Empire: British Policy on the South African Frontier, 1834–1854*. Los Angeles: University of California Press, 1963.

"Gandar Trial: Ex-Prisoner Describes Torture by Warder." *IPI Report*, May–June 1969, pp. 14–15.

Gann, L. H., and Duigan, Peter. *Why South Africa Will Survive: An Historical Analysis*. London: St. Martin's Press, 1980.

Garrett, F. E., and Edwards, E. J. *The Story of an African Crisis: Being the Truth about the Jameson Raid and Johannesburg Revolt of 1896*. London: Archibald Constable, 1897.

Geyser, D., and Marais, A. H. *Die Nasionale Party: Agtergrond, Stigting en Konsolidasie*. Pretoria: Academica, 1975.

Giffard, C. A. "Censorship by Intimidation: The Saga of the South African Press Council." University of Wisconsin, Madison, November 4, 1975.

Giffard, C. A. "Circulation Trends in South Africa." *Journalism Quarterly*, Spring 1980, pp. 86–91, 106.

Giffard, C. A. "The Impact of Television on South African Daily Newspapers." *Journalism Quarterly*, Summer 1980, pp. 216–23.

Giffard, C. A. "Keeping Terrorism under Wraps: The Special Case of South Africa." Paper delivered at Association for Education in Journalism, Corvallis, Ore., August 1983.

Giffard, C. A., "Media Trends in South Africa." Paper presented at "The Road Ahead" Conference, Grahamstown, South Africa, July 1978.

Giffard, C. A. "South African Attitudes toward News Media." *Journalism Quarterly*, Winter 1976, pp. 653-60.

Giffard, C. A., ed. *The Reminiscences of John Montgomery*. Cape Town: A. A. Balkema, 1981.

Ginwala, Frene. "The Press in South Africa." *Index on Censorship*, no. 3, 1973, pp. 27–43.

Gordimer, Nadine. "New Forms of Strategy—No Change of Heart." *Critical Arts*, June 1980, pp. 27–33.

Gordimer, Nadine. "The South African Censor: No Change." *Index on Censorship*, February 1981, pp. 4–10.

Gordimer, Nadine; Dugard, John, et al. *What Happened to Burger's Daughter, or How South African Censorship Works*. Johannesburg: Taurus, 1980.

Green, G. A. L. *An Editor Looks Back*. Westport, Conn.: Negro Universities Press, 1970.

Greig, G. *Facts Connected with the Stopping of the South African Commercial Advertiser*. Cape Town: Africana Connoisseurs Press, 1963.

Gunter, C. F. G. "Die Eerste Nuusblaaie Aan die Kaap (1830–1833) en die

Stryd vir die Vryheid van die Pers (1823–1829)." M.A. thesis, University of South Africa, 1930.

Hachten, William A. "The Black Journalist under Apartheid." *Index on Censorship*, May/June 1979, pp. 43–48.

Hachten, William A. "The Future of Mass Communication in Africa." Paper presented at "The Road Ahead" Conference, Grahamstown, South Africa, July 7, 1978.

Hachten, William A. *Mass Communications in Africa: An Annotated Bibliography*. Madison, Wis.: Center for International Communication Studies, 1971.

Hachten, William A. "Mass Media in South Africa: The View from Without." Paper presented at "English-Speaking South Africa: An Assessment" Conference in Grahamstown, South Africa, 1974.

Hachten, William A. *Muffled Drums: The News Media in Africa*. Ames: Iowa State University Press, 1971.

Hachten, William A. "Policies and Performance of South African Television." *Journal of Communication*, Summer 1979, pp. 62–72.

Hallett, Robin. "The South African Intervention in Angola, 1975–75." *African Affairs*, July 1978, pp. 347–86.

Harrington, A. L. *The Grahamstown Journal and the Great Trek, 1834–1843*. M.A. thesis, University of South Africa, 1968.

Harrison, Randall, and Ekman, Paul. "TV's Last Frontier: South Africa." *Journal of Broadcasting*, Winter 1976.

Hattersley, A. F. *Portrait of a Colony: The Story of Natal*. London: Cambridge University Press, 1940.

Head, Sydney. "African Mass Communication: Selected Information Sources." *Journal of Broadcasting*, Summer 1976, pp. 318–415.

van den Heever, C. M., ed., and Pienaar, P. de V. *Kultuurgeskiedenis van die Afrikaner*. Cape Town: Nasionale Pers, 1945.

Hepple, Alex. *Censorship and Press Control in South Africa*. Johannesburg, 1960. Published by the author.

Hepple, Alex. *Press under Apartheid*. London: International Defence and Aid Fund, 1974.

Herbst, D. A. S. "Die Dilemma van die Moderne Koerant: 'n Historiese Ondersoek met Toespitsing op Maatskaplike, Ekonomiese en Politieke Aspekte." D. Phil. diss., Potchefstroom University, 1966.

Hoagland, Jim. *South Africa: Civilizations in Conflict*. Boston: Houghton Mifflin, 1972.

Hobson, J. A. *The War in South Africa: Its Causes and Effects.* New York: Garland, 1972.

Hockly, J. A. *The Story of the British Settlers of 1820 in South Africa.* Cape Town: Juta, 1966.

Hopkinson, Tom. *In the Fiery Continent.* New York: Doubleday, 1963.

Hotz, L. "The Press: Thomas William Mackenzie," in R. M. de Villiers, ed., *Better Than They Knew.* Vol. 2. Cape Town: Purnell, 1974.

"How Ideology Weakened a News Chain." *Business Week,* August 25, 1980.

"Into the TV Age." *Time,* January 19, 1976, p. 41.

"Is This Act Really Necessary?" *Black Sash* 23, no. 4 (February 1981): 14–17.

van Jaarsveld, F. A. *Afrikaner Quo Vadis?* Johannesburg: Voortrekkerspers, 1971.

van Jaarsveld, F. A. *The Awakening of Afrikaner Nationalism, 1868–1881.* Cape Town: Human and Rousseau, 1961.

Jackson, Gordon. "TV2: The Introduction of Television for Blacks in South Africa." Paper presented to Association for Education in Journalism, Michigan State University, August 1981.

Jenkins, G. A. *Century of History: The Story of Potchefstroom.* Cape Town: A. A. Balkema, 1971.

Kahn, Ellison. "Where the Lion Feeds—and the Censor Pounces: A Disquisition on the Banning of Immoral Publications in South Africa." *South African Law Journal* 83 (1966): 278–336.

Kane-Berman, John. *Soweto: Black Revolt, White Reaction.* Johannesburg: Ravan Press, 1978.

Kitchen, Helen. *The Press in Africa.* Washington: Ruth Sloan Associates, 1956.

Kitchen, Helen. "Some Observations on U.S. Media Coverage of South Africa in the 1980's." *International Affairs Bulletin* 4, no. 3 (1980): 10–17.

Kleu, Sebastian. "The Afrikaans Press: Voice of Nationalism." *Nieman Reports,* October 1961, pp. 9–11.

Kruger, D. W. *The Making of a Nation: A History of the Union of South Africa, 1910–1961.* Johannesburg: Macmillan, 1969.

Kuper, Leo. *An African Bourgeoisie: Race, Class and Politics in South Africa.* New Haven: Yale University Press, 1965.

Lacob, Miriam. "South Africa's 'Free' Press." *Columbia Journalism Review,* November/December 1982, pp. 49–56.

Laurence, John. "Censorship by Skin Colour." *Index on Censorship*, March/
April 1977, pp. 40–43.

Laurence, John. *The Seeds of Disaster*. London: Victor Gollancz, 1968.

Lelyveld, Joseph. "Breakup of a Community." *New York Times Book Review*, May 17, 1981, pp. 3, 29–30.

Lelyveld, Joseph. "And Now, Separate TV for South Africa Blacks." *New
York Times*, December 9, 1981, p. 8.

Lelyveld, Joseph. "South Africa's Censors Relax Some Ground Rules." *New
York Times*, December 4, 1980, p. 4.

Le May, G. H. L. *British Supremacy in South Africa, 1899–1907*. Oxford
University Press, 1965.

Le Roux, N. J. *W. A. Hofmeyr, Sy Werk en Waarde*. Cape Town: Nasionale
Boekhandel, 1953.

Le Sueur, G. *Cecil Rhodes: The Man and His Works*. London: John Murray,
1913.

Leyds, W. J. *The First Annexation of the Transvaal*. London: T. Fisher
Unwin, 1906.

Lighton, C., and Harris, C. B. *Details Regarding the Diamond Fields Advertiser
(1878–1969)*. Kimberley: Northern Cape Printers, 1968.

Lloyd, A. C. G. *The Birth of Printing in South Africa*. London: Alexander
Moring, 1914.

MacDonald, T. *Transvaal Story*. Cape Town: Howard Timmins, 1961.

Magubane, Peter. *Magubane's South Africa*. New York: Knopf, 1978.

Malan, D. F. *Afrikaner Volkseenheid en my Ervarings op die Pad Daarheen*.
Cape Town: Nasionale Boekhandel, 1959.

Mandelbrote, J. C. *The Cape Press, 1838–1850: A Bibliography*. Cape Town:
School of Librarianship, University of Cape Town, 1945.

Marais, J. S. *The Fall of Kruger's Republic*. Oxford University Press, 1961.

Marquard, Leo. *The Peoples and Policies of South Africa*. London: Oxford
University Press, 1969.

Mathews, Anthony. "Banned." *Sunday Tribune* (Durban), January 4, 1981.

Mathews, Anthony. "Censorship, Access to Information and Public Debate." *Theoria* 55 (October 1980): 21–31.

Mathews, Anthony. *The Darker Reaches of Government*. Johannesburg: Juta,
1978.

Mathews, Anthony. *Law, Order and Liberty in South Africa*. Cape Town:
Juta, 1971.

McKay, Vernon. "The Propaganda Battle for Zambia." *Africa Today*, April 1971, pp. 18–26.

McKay, Vernon. "South African Propaganda: Methods and Media." *Africa Report*, February 1966, pp. 41–46.

McKay, Vernon. "South African Propaganda on the International Court's Decision." *African Forum*, Fall 1966, pp. 51–64.

McKinnell, R. T. "The Printing and Newspaper Industry of South Africa, with Special Reference to Natal." M.A. thesis, University of Natal, 1951.

Mervis, Joel. "The Nightmarish World of South Africa's Journalists." *IPI Report*, November 1979, pp. 12–14.

Meurant, L. H. *Sixty Years Ago*. Cape Town: Africana Connoisseurs Press, 1963.

Muller, C. F. J., ed. *Five Hundred Years: A History of South Africa*. Pretoria: Academica, 1969.

Muller, W. A. "Dr. H. F. Verwoerd se Joernalistieke Bydrae tot die Republikeinse Idee." M.A. thesis, University of Pretoria, 1973.

Munger, Edwin S., ed. *The Afrikaners*. Cape Town: Tafelberg, 1979.

Mybergh, Tertius. "The South African Press: Hope in an Unhappy Land." *Nieman Reports*, March 1966, pp. 3–6.

Natal Mercury. "The Natal Mercury Centenary Souvenir: One Hundred Years of Service, 1852–1952." November 25, 1952.

Natal Witness. Centenary Number, Pietermaritzburg, 1924.

Neame, L. E. *Today's News Today: The Story of the Argus Company*. Johannesburg: Argus, 1956.

Neier, Aryeh. "Selling Apartheid." *Nation*, August 11, 1979, pp. 104–6.

van Niekerk, A. P. "Die Kaapse Pers en die Groot Trek, 1834–1842." M.A. thesis, University of South Africa, 1966.

Nienaber, P. J. *'n Beknopte Geskiedenis van die Hollands-Afrikaanse Drukpers in Suid-Afrika*. Cape Town: Nasionale Pers, 1943.

Nienaber, P. J. *Mylpale in die Geskiedenis van die Afrikaanse Taal en Letterkunde*. Johannesburg: Afrikaanse Pers Boekhandel, 1951.

Nixon, J. *The Complete Story of the Transvaal*. Cape Town: C. Struik, 1972.

Nixon, Ray, and Hahn, Tae-Youl. "Concentration of Press Ownership: A Comparison of 32 Countries." *Journalism Quarterly*, Spring 1971, pp. 5–16.

O'Brien, Conor Cruise. "How Long Can They Last?" *New York Review of Books*, November 5, 1982, pp. 17–31.

Oliver, G. D. "South Africa: An Inquiry Which Ridicules Its Authors." *IPI Report*, July 1964, pp. 1–5.

O'Meara, Patrick. "South Africa's Watergate: The Muldergate Scandals." *American Universities Field Staff Reports*, Africa Series, no. 43, 1979.

Oppenheimer, H. F. "The Press and South African Society," in *Communications in Africa* 1, no. 4 (December 1972). Grahamstown: Department of Journalism, Rhodes University.

Orlik, Peter B. "Co-Opting the Messenger: The Afrikaner Take-Over of the South African Broadcasting Corporation." Unpublished and undated paper.

Orlik, Peter B. "Under Damocles' Sword—The South African Press." *Journalism Quarterly*, Summer 1969, pp. 343–48.

Orlik, Peter B. "South Africa: How Long without TV?" *Journal of Broadcasting*, Spring 1970, pp. 145–58.

Orlik, Peter B. "The South African Broadcasting Corporation: An Historical Survey and Contemporary Analysis." Ph.D. diss., Wayne State University, 1970.

Orlik, Peter B. "Southern Africa," in Sydney W. Head, ed., *Broadcasting in Africa*, pp. 140–51. Philadelphia: Temple University Press, 1974.

Pachai, B. "Gandhi and His South Africa Journal *Indian Opinion*." *Africa Quarterly*, July–September 1969, pp. 76–82.

"Pandora's Box." *Newsweek*, May 26, 1975, p. 63.

Patterson, S. *The Last Trek: A Study of the Boer People and the Afrikaner Nation*. London: Routledge and Kegan Paul, 1957.

"Percy Qoboza Case." *Nieman Reports*, Winter/Spring 1978, pp. 34–37.

Pienaar, S. W. *Schalk Pienaar: 10 Jaar Politieke Kommentaar*, compiled by Ton Vosloo. Cape Town: Tafelberg: Uitgewers, 1975.

du Plessis, Deon. "White Liberals Getting It from All Sides." *Sunday Tribune* (Durban), January 25, 1981, p. 8.

du Plessis, J. H. D. "Die Afrikaanse Pers: 'n Studie van die Onstaan, Ontwikkeling en Rol van die Hollands-Afrikaanse Pers as Sosiale Instelling." D. Phil. diss., University of Stellenbosch, 1943.

Pogrund, Benjamin. "Color Line." *New Republic*, December 17, 1977, pp. 15–17.

Pogrund, Benjamin. "The South African Press." *Index on Censorship*, August 1976, pp. 11–16.

Pollak, Richard. *Up against Apartheid: The Role and the Plight of the Press in South Africa*. Carbondale: Southern Illinois University Press, 1981.

Pollock, Francis. "America's Press on Safari." *Nation*, November 7, 1966, pp. 479–81.

Potter, Elaine. *The Press as Opposition: The Political Role of South African Newspapers*. Totowa, N.J.: Rowman and Littlefield, 1975.

Preller, G. S. "Oudste koerante Kroniek—'n interessante kroniek oor die alleroudste nuusblaaie in die noordelike provinsies." *De Volkstem*, October 1, 1924.

"Press Commission Report." *Africa Digest*, August 1964, pp. 26–27.

Pringle, T. *Narrative of a Residence in South Africa*. London: Edward Moxon, 1835.

Prior, M. *Campaigns of a War Correspondent*. London: Edward Arnold, 1912.

"Publishing under Seige." *South*, April 1981, pp. 34–35.

"Qoboza." In Notes and Comments, *New Yorker*, November 28, 1977, pp. 41–42.

Rand Daily Mail. "Our First Fifty Years, 1902–1952." September 22, 1952.

Rand Daily Mail. "The Story of a Newspaper Enterprise," August 26, 1911.

Rand Daily Mail. "The Story of the *Rand Daily Mail*, 1902–1923." September 23, 1923.

Rees, Mervyn, and Day, Chris. *Muldergate*. Johannesburg: Macmillan, 1980.

Regan, F. W. *Boer and Uitlander: The True History of the Late Events in South Africa*. London: Digby, Long, 1896.

"Reluctant Witness Tells of Trap for Newsman." *IPI Report*, February 1969, pp. 5–6.

van Rensburg, J. J. "Hollandse Joernalistiek in die Oranje Vrystaat, Meer Bepaald in Bloemfontein voor 1900." M.A. thesis, University of South Africa, 1937.

Report of the Commission of Inquiry into Matters Relating to Television. Pretoria: Government Printer, 1971.

Report of the Commission of Inquiry into the Mass Media, PR 89, 3 vols.; and *Supplementary Report of Commission of Inquiry into the Mass Media*, PR 13. Pretoria: Government Printer, 1981, 1982.

Report of the Commission of Inquiry into the Reporting of Security News from South African Defense Force and Police. PR 52. Pretoria: Government Printer, 1980.

"Rewards of Moderation: Suppression of the *World*." *New Republic*, October 19, 1977, pp. 5–6.

Robertson, Ian, and Whitten, Phillip, eds. *Race and Politics in South Africa.* New Brunswick, N.J.: Transaction Books, 1978.

Robinson, A. M. L. *None Daring to Make Us Afraid: A Study of English Periodical Literature in the Cape Colony from Its Beginnings in 1824 to 1835.* Cape Town: Maskew Miller, 1962.

Ronan, B. *Forty South African Years: Journalistic, Political, Social, Theatrical and Pioneering.* London: Heath Cranton, n.d.

Rose, E. B. *The Truth about the Transvaal: A Record of Facts Based upon Twelve Years' Residence in the Country.* London: E. B. Rose, 1902.

Rose, P. H. "The Progress of the Press," in *A Century of Progress in Natal, 1824–1924.* Centenary number of the *Natal Witness*, Pietermaritzburg, 1924.

Rosenthal, E. *Gold! Gold! Gold! The Johannesburg Gold Rush.* London: Macmillan, 1970.

Rosenthal, E. *160 Jaar van Drukwerk in Kaapstad.* Cape Town: Cape Town Association of Printing House Craftsmen and the Kaapse Kamer van Drukwerk, 1960.

Rotberg, Robert I. *Suffer the Future: Policy Choices in South Africa.* Cambridge: Harvard University Press, 1980.

Rothmyer, Karen. "The McGoff Grab." *Columbia Journalism Review*, November/December 1979, pp. 33–39.

Rothmyer, Karen. "The South African Lobby." *Nation*, April 19, 1980, pp. 455-58.

Rubin, Barry. "Media under Pressure." *IPI Report*, January 1981, pp. 8–9, 15.

Rubin, Barry. "The Press Divided." *IPI Report*, March 1981, pp. 8–10.

Rubin, Barry. "Press under Apartheid." *IPI Report*, February 1981, pp. 8–9, 15.

Rubin, Barry. "The Uncertain Future of South Africa's Press." *Washington Journalism Review*, November 1980, pp. 41–45.

Sachs, Albie. "The Instruments of Domination in South Africa," in Leonard Thompson and Jeffrey Butler, eds., *Change in Contemporary South Africa*, pp. 223–49. Berkeley: University of California Press, 1975.

St. Leger, F. Y. *The African Press in South Africa.* Ph.D. diss., Rhodes University, South Africa, 1974.

Sampson, Anthony. *Drum: The Newspaper That Won the Heart of Africa.* New York: Houghton Mifflin, 1957.

Scannell, F. P. *Keeromstraat 30: Gedenkbundel vir die Vyftigste Verjaardag van Die Burger.* Cape Town: Nasionale Boekhandel, 1965.

Schecter, Daniel. "Media Myopia: U.S. Press Coverage Distorts Economic Issues, Black Views." *More,* December 1977, pp. 26–31.

Scholtz, G. D. *Dr. Hendrik Frensch Verwoerd, 1901–1966.* Johannesburg: Perskor, 1974.

Schonfrucht, R. M. *The Cape Press, 1851–1855: A Bibliography.* Cape Town: School of Librarianship, University of Cape Town, 1955.

van Schoor, M. C. E., and Van Rooyen, J. J. *Republieke en Republikeine.* Cape Town: Nasionale Boekhandel, 1960.

Seiler, John. "World Perspectives of South African Media." *Communications in Africa,* January 1973, pp. 26–30.

"The Selling of Apartheid." *Africa,* June 1978, pp. 71-73.

Serfontein, J. H. P. "The Afrikaner Mafia." *Africa,* December 1978, pp. 67–70.

Serfontein, J. H. P. *Brotherhood of Power.* London: Rex Collings, 1979.

Serfontein, J. H. P. "Press War in South Africa." *Africa,* February 1981, p. 64.

Shaw, G. *Some Beginnings: The Cape Times, 1876-1910.* Cape Town: Oxford University Press, 1975.

Shorten, J. R. *The Johannesburg Saga.* Johannesburg: John R. Shorten, 1970.

Silk, Andrew. "Black Journalists in Johannesburg." *Nation,* November 5, 1977, pp. 454–56.

Silk, Andrew. "Vorster Bullies the Press." *Nation,* May 21, 1977, pp. 18–21.

Silver, Louise. "Criticism of the Police: Standards Enunciated by the Publications Appeal Board." *South African Law Journal* 95 (1978): 580–83.

Silver, Louise. "The Statistics of Censorship." *South African Law Journal* 96 *Journal* 97 (1980): 125–37.

Silver, Louise. "The Statistics of Censorship." *South African Law Journal* 96 (1979): 1120–126.

Smith, A. H. *The Spread of Printing: South Africa.* Amsterdam: Vangende, 1971.

Smith, E. *Fields of Adventure: Some Reflections of Forty Years of Newspaper Life.* London: Hutchinson, 1923.

Smith, H. Lindsay. *Behind the Press in South Africa*. Cape Town: Stewart, 1945.

"South Africa: IPI Member Faces Trial." *IPI Report*, December 1968, pp. 6–7.

"South Africa: Report on Introduction of TV." *EBU Review*, July 1971, pp. 51–52.

South Africa: Time Running Out. Report of the Study Commission on U.S. Policy toward Southern Africa. Berkeley: University of California Press, 1981.

"South Africa after Muldergate." *Atlas*, August 1979, pp. 17–20.

South African newspapers available on microfilm. State Library, Pretoria, 1975.

S.A. Press Commission, 1950–1964. *First Portion of the Report of the Commission of Inquiry into the Press*. S.A. Department of the Interior, 1962–64.

The Star. "Diamond Jubilee of The Star." October 17, 1972.

The Star. "The Press, Printing and Publishing in South Africa." October 7, 1936.

The Star. "The Star Celebrates Its Golden Jubilee." October 17, 1947.

Strauss, S. "Beriggewing in *De Volksstem* en *The Star* gedurende die Tydperk 1896 tot 1899 oor die Gebeurtenisse wat gelei het tot die Tweede Vryheidsoorlog 1899–1902." M.A. thesis, University of Pretoria, 1964.

Strauss, S. A.; Strydom, M. J.; and van der Walt, J. C. *Die Persswese en die Reg*. Pretoria: J. L. van Schaik, 1964.

Stuart, K. W. *The Newspaperman's Guide to the Law*. 3d ed. Durban: Butterworth, 1982.

Stuart, K. W., and Klopper, W. *The Newspaperman's Guide to the Law*. Johannesburg: Mainpress, 1968.

Stulz, N. W. *Afrikaner Politics in South Africa, 1934–1948*. New York: 1969.

Subramoney, Marimuthu. "I Don't Think I'll Last Much Longer." *Index on Censorship*, June 1981, pp. 35–38.

Sunday Times. "Sunday Times Golden Jubilee, 1906-1956." Johannesburg, February 5, 1956.

Sunday Times. "Then and Now: 21 Years of the Sunday Times." Johannesburg, February 6, 1927.

Survey of Race Relations in South Africa. Annual Publication. Johannesburg: South African Institute of Race Relations, 1979.

Sussens, Aubrey. "The English Press under Apartheid." *Nieman Reports*, October 1961, pp. 8–9.

Suzman, Arthur. "Censorship and the Courts." *South African Law Journal*, 1972, pp. 191–206.

Switzer, L. S. "Politics and Communication in the Ciskei, an African Homeland in South Africa." Occasional Paper No. 23, Institute of Social and Economic Research. Grahamstown, South Africa: Rhodes University, 1979.

Switzer, L. S. "Steyn Commission 1: The Press and Total Strategy." Rhodes University, 1980.

Switzer, L. S., and Switzer, Donna. *The Black Press in South Africa and Lesotho*. Boston: G. K. Hall, 1979.

Thompson, L. M. *The Unification of South Africa, 1902–1910*. London: Oxford University Press, 1960.

Thompson, L. M., and Prior, Andrew. *South African Politics*. New Haven: Yale University Press, 1982.

Tomaselli, Keyan. *The South African Film Industry*. 2d ed. Johannesburg: African Studies Institute, 1980.

Treurnicht, A. P. *Credo van 'n Afrikaner*. Cape Town: Tafelberg Uitgewers, 1975.

Union List of South African Newspapers. November 1949. South African Public Library, Cape Town, 1950.

Die Vaderland. Die Vaderland se 21e Verjaardag as Dagblad—July 2, 1957. Johannesburg: Afrikaanse Pers, 1957.

Varley, D. H. *A Short History of the Newspaper Press in South Africa, 1642–1952*. Cape Town: Nasionale Pers, 1952.

Viljoen, J. M. H. *'n Joernalis Vertel*. Cape Town: Nasionale Boekhandel, 1953.

de Villiers, J. "South African Community and its Newspapers: A Socio-Historical Study." Ph.D. diss., University of the Orange Free State, 1976.

de Villiers, Les. *Secret Information*. Cape Town: Tafelberg, 1980.

de Villiers, René. "The Press and the People." Address before the South African Institute of Race Relations, Johannesburg, November 1967.

Visser, R. P., ed. *Die Vaderland Gedenkalbum*. Johannesburg: Afrikaanse Pers Boekhandel, 1957.

van der Vyver, J. D. "The Function of the Press in the Face of Excessive

Governmental Powers." Paper presented at Survival of the Press Conference, Rhodes University, Grahamstown, South Africa, 1978.

van der Vyver, J. D. "General Aspects of the South African Censorship Laws." Paper presented at conference on censorship, University of Cape Town, April 1980.

Walker, E. A. *A History of Southern Africa*. London: Longmans, Green, 1965.

de Wet, C. R. *Die Stryd tussen Boer en Brit*. Cape Town: Tafelberg-Uitgewers, 1959.

Whitehead, Marion. "The Black Gatekeepers: A Study of Black Journalists on Three Daily Newspapers Which Covered the Soweto Uprising of 1976." Honours thesis in journalism, Rhodes University, South Africa, January 1978.

Whitten, Leslie H. "South Africa on Madison Avenue." *Progressive*, October 1969, pp. 30–32.

Wilkins, Ivor, and Strydom, Hans. *The Super Afrikaners*. Johannesburg: Jonathan Ball, 1978.

Woods, Donald. *Asking for Trouble—An Autobiography of a Banned Journalist*. New York: Atheneum, 1981.

Woods, Donald. *Biko*. New York and London: Paddington Press, 1978.

Woods, Donald. "South Africa: Black Editors Out." *Index on Censorship*, June 1981, pp. 32–34.

Zille, Helen. "South Africa Gags 2 Student Journalists, Bans Their Anti-Apartheid Paper." *Chronicle of Higher Education*, April 28, 1982, p. 12.

Zille, Helen. "Student Press Is the Chief Victim of South Africa's Censorship Law." *Chronicle of Higher Educaiton*, November 1979, p. 19.

van Zyl, J. A. F., and Tomaselli, K. G. *Media and Change*. Johannesburg: McGraw-Hill, 1977.

Index

SPRING 1989